Robert William Dale

Fellowship with Christ,

And Other Discourses Delivered on Special Occasions

Robert William Dale

Fellowship with Christ,
And Other Discourses Delivered on Special Occasions

ISBN/EAN: 9783337167295

Printed in Europe, USA, Canada, Australia, Japan

Cover: Foto ©Lupo / pixelio.de

More available books at **www.hansebooks.com**

FELLOWSHIP WITH CHRIST

AND OTHER DISCOURSES

DELIVERED ON SPECIAL OCCASIONS

BY

R.^d W. DALE, LL.D.,

BIRMINGHAM

THIRD THOUSAND

London:
HODDER AND STOUGHTON,
27, PATERNOSTER ROW.

MDCCCXCII.

BUTLER & TANNER,
THE SELWOOD PRINTING WORKS,
FROME, AND LONDON.

To the
CHURCH AND CONGREGATION
MEETING IN CARR'S LANE, BIRMINGHAM,
IN GRATEFUL ACKNOWLEDGMENT
OF THE UNMEASURED AFFECTION AND
GENEROUS CONSIDERATION
SHOWN TO
THEIR PASTOR
DURING SERIOUS ILLNESS AND MANY MONTHS
OF WEAKNESS.

TREBORTH,
September, 1891

CONTENTS.

I.
FELLOWSHIP WITH CHRIST . . . . . . PAGE 1

II.
THE RISEN CHRIST 31

III.
THE CHRISTIAN GOSPEL AND THE SPIRIT OF GOD . 57

IV.
THE FAITH ONCE FOR ALL DELIVERED UNTO THE SAINTS 88

V.
GOD'S GREATNESS AND CONDESCENSION . . . 116

VI.
SOCIAL SCIENCE AND THE CHRISTIAN FAITH . . 147

VII.
FAITH AND PHYSICAL SCIENCE 171

VIII.
CHRIST AND THE STATE 192

IX.

THE THEOLOGY OF JOHN WESLEY 216

X.

THE MINISTRY REQUIRED BY THE AGE . . . 247

XI.

THE CONGREGATION HELPING THE MINISTER . . 278

XII.

THE UNITY OF THE CHURCH 304

XIII.

PROPITIATION 324

XIV.

THE DIVINE LIFE IN MAN 343

I.

FELLOWSHIP WITH CHRIST.[1]

"God is faithful, through whom ye were called into the fellowship of His Son Jesus Christ our Lord."—1 *Cor.* i. 9.

YE were "called into the fellowship of His Son," and since "God is faithful," He will "confirm you unto the end, that ye be unreprovable in the day of our Lord Jesus Christ." That is, our fellowship with Christ begins in the fleeting years of this mortal life; it will last through the endless ages of the life of Christ in God. This is Paul's account of the Christian redemption. He gives the same account of it elsewhere. He tells the Thessalonian Christians that God has "called" them through the Gospel "to the obtaining of the glory of our Lord Jesus Christ." To the Romans he says: "The Spirit Himself beareth witness with our spirit that we are children of God; and if children then heirs, heirs of God"; but with no separate, independent, personal rights in our inheritance—"heirs of God and joint-heirs with Christ."

---

[1] The Annual Sermon preached on behalf of the London Missionary Society, in the City Temple (Rev. Dr. Parker's) on Wednesday morning, May 14th, 1884.

The inheritance is Christ's, and therefore it is ours. His vision of God ; His righteousness ; His eternal and infinite blessedness in the Father's love; His glory as the Son of God ; these are the inheritance ; we are to share the inheritance with Him. Paul says again : " If we died with Him, we shall also live with Him ; if we endure, we shall also reign with Him " : " Your life is hid with Christ in God. When Christ, who is our life, shall be manifested, then shall ye also with Him be manifested in glory " ;—the final revelation of the glory of Christ must include the revelation of the glory of all who are in Christ. The Apostle John lived under the inspiration of the same hope : " Beloved, now are we children of God ; and it is not yet made manifest what we shall be. We know that if He shall be manifested, we shall be like Him, for we shall see Him even as He is." And this truth was revealed by our Lord Himself during His earthly ministry. In the prayer which He offered during the night in which He was betrayed, He said : " The glory which Thou hast given Me I have given unto them, that they may be one, even as We are one ; I in them, and Thou in Me, that they may be perfected into one."

God has called us "into the fellowship of His Son Jesus Christ our Lord." So great a future transcends the measures of our faith. When we consider who Christ is,—the Eternal Son of God ; when we remember that His humanity, in which He accepted the limitations and hard conditions of our earthly life, has passed through changes so wonderful that, though still remaining man, He has returned to the glory which He had with the Father before the world was, we shrink with awe and fear from the greatness of our destiny. These heights are inaccessible to us. They lie beyond the reach of our strength. We should be content with inferior honours and with a humbler blessedness. To be among the nations of the saved in the City of God would be more than enough; this, through the infinite grace of Christ, may be possible to us; but that we should have fellowship with Christ in His glory, that His glory should in any sense be ours, is more than we are willing to hope for. There would be irreverence, we are ready to think, in hoping for it.

My brethren, the great work which has drawn us together this morning is a decisive and startling confirmation of the reality of the boldest and most daring conceptions of the grandeur of our eternal future. We are in fellowship—in partnership—with Christ, already. Our greatness has begun; and the proof of it is to be found in every mission-station that we have planted in heathen countries, in every missionary that sails from our shores, in every meeting that is held, and in every sermon that is preached, to enforce our responsibility and to increase our enthusiasm for the evangelization of the world. How great a place the salvation of mankind holds in the heart of God, who can tell? To achieve it, the Eternal Son of God laid aside His glory, endured

sorrow and pain and the unknown desolation of the
Cross. But in the divine order we share with Christ
the work of restoring the human race to God. Christ
has His place; we have ours. God has called us
into the fellowship of His Son. Jesus Christ is the
Saviour of the world; we share with Him the work
of saving it.

I.

The root of this fellowship with Christ in His
supreme work and in His eternal glory is to be found
in Christ's original and normal relations to the human
race. There is a remarkable passage in the Epistle
to the Hebrews, which all of you will remember:
"It became Him for whom are all things, and through
whom are all things, in bringing many sons unto
glory to make the Author of their salvation perfect
through sufferings." "Many sons"—that seems to
require explanation. For the writer of this epistle
has rested his whole argument for the unique greatness of Christ—a greatness transcending that of
prophets and of angels—on His wonderful title 'the
Son' of God. How is it that he now describes men
—men who needed salvation—as being also "sons"
of God? He anticipates the objection: "for both
He that sanctified"—that is Christ—"and they that
are sanctified"—ourselves—"are all of one"—are of
one Father—"for which cause He is not ashamed
to call them brethren." "Since, then the children
are sharers in flesh and blood, He, the Eternal Son

of God, "also Himself in like manner partook of the same." "It behoved Him in all things to be made like unto His brethren." That is, the brotherly relation between Christ and us did not begin when He was born at Bethlehem. Before His incarnation He was our Brother, and when things went wrong with us it was a brotherly act—an act done at the impulse of brotherly affection, to come and share our troubles that He might deliver us from them. We are not the brethren of Christ because Christ has assumed our nature; Christ assumed our nature because we were His brethren.

I suppose that, if we had fulfilled the Divine idea of human righteousness, Christ would still have become man. He would have become man, not to atone for human sin, but to achieve a transcendent form of human perfection, and to open for us an access to transcendent heights of blessedness and glory. The incarnation was not an after-thought, a Divine expedient to meet contingencies foreseen or unforeseen. It was involved in the creation of man. We were created in Christ. What this meant, what it included, we discover in His temptation in the wilderness, His agony in Gethsemane, His desolation and death on the Cross.

We may approach this great mystery through the facts which illustrate the unity, or, as it is described with closer accuracy, the solidarity of the human race. We are all partners, without our choice, in each other's health and sickness, joy and sorrow, fully and wisdom, righteousness and sin. Our fortunes are in the keeping of other men ; their fortunes are in ours. It is not our contemporaries alone that make life blessed or sad for us, that augment our strength or crush our weakness. It is not our contemporaries alone to whom we, in our turn, may be a blessing or a curse. We are heirs of all the past, and the entail cannot be cut off. We are trustees for all the future, and we cannot decline the trust. We are the poorer or the richer for the indolence or the industry of countries which lie beyond the ocean, of nations which perished in the very morning of human history. The sins of ancient eastern empires cast their shadow upon the civilization of modern Europe, and the penalty of their crimes is being paid by populations that are ignorant both of their glory and their shame. Their palaces and temples have crumbled into dust ; the very names of their sovereigns, their statesmen, their famous soldiers are almost forgotten : but the evil which they did remains, and for many centuries to come we are not likely to escape from it.

There is a vivid illustration before us at this moment. The long oppression by which the moral vigour of the inhabitants of the wealthy valley of the Nile has been destroyed complicates the domestic policy of England, and troubles the friendly relations of the great powers of Europe. It has been the design of English statesmen to restore to Egypt national independence, and to lay there the foundations of free institutions. Had that policy achieved immediate success, our troubles would have ceased both at Cairo and Khartoum. But it still remains doubtful whether the history of five or six thousand years has not rendered the people incapable of the tasks of freedom. The sins of the Pharaohs and the Ptolemies, of the Caliphs and the Sultans, are delaying a measure for the political enfranchisement of two millions of men in England, Scotland, and Ireland; and, in the absence of generosity, courage, and self-control in the statesmen and nations of Europe, may issue in a great European war.

It is wonderful how far this solidarity of the race extends, binding together in a partnership indissoluble, the richest and the poorest, slaves and princes, the tents of the desert and the palaces of cities, sinner and saint, executioner and martyr, Christian and pagan, the earliest and the latest centuries of human history. It extends—this is one of the great discoveries of the Christian Gospel,—it extends from earth to heaven, from the sins and miseries of our mortal life to the blessedness and glory of the eternal Son of God. When we were created in Christ, the fortunes of the human race for good or for evil became His. The Incarnation revealed and fulfilled the relations which already existed between the Son of God and mankind. From the beginning, Christ had entered into fellowship with us. When we sinned, He remained in fellowship with us still. He was in partnership with us; the miseries of the race were His, His by His own choice, and He endured them all. It "behoved" the eternal Son of God to share the fortunes of God's earthly children. He not only became man, but submitted to all the sufferings and humiliations of our earthly condition. He endured the pains which are common to man and to inferior races. He was tried by hunger, thirst, weariness, and physical torture. He endured the sharper agonies, the deeper sorrows, which are man's special and separate inheritance, as the result of his revolt against God. He was tempted by the Devil; He was suspected, hated, slandered. His friends were not always faithful; one of them betrayed Him. The most appalling woe—the woe which we might have thought could never have come on the Son of God, and which to many of us seems incredible—fell upon Him; in the mysterious darkness of his last hours, He cried, "My God, My God, why hast Thou forsaken Me?" That sorrow broke His heart, and He died. He clung to us through death, and so He saved us. Through His blood we have remission of sins; in His resurrection we rise to the eternal life of God. There is solidarity between the human race and Christ. His fellowship with us is real; our fellowship with Him is not less real. That relationship between the Eternal Son of God and us which made it possible for Him to share our weakness and the desolation which was the result of our sin, also makes it possible for us to share His work in this world and His glory in the next. His fellowship with us is the foundation of our fellowship with Him.

II.

The relationship between Christ and the human race is illustrated in the Divine idea of human perfection. It has been the habit of theologians to express what they have believed to be the true and original relationship between man and God in terms of Law. They have assumed, not only that we were created to obey the eternal law of righteousness, but that, had we obeyed it, our eternal blessedness would have been the natural result and the just reward of our personal perfection. Having made this initial assumption, they have concluded that it is only because we have sinned that we have to find eternal life, eternal righteousness, and eternal blessedness in Christ. But this is an inversion of the true relations between Grace and Law. We came under Law only because we fell away from the ideal of Grace, or declined the path which would have led to the attainment of it. It was not the Divine thought that our righteousness should have no deeper, surer root than our own freewill; or that its possibilities of growth and expansion should be determined by the limitations of our personal life. Nor was it God's purpose that the measures of our eternal blessedness, the nearness of our access to Himself, our rank, if I may call it so, in His eternal kingdom, should be nothing more than the natural fruit and the equitable recompense of our personal obedience. We were not created under Law. We were never meant to be mere servants in the household of God, with no wealth but the wages we might earn. We were meant to be God's children, not His servants; and, according to the Divine idea of human nature, man was created for an inheritance of greatness and of glory, which no obedience of his own, though prolonged through millennium after millennium of faultless righteousness, could ever have purchased.

We were created in Christ; God "hath blessed us with every spiritual blessing in Christ, even as He chose us in Him,"—the whole race, men of every nation and kindred and people and tongue,—"before the foundation of the world, that we should be holy and without blemish before Him in love, having fore-ordained us unto adoption as sons, through Jesus Christ, unto Himself, according to the good pleasure of His will, to the praise of the glory of His grace, which He freely bestowed on us in the Beloved." That was the Divine idea in the creation of man. We were created to be "heirs of God," not servants merely—to illustrate the riches of His grace, not merely the equity of His law; "heirs of God, joint-heirs with Christ." Now that we have broken with the Divine purpose, and lost the fair paradise which God meant to be our home, fairer than the fairest scenes of any earthly land, it is in Christ "that we have our redemption through His blood; the forgiveness of our trespasses according to the riches of His grace."

The Incarnation was no after-thought; and that

we should have eternal life and blessedness in Christ —not in ourselves—was no after-thought. The incarnation was no mere Divine expedient for recovering us from the loss and ruin which had come upon us through our sin. Nor is it simply because we have failed to achieve a righteousness of our own that we have to find eternal righteousness in Christ.

Faith in Christ was the original law of our perfection. The life of faith in the Son of God is the ideal life of man. According to the original constitution of human nature, human righteousness was to be the revelation of forces which have their fountains beyond the limits of humanity. It was to be the expression of the energy and perfection of the righteousness of Christ. Our place in the Divine kingdom was to be determined, not by our personal merits; it was determind for us by the infinite love which made the Sonship and the glory of Christ the inheritance of our race. Christianity is as "old as the Creation," in another sense than that in which the words were used in the last century. When God calls us into the fellowship of His Son Jesus Christ our Lord, He calls us back to those Divine heights which are native to us, and restores us to our original place in the Divine household. We may almost venture, each one of us, to speak to Christ in the words which Christ Himself addressed to the Father: "All things that are Mine are Thine, and Thine are Mine." His life of varied suffering, His awful death, illustrated the reality of His fellowship with us. The illustration of the reality of our fellowship with Him will come when we share His eternal glory. Our partnership with Him in His blessedness will be as complete as His partnership has been with us in our suffering. He shared our weakness; we shall share His strength: He took "the form of a servant"; we shall reign with Him. He descended into the awful darkness which deepens round the man who has lost the sense of God's presence; and since, through eternity, He will be the Way as well as the Truth and the Life, we shall have access to the Father in Him and through Him; and His fellowship with the Father will be ours.

III.

The relations between Christ and man, between man and Christ, determine the law of the personal Christian life. They are the ground of Christian morals. The ethics of the Sermon on the Mount have their root in the mystical relations between Christ and His people, which are illustrated in the parable of the vine. But to pursue that line of thought would lead us away from the great work which should command our thoughts and fill our hearts this morning.

The life that is in Christ has been revealed in many wonderful and glorious forms. For us, at least, its most wonderful and most glorious revelation is in what He has done and endured for the salvation of the human race. It is because we share His life, because there is solidarity between Him and us, that we share with Him the work of saving the world. From the very first, Christ took men into partnership, into real and effective partnership, with Himself in this work; and the results of His Incarnation, Ministry, and Death were rested on their fidelity.

That He might save men, He revealed God. The revelation was made to those who saw and heard Him during His earthly ministry. It was made most fully to the men whom the Father had given Him out of the world, and whom He appointed to be apostles. They were devout Jews, and they had been prepared by the traditions of their race, by the worship of the temple, by the instruction of the synagogue, by the songs of psalmists and the visions of prophets, to receive the new revelation of God through Christ. During the two or three years that they lived with Him, the affection and reverence and faith which He inspired, and the power of His life over theirs, increased their moral and spiritual sensitiveness to His teaching. Even at the last, however, their knowledge of His true greatness, and of the real nature of His work, was imperfect. But, imperfect as it was, it gave them an immense personal value, both to Him and to the world. They were in fellowship with Him, and apart from them the great purpose for which He had become man could not be accomplished. Through them the revelation of God through Him was to be made known to the human race. New knowledge, new powers, came to them after He had passed into the heavens; and they discharged their trust with the noblest fidelity. The trust was real, and everything depended on the spirit and power with which they fulfilled it.

In the greatness of their position the apostles stand alone. But the Church of every subsequent generation has inherited apostolic duties; these duties have descended to ourselves, and we feel the pressure of our obligations this morning. Christ has revealed God; we are in fellowship with Christ; and the uncounted millions of men belonging to heathen races are to receive the revelation through us.

Christ has revealed God—and if I may turn aside for one moment from the work of Christian missions —we have not only to make known what Christ has revealed, but we have fellowship with Christ in the very process of revelation. For the revelation did not receive its final expression from Himself in any series of theological definitions, beyond which no further discoveries of God were possible. His words are preserved for all ages in the four Gospels, but they are not formal and final statements of truth; they are "spirit and life." The theology of no Church, of no age, can exhaust their meaning. The range of Divine truth which the words of Christ reveal is extended, the ideal of Christian perfection which they present is heightened and ennobled, as the intellectual wealth of the Church is augmented by the new intellectual triumphs of every new generation; as the morality of the Church receives a more varied discipline from the increasing complexity and delicacy of the social relations in every civilized Christian State; as the Christian life is developed into new forms of sanctity by the vicissitudes of the fortunes of the Church, and by the changes which pass upon the relations of the Church to the general condition of mankind. Christ revealed God; but He Himself described the Divine Word which came through Him as seed, of which He was the Sower. The seed itself is the revelation; but for the revelation which it contains to be actually unfolded, it requires soil and air, moisture, heat and light. The good ground is necessary to the good seed. In us, in some of us, let us hope that it is bringing forth fruit thirty, sixty, and a hundred fold. The revelation of God through Christ is expanded, enlarged, prolonged through the life of the Church. In the Church, the Word of God liveth and abideth for ever, and while it lives it grows. The contents of the Christian revelation are richer and more varied to-day than they were in any past age. We have fellowship with Christ in revealing God.

If this is true, then by sending the Christian Gospel to heathen nations, we are not only making known to them what God has made known to us; we are rendering possible an enlargement, an immense development, of the Christian revelation. The intellectual genius of these nations is different from ours; their moral temperament is different, their civilization is different, their social organization is different. The Divine Word, when it strikes root in these new soils and under these new skies, will have new and unexpected growths. There is a kind of Christian perfection possible to the East which is not possible to the West, and there is, therefore, a kind of Divine knowledge accessible to the East which the West will never discover for itself. The ear of the East is sensitive to Divine voices that have been speaking through Christ for eighteen centuries, but which our ear has not recognised. And when our missions begin to achieve their great triumphs, the saints and theologians of India and of China will tell us truths concerning the revelation of God in Christ which we have never learnt. To them, whole provinces of wonder and glory will be revealed, of which the Churches of the West know nothing. Christ revealed God; we are in fellowship with Christ, and through the success of Christian missions the revelation itself will become richer and more wonderful.

Christ came to redeem and to save the human race; and God has called us into fellowship with Christ. Christ and Christ alone could atone for human sin; to attribute to the merits and sufferings of saints any atoning virtue, to regard them as constituting any reason for the remission of either the eternal or the temporal penalties of sin, is to obscure Christ's unique glory. The Lord hath laid on Him the iniquity of us all, and He bore the awful burden alone. He atoned for the sins of all men—for the sins of the penitent and the impenitent, of those who receive the Gospel, of those who reject it, of those to whom the Gospel was never preached. He atoned for the sins of heathen as well as of Christian nations. By His incarnation, death, and resurrection, He brought the human race into new relations to God; or, rather, He restored and confirmed the original and normal relations which had been disturbed by sin. Christ is the Propitiation for the sin of the world. Therefore the whole world is not under Law, but under Grace.

But the death of Christ is not only the objective ground on which God grants the remission of sin. It contains the strongest motives to penitence and to faith in the infinite mercy of God. As an atonement, its power reaches the whole race, apart from any co-operation of ours. As a revelation of the righteousness and love of God to the human conscience and heart, its power can be felt only where it is known, and we have been called into the fellowship of Christ that we may make it known to all mankind.

This is our place. Christ has descended from the glory which He had with the Father before the world was, to the limitations of human weakness, to suffering, agony and death, that He might restore men to God. He has done His part; it is for us to do ours. This wonderful appeal of the infinite love of God to mankind has been intrusted to you and to me, and to our Christian brethren in all the Churches. It is our place to fill the hearts of men with wonder, with joy, with infinite hope, by telling them of the almost incredible sufferings of the Son of God for their salvation. It is our place to bring home to the hearts of God's children the final proof of how dear they are to the Father, whom they have forgotten. This is the true measure of the grandeur of our position ; we have to give effect to the appeal of the infinite love of God, in the life and death of Christ, to the faith, affection, and loyalty of the human race. It is natural for us to shrink from these immense responsibilities, but they are inseparable from that relationship to Christ, which is the condition and assurance of our personal salvation.

It is our habit to think of all that we ourselves receive from our fellowship with Christ ; nor can we think of this aspect of our fellowship with Him too much, if only we think enough of another aspect of it, which perhaps we are in danger of overlooking.

Take our Lord's own illustration of the fellowship between us : "I am the vine, ye are the branches," "as the branch cannot bear fruit of itself except it abide in the vine, so neither can ye except ye abide in Me." " Apart from Me ye can do nothing." That is true ; and we know it. But look at the illustration a little closer ; the branches, apart from the vine can do nothing ; but what are we to say of the vine apart from the branches ? A branch cannot bear fruit of itself ; if it is separated from the vine it withers and perishes. But can the vine bear fruit without the branches ? If the branches are separated from the vine, if the branches which remain in it are dead branches, where will the fruit be ? If some branches wither and are removed, other branches must be created by the living force of the vine, or the vine will be bare of blossoms in spring, and of clustering grapes in autumn. The vine bears fruit through the branches; this is just as true as that the branches bear fruit because they are in the vine.

Take Paul's illustration of our fellowship with Christ. We are the body of Christ. This is an illustration to which he recurs several times. He uses it in the Epistle to the Romans, in the first Epistle to the Corinthians, in the Epistle to the Ephesians. It seemed to him to represent one of the great realities of Christian faith and life. We are "the body of Christ and severally members thereof." Apart from Him we have no life, no energy, and all our functions cease. Apart from Him the hand has no strength, the eye no vision, and the ear is no longer sensitive to the voice of God. But if we are the body of Christ, we are the organization through which Christ acts. To every one of us, as a separate member of His body, there is destined a special function; and upon the manner in which we discharge it depends the health and vigour of the whole body of Christ, and the effectiveness with which it serves His will.

Through us—for we are the hands of Christ—He gives bread to the hungry, clothes the naked, smoothes the pillow of the sick and the weary, builds homes for the homeless, breaks the chains of the slave, opens the prison-doors for the oppressed, lightens the heavy burdens of the poor and the wretched. If His hands are paralysed and refuse their office, how shall He do these works of mercy? Through us—for we are the voice of Christ—He speaks words of comfort and peace to the penitent, and of menace to those who are in daring revolt against God—words of courage to the desponding, of compassion to the broken-hearted, of immortal hope to the dying. The voice may be clear or indistinct, musical as the songs of angels, or harsh as the rudest of earthly discords: Christ can but speak with the voice He has. The voice may be lost altogether; and then, how is He to speak at all?

I do not say that, in the nature of things, Christ could not have revealed His life and given effect to His will without us. I do not say that in fact Christ has no other modes of blessing and saving men than through the Church; that He does not command other forces than those which act through the righteousness, the sanctity, the compassion for human suffering, the mercy for human sin, the zeal for the Divine honour of those who have already been drawn into fellowship with Him. But I do say that, in the Divine order for the salvation of the world, we have our place, and that our responsibilities and powers are not apparent only, but real.

There was a rough method of representing the Calvinistic doctrine concerning the relations between man and God, which even those of us who reject Calvinism must see was false and unjust. It used to be said that, according to Calvin, a man if he is among the elect will be saved, do what he may; that if he is not among the elect, he will be lost, do what he can. If that had been a true representation, Calvinism would have taken the life out of every motive to repentance, to prayer, to patience in well-doing. But the fatalism which was falsely attributed to that august system of theology actually infects some prevailing opinions concerning the relations of the Church to the heathen world. It seems to be tacitly assumed that the moral and spiritual interests of the rest of mankind cannot have been intrusted, in any real sense, and to any serious extent, to the keeping of those who are in fellowship with the Lord Jesus Christ. It is thought incredible that the condition —the moral and spiritual condition—of unnumbered millions of men should be much the better for our energy and zeal, or much the worse for our unfaithfulness and indifference. This is the old fatalism in a worse and more malignant form. An immoral inference from the doctrine of the Divine decrees only prevented a man from making sure of his own salvation. This indolent and presumptuous reliance on the Divine goodness would prevent the Church from using its strength for the salvation of the world. It quenches the fire of missionary enthusiasm, relaxes the energy of every kind of evangelistic work, both at home and abroad.

From speculations I appeal to facts. We are in possession of the revelation of God through Christ. If heathen men are to receive it, they must receive it through us. Will it make no difference to them whether or not we teach them to regulate their ethical life by the Sermon on the Mount? Will it make no difference to them whether or not they hear from us the parable of the prodigal son, and are told that it was spoken by the Son of God, who came to seek and to save the lost? Will it make no difference to them whether or not they learn—and they must learn it from us, if in this world they are to learn it at all—that the Lord Jesus Christ, the Creator of all things, has made their sorrows, their infirmities, their temptations, and in a wonderful sense their very sins His own, that they may receive the remission of sins through Him, and share His strength for doing the will of God? We maintain with passionate earnestness, we assert it as the glory of our faith, that the love of God is a love for all mankind ; and heathen nations do not know it ; will it make no difference to them if we tell them the blessed news that they have a Father in heaven, and that it is His will that beyond death they should live with Him in eternal glory? Has the knowledge of these great truths made so little difference to yourselves that you cannot believe that the knowledge of them would make much difference to the people of India and China, of Central Africa and New Guinea? Have they done nothing to ennoble your character, to raise you to new heights of power, to give you the vision of God, to transfigure the sorrows and the duties of these mortal years, as well as to inspire the hope of immortality ? You know that, if the Christian Gospel had never reached you, your life would have missed what constitutes its dignity, its strength, its security, and its glory.

But you tell me that you are confident that if the supreme revelation of God's love does not reach men in this world, it will reach them in the next. I will not stay to discuss the suggestion. I want to ask—Would you have been content to live and die without knowing Christ? For yourselves it would have been an immeasurable loss if the revelation had not reached you here. And, by delaying to give to heathen nations the Christian Gospel, you are inflicting this immeasurable loss upon them.

But still you urge that the eternal future of the heathen is safe; for there are no limits to the mercy of God. "No limits to the mercy of God!" Are you sure of it?—sure of it in the sense which, for the purposes of this discussion, the words must bear? In one direction, at least, there are limits. Have you forgotten the rich man who was clothed with purple and fine linen, and fared sumptuously every day, and who cared nothing for the beggar lying at his gate? Has not the parable a wider application than that which is commonly given to it? We, too, are rich beyond all hope and thought in the divinest wealth, and the heathen Lazarus lies at our very gate full of sores, hardly receiving the crumbs that fall from our table. It may be, as you tell me, that Lazarus when he dies will be carried by the angels into Abraham's bosom. But what will be our doom if, with treasures infinitely more precious than those of Dives, we are guilty of a more cruel selfishness? It will not do for us to presume that there are no limits to the Divine mercy.

God's mercy is infinite—True. But it is perilous logic when you are drawing conclusions from infinite premisses. "There are no limits to the mercy of God." What do you infer from it? As soon as the infinite glories and energies of the Divine life are manifested in the actual order of the world, and in the actual course of human affairs, they seem to submit to limitations. There is your brother, your playmate at home, your comrade at school; misfortune has fallen upon him, he has lost everything; you have the power, ample power, to help him; his claims upon you are direct, indubitable, sacred. For him you are the elect minister of the Divine compassion, and the Divine compassion is infinite. But the infinite compassion of God having appointed you to relieve your brother's distress is limited by your willingness to relieve him.

In every condition of human life the fatalism which releases itself from duty by appealing to the infinite goodness of God is contradicted by the sternest facts. If those who have bread do not feed the hungry, God is pitiful; but no manna falls from heaven—they starve. If the strong do not care for the sick, God is pitiful; but no angelic messengers descend to cool the fires of fever—they die. If Christian men do not send the Gospel of Christ to the heathen, God's love is infinite, but tell me, why are you so sure that the heathen will be none the worse for our neglect? "No limits to the mercy of God!" The limitations are real, obvious, appalling. He, in His infinite love, intended the Gospel for all mankind. Through the want of faith, of courage, of enthusiasm in the Church, it remains unknown, through generation after generation, to millions upon millions of the race.

To those of us who hold the Evangelical faith in its historic form, it is no recent discovery that, through the grace of God, men who have never heard of Christ may share the blessedness of the Christian salvation.

> "Ten thousand sages lost in endless woe,
> For ignorance of what they could not know?
> That speech betrays at once a bigot's tongue;
> Charge not a God with such outrageous wrong!"

Those are the indignant words of a poet of our own. It is more than a hundred years since they were written. And kindling with a generous fervour, Cowper went on to say:

> "The partial light men have,
> My creed persuades me, well employed may save;
> While he that scorns the noon-day beam, perverse,
> Shall find the blessing unimproved a curse."

Yes; there is a light which lighteth every man, and which is not completely obscured by the grossest forms of heathenism. That Light is Christ Himself, and those who follow Him in heathen or in Christian lands "shall not walk in the darkness, but shall have the light of life." But it lies with us to determine,— and the responsibility is overwhelming,—whether men shall have the faint glimmering of a doubtful dawn struggling with the heavy clouds of night, or the noon-day glory that shines through the Gospel of the Lord Jesus Christ.

It may be—for myself I have never discovered any sure grounds for the belief—that, even for those who in this life love the darkness rather than the light, there will be the possibility of repentance beyond death. Heathen men who felt no reverence for the authority of conscience, and were untouched by the nobler elements of heathen tradition and faith, but who might have been drawn to God by the revelation of His love through Christ, may perhaps in other worlds be filled with awe by the majesty of God's righteousness and inspired with trust and loyalty by His infinite grace. We know too little of the conditions of the moral life of man beyond death to be peremptory in our conclusions. After death, all that we can see in the New Testament is "judgment," with eternal life for those who have loved the light, and eternal death for those who have hated it. But it may be, as you say, that after all God will—do what?—remedy the miserable results of our neglect. We may find shelter in this when it is too late to remedy the miserable results of our neglect ourselves. But to retreat to this refuge before we have strained every energy to achieve the present salvatior of men, is to tempt the mercy of God and to betray the supreme interests of the human race.

Let us acknowledge that the position in which we

stand, in relation to all men, whether in our own country or in other countries, that have not yet received the Christian redemption, is appalling. If there is glory in it, there is terror. It raises questions which, as far as I can see, have received no adequate solution. But mystery surrounds all the sublimer heights of human greatness. The valleys are clear, but the mountain-peaks are in the clouds.

The moral freedom of man gives him his characteristic dignity in relation both to the universe and to God; and yet it is because the moral freedom of man is so real that some of the aspects of man's present condition and future destiny are covered with such oppressive gloom. If he were not free, really free, the darkest evils of his condition would disappear; but with the darkness, the splendours too would pass away, the mystery of life would be over.

It is the reality of our fellowship with Christ which makes our responsibility so immense, and, as we sometimes think, so unendurable. We share—we really share—His solicitudes and sorrows, His labours and conflicts, His joy and triumph in saving the world. The position is terrible; but the greatness of the service we are called to render to mankind is inseparable from the glory of our relations to Christ. We might be relegated to inferior tasks, but then the reality of our fellowship with Christ would cease.

Our true course is, not to suffer ourselves to be paralysed by the contrast between our personal weakness and the duties to which we are appointed, but to accept with courage God's estimate of our possible achievements rather than our own. Instead of becoming entangled in speculations on what will happen to men if we fail to discharge our trust, and how God will remedy the calamitous results of our failure, we should resolve, that up to the limits of our strength—or, rather, of the strength which God gives us—we will not fail. The grandeur of our task should give to weakness heroic strength, and kindle in the coldest hearts the fires of a Divine enthusiasm.

But the fires of enthusiasm die down, and the passionate strength which suddenly rises to the height of a great enterprise is soon exhausted. Nor can work like ours be done under the iron constraint of duty. We must find our inspiration in Christ. It was free spontaneous love for man that brought Him from Divine glories to the darkness and desolation of the cross; and we must have fellowship with Christ in His love for the race, or we can have no fellowship with Him in saving it. This alone will sustain our courage, our fortitude, our constancy, through the vicissitudes of hope and disappointment, of defeat and triumph, which are incident to a work like this. This alone will make us equal to its immense demands, and enable us to endure the loss of all things, not that we ourselves, but that other men may come to the knowledge of Christ, may be found in Him, may know the power of His resurrection, and rise through Him to an eternal life in God. This alone can give to our words concerning Christ any persuasive power.

Nothing but the strength and tenderness of our own love for men can render credible what we tell them concerning the love of Christ.

To have fellowship with Christ in His work, the life of Christ must be ours. His love for the human race must be shed abroad in our hearts. He is the vine, we are the branches; apart from Him we can do nothing. The missionary spirit cannot be suddenly created in assemblies like this. We may be deeply moved for a time by dark and appalling descriptions of the miseries of the heathen, by animating accounts of the light and joy which have come to heathen men who have received the Christian Gospel; by vehement appeals to our loyalty to Christ and our pity and compassion for mankind; but the true and enduring inspiration is to be sought elsewhere. Its eternal fountains are in the eternal love of God for the human race, revealed in Christ Jesus our Lord. Only as we abide in Christ, and Christ abides in us, can the spirit we need for this work become ours. Christ Himself has taught us the conditions on which success depends. "Neither for these only do I pray, but for them also that believe through their word; that they may all be one; even as Thou, Father, art in Me, and I in Thee; that they also may be in Us; that the world may believe that Thou didst send Me." That majestic vision of a great society of men, of all races and of all lands, inspired with the life of God, living in the light of God, blessed in the love of God, and governed in the greatest and obscurest of earthly conditions by the laws of God's eternal kingdom, will be a more wonderful and decisive proof of the Divine authority of Christ than the greatest of His miracles. But it will not be merely by the vision of this triumphant achievement of His power and grace that the revolt of the world will be subdued. When the Church is drawn into this perfect union with Christ, and with God through Him, the fires of an infinite love for mankind will burn in all Christian hearts; and all that bear the name of Christ, being one with Him, will share His passion for the salvation of men. The generous pity, the brotherly affection, the zeal of confederated millions inspired with enthusiasm for the restoration of the human race to God, the world will be unable to resist; and the final victory of the love of God over the miseries and sins of men will be achieved. But we ourselves are one with Christ, and, though the days may yet be remote when the whole earth will be filled with the glory of God, we share with Christ the work of saving the world, that we may share His eternal joy and blessedness in its salvation. We are greater than we thought. We know not what we shall be; we know not what we are; but this we know—that in this life, and in the life to come, God has called us "into the fellowship of His Son Jesus Christ our Lord." Fellowship with Christ is the ultimate ground of missionary duty; fellowship with Christ is the ultimate secret of missionary success.

II.

THE RISEN CHRIST.[1]

" Wherefore we henceforth know no man after the flesh : even though we have known Christ after the flesh, yet now we know Him so no more."—2 *Cor.* v. 16.

THIS epistle is one of the earliest pieces of missionary literature. It was written by the first and the greatest of Christian missionaries to heathen nations, and written to a Christian Church the large majority of whose members were recent converts from heathenism. The words which I have read reveal part of the secret of Paul's own intense life, and part of the secret of the energy and success of his work as a missionary. We who are assembled here this morning have inherited the awful, the glorious trust which he received from God ; to us, in these last days, is " this grace given, to preach unto the Gentiles the unsearchable riches of Christ " ; and it will be well for us to inquire whether, like Paul, we can say that " *we* know no man after the flesh," and that " even though

---

[1] The Annual Sermon preached on behalf of the Wesleyan Missionary Society, in Great Queen Street Chapel, London, on Friday morning, April 26th, 1889.

we *have* known Christ after the flesh, yet now we know Him so no more." It may be that through this inquiry we shall discover new sources of strength for our work among heathen people; and whatever increases our strength for work among them will also increase our strength for work among our own countrymen.

And as I am much more anxious that you should receive into your very hearts the account which Paul gives of himself than that you should listen to any arguments or appeals of mine, I propose to attempt a somewhat extended exposition of his meaning.

The words are part of a most pathetic and moving piece of autobiography; and it will be necessary to recall some of the disclosures of Paul's personal life that precede them. There is something profoundly affecting in these disclosures. When we are in some moods it is hardly possible to read them without tears. It is as if Paul were with us still. The eighteen hundred years which separate him from us disappear. We know him better than we know the oldest and dearest of our friends. We can see deeper into his life; for he lays it all open. His sorrows, perplexities, and wounded love, his indignation, his consciousness of weakness, his consciousness of integrity, the depression occasioned by his physical exhaustion, the courage and hope and energy drawn from Divine fountains of life and strength, his eager longing for the perfect salvation and the vision of God, his awe in anticipation of the judgment-seat of Christ—they are all here; he speaks of them all as he might have spoken of them to Timothy when spending a long sleepless night with him on shipboard or in prison.

But we must limit ourselves to those parts of the wonderful confession which are most intimately and vitally connected with the text.

I.

In the third chapter of this epistle Paul contrasts his own ministry, which he calls the ministry of righteousness and the ministry of the Spirit which giveth life, with the ministry of Moses, which he calls the ministry of condemnation and the ministry of death. His own, he says, is far more glorious. What those words meant on the lips of a Jew, to whom Moses was the august and venerable deliverer and legislator of the elect race, who had received the reverence of sixteen centuries, it is hardly possible for us to imagine. But his exultation soon begins to sink. He might have gone on to say that a ministry so great—a ministry through which the human race were to receive righteousness and eternal life, and were to enter into the very blessedness of the Eternal—challenged and provoked into energetic activity all the forces of his nature, and inspired him with the strength and courage which its immense and perilous tasks demanded. It was something like this that he did say, but he said it in quite another form: "Seeing we have this ministry, even as we obtained mercy, *we faint not*"—we do not become cowardly, we do not give way:—that is all! He is thinking of his personal weakness as it was brought home to him, on the one hand by the greatness of his work, and on the other by the dangers, the sorrows, and the sufferings in which it involved him. And, a little further on, this latent thought breaks out into most pathetic expression: "We have this treasure in earthen vessels"—frail, perishable vessels—and the life we are living consumes our strength. On every side we are pressed, perplexed, hunted down, smitten to the earth, and yet we are not crushed; we do not despair; we are not forsaken; we are not destroyed. And now comes the first approach to the words which we have specially to consider this morning: "We who live are always delivered unto death for Jesus' sake"—that is, our life is little better than a continual dying, that another life than ours, the life of Jesus, "may be manifested in our mortal flesh."

Let us pause there for a moment. What Paul means is, that his incessant labours and anxieties, the hardships and persecutions he had to endure, were wearing him away. The elasticity, the alertness, the animation, the consciousness of vigour, which I suppose he had in his earlier years, were all gone. Yes; but he does not faint, for the life which came to him from Christ had courage in it, and hope, and resolute force, and made continued activity possible to him. How often have I heard a testimony just like Paul's from poor men and women who had no suspicion of the mystical depth and the infinite grandeur of their words! They had lived a hard, anxious, cheerless life; had suffered from poverty and ill-health; in some cases had been tortured with physical disease; had been treated coldly, and even with cruel unkindness, by those who ought to have been their consolation and support; their sorrows were more than mortal strength could bear; but they said that their strength was not their own, their courage did not fail, nor their cheerful trust in the love of God—a force, a life, higher than their own was manifested in their mortal flesh. And this has been the experience of sixty generations of saints.

I confess that I find very little satisfaction in any attempts—whether of my own or of other men—to solve the mystery of pain and sorrow. Such knowledge is too wonderful for me; it is high, I cannot attain unto it. But this seems clear from the common experience of men: In years of health, vigour, and prosperity, our native strength seems sufficient for us; we are equal to every task, and can bear every burden; we are confident, sanguine, victorious. But with diminishing vigour there are sometimes heavier troubles, and when we have lost the light-heartedness of early years we have to pass through regions of desolation which would have sunk our spirits even in the buoyancy of youth. Or the exhaustion may come, not from accumulating years, but from labour and oppressive responsibilities, from sickness and disappointments and bereavements. And then, if we are in Christ, we discover that there are springs of energy within us of which we knew very little when we were subjected to no real strain. As things are—in the actual moral conditions which we have to reckon with—the sharp agonies, or the waste and weariness of our earthly life, liberate the diviner life which is given us in Christ. It is in the extremity of mortal weakness that we become conscious of immortal strength. We die while we live, that we may live indeed. Or, to quote Paul's words again, it is when the "outward man is decaying"—strength sinking, all earthly springs of delight running dry, human ties dissolving, darkness falling on our homes, friends failing us or passing into the unseen world, and leaving us lonely when most we need their support—it is when the "outward man is decaying," through the loss of all the natural supplies of power and joy, that the "inward man" becomes vividly conscious that it is being "renewed day by day." That is the first truth we have to remember if we are to master what Paul meant in the text.

And the second is this: When we become conscious that our enduring strength, our true life, is not drawn from the visible and temporal order, we set our minds and hearts on the invisible and eternal order; "we look not at the things which are seen, but at the things which are not seen; for the things which are seen are temporal, but the things which are not seen are eternal." As we have learnt that earthly strength and joy and peace are transient and earthly sorrows transient, our thoughts pierce the visible forms of things which conceal God's eternal kingdom. And that vision of the Divine order gives a new interpretation to earthly troubles. The inward man is being renewed, while the outward man is decaying, and so the earthly troubles are working for us "more and more exceedingly an eternal weight of glory."

There is a triumph in these words to which few of us can rise. It is as if Paul had said: The worst things that happen to me are the best; everything that seems most hostile is most friendly. Let the transient sorrows come; let them come thick, without intermission; they are compelled into the service of the Eternal Love—they are working *for* me while they seem to work *against* me—wasting my mortal strength, increasing my heavenly vigour; desolating my brief earthly life, adding to the power and fulness of my eternal life in God—working for me "more and more exceedingly an eternal weight of glory."

He is living already among eternal things. His higher life is growing in strength as his lower life is failing. He is conscious that his true home is in a fairer and diviner world than this. He is longing for the time when his earthly limitations will fall away, and he will be translated completely into the native land of the sons of God. He has a passionate desire for final emancipation, whether by death and resurrection, or, better still, by that sudden entrance into eternal glory which he is expecting for those who live till the hour of Christ's appearing. But he belongs already to the eternal order. *That* is his true home.

And he has discovered that it is the true home of all men. For Christ, the Head of the race, who had become flesh and who had lived the earthly life, had not only died—He had risen from the dead, had passed away from this visible world, and with His human nature enlarged, transfigured, glorified, had ascended to a higher region of life. "One died for all, therefore all died;" according to God's thought and purpose the whole race, when Christ died, ceased to belong to this world, and we, entering into the thought of God, "henceforth know no man after the flesh."

In death all earthly distinctions disappear; the rich man is rich no longer, and the poor man is poor no longer; the unfortunate are no longer oppressed by their earthly troubles, and the successful are no longer happy in their earthly prosperity; the authority of the master comes to an end, and the bondage of the slave. And for me, says Paul, all men died in Christ. I see them environed by the invisible and eternal order to which they now really belong. I, for my part, henceforth know no man after the flesh. How that affects our missionary work will become apparent before I close.

But now there is another and still more important revelation of the secret of Paul's life and power: "Even though we *have* known Christ after the flesh, yet now we know Him so no more."

There were Christian people then living who had

known the Lord Jesus Christ in Nazareth, in Capernaum, in Jerusalem; and this was surely a great distinction and a great blessedness. But the very distinction, the very blessedness, may have been a peril to them. I can imagine them making a great deal too much of it, and assuming a certain superiority over their Christian brethren. I can imagine them saying, "We remember how the Lord Jesus Christ looked; we remember the tones of His voice; we remember when He came to the village in which we used to live; we saw Him work miracles there; we were in the crowd and shouted "Hosanna" when He entered Jerusalem in triumph; we often heard Him teach in the Temple; we did not receive the Christian Gospel from Paul or Apollos or Peter, but from the Lord Jesus Christ Himself." And I can also imagine that many other Christian people in apostolic times, when the memory of our Lord's earthly history was so fresh, would feel an absorbing and exclusive interest in all that they could learn about Christ as a man among men, and would come to think of Him always under the common conditions of human life and in the place which He filled for a time in the visible, natural order of the world.

There are some of us, Paul seems to say, who have known Christ after the flesh; but now, if we have really passed into the eternal kingdom, we know Him in quite another way. What does it matter that we remember His face, His voice, His manner, His dress? To us He is not, first of all, a fellow-countryman, a fellow-townsman, a man who lived in the next street, whom we used to see in the synagogue on the Sabbath, and whose brothers and sisters and friends we knew; or a wonderful religious teacher who in our presence said many wonderful things and did many wonderful works; He is the Eternal Son of God; Brother of all men. His earthly life has passed into a larger, mightier, and more glorious life. It may be a source of joy to some of us to remember that we were in the crowd on the mountain side when He delivered His great discourse on the blessings which men were to find in His kingdom and on the laws of the perfect life; or that we sat on the green grass when He multiplied the loaves and the fishes; but *now*, when we and other Christian men gather together in His name, we meet Him, not in the weakness of His flesh, but in the power of His eternal glory. Paul's Gospel began where the gospel of those who knew Christ after the flesh ended; it began with the sufferings and death of Christ. " I delivered unto you *among the first things* that Christ died for our sins according to the Scriptures; and that He was buried; and that He hath been raised the third day according to the Scriptures." All that went before, Paul passed over very lightly. These were the critical events in Christ's history;— He died for the sins of men; He rose again; and as the Head of the human race—and, according to the thought and purpose of God, carrying the race with Him—passed into that eternal kingdom to which the race was destined from the beginning, and in which alone the life of man, which is akin to the life of God can reach the height of its power, its greatness, its perfection, and its joy.

II.

To Paul, then, Christ was infinitely more than an august and pathetic tradition. Christ must be infinitely more than an august and pathetic tradition to us if we are to preach the Christian Gospel with any effect either to our countrymen at home or to the heathen. We shall miss the substance of our message if we know Christ after the flesh, and have nothing more to tell men than the story of His earthly life and ministry. From the materials given to us in His teaching and in His personal history we may construct a beautiful system of ethics and a noble conception of God, but we shall still miss a great part—and the most animating and effective part—of the Gospel of Christ. The Christian religion is for several reasons very properly described as an historical religion. It is founded on the history of Jesus of Nazareth, in whom the Eternal Word—the Son of God—became flesh and revealed the very life and glory of the Father. But the history on which our faith rests did not come to an end eighteen hundred years ago when Jesus of Nazareth was crucified; nor even when He rose from the dead; nor even when He ascended to the Father. "Even though we *have* known Christ after the flesh, yet now we know Him so no more." Through sixty generations men of every tongue and of every land and of every Church have discovered for themselves that He is living still. Penitents have received absolution from His lips. At His word an evil passion has sometimes withered to its roots; at the touch of His hand evil habits have sometimes fallen away from men as the fetters fell away from Peter at the touch of the angel. More commonly He has given to those who have trusted Him strength to struggle with their baser life and to subdue it—strength to achieve by vigilance and self-discipline a righteousness which they knew was impossible to them apart from Him. He has given them peace in times of great trouble, courage in the presence of great dangers; and they knew that the peace and courage came from Him. In prisons and solitary places they were not alone, for He was with them. In Christ—not in the remembrance of Christ—but in the living, personal Christ, a great multitude that no man can number have found God. Those who deny His supernatural power have only begun their task when they have stated the case against the miracles which are recorded in the narratives of His earthly life. They have to descend through the Christian centuries and to destroy the trustworthiness of the long succession of penitents and saints who have testified, on their own knowledge, that He was living still, and that His compassions failed not, and that His power was unspent. For the life of every Christian man adds to the great story of Christ new miracles of mercy and of power. The canon is not closed. Every age contributes materials for new

Gospels. Four brief narratives contain the record of Christ's earthly ministry, and they are incomplete, for "many other signs did Jesus in the presence of His disciples," and many other discourses were spoken by Him of which the evangelists have said nothing; but if the history were to be told of the greater miracles of grace which He has wrought since He ascended to the throne of God, " I suppose that even the world itself would not contain the books that should be written."

And we miss, I repeat, a large part of the substance of the Gospel which we have to deliver to all men if we tell them nothing more than the story of His earthly ministry. We have not to give men merely a system of ethics constructed from the teaching of Christ and from the example of His perfect life; we have to tell them that Christ lives, that He is the King of the human race, and that to submit to His personal authority is the first and supreme duty of every man and the condition of all perfection. We have not merely to teach men a great system of theological truth founded on the earthly manifestation of God in Christ and on all that Christ taught concerning the Father; we have to tell them that Christ lives, and that they are to find the living God in Him. We have not to teach men a mere method of salvation revealed by Christ eighteen centuries ago —a method by which, if they understand it and use it, they can save themselves; the Christian method of salvation is the method by which Christ Himself saves men; and we have to tell them that Christ is alive—that from His own lips they are to receive the pardon of sin, and that from His own volition they are to receive the gift of eternal life. With a dead Christ—a Christ belonging to a remote age of human history, and not able and eager to save men now—the Christian method of salvation would be worthless. It all depends on Him.

I say that we shall miss a great part of the substance of our message if we know Christ only after the flesh. And, therefore, we shall be wanting in a necessary qualification for delivering our message unless we are able to say, with Paul—"even though we have known Christ after the flesh, yet now we know Him so no more." To have seen the Lord after He had risen from the dead was one of the qualifications for the apostleship; and the Apostles were not merely witnesses who could declare on their own knowledge that Christ had died and had risen again, as the friends of Lazarus at Bethany could declare on their own knowledge that Lazarus had died and risen again; for the testimony of the apostles concerning Christ contained an element which was not present in the testimony of the friends of Lazarus. When Lazarus came out of the grave, he took his place once more in the visible and natural order of the world. When Christ rose, he passed into new and higher regions of life. The friends of Lazarus could say that the dead man lived again and had come back to the common paths in which he had walked before;

they knew him once more "after the flesh." The
Apostles said that Christ lived again, but that He
lived after another manner; that He lived again, but
under conditions which were wholly new, and which
surrounded Him with mystery. He was the same,
yet different. They had known Him after the flesh;
now they knew Him so no more. His appearances
during the forty days after the Resurrection had this,
among other purposes—to bring home to them the
immense change through which He had passed, and
to discipline their faith in the reality of His presence
in the invisible and eternal order. He became visible
at unexpected times and in unexpected places, and
they learnt that He was always near; near when no
visible appearance assured the senses of His nearness.
They saw that the limitations of His human life had
been dissolved, and they were gradually prepared to
receive His own wonderful words—"All authority
hath been given unto Me in heaven and on earth."
Not until they had this new knowledge of Christ in
His glory could they be sent to make disciples of all
nations.

III.

It may be well for us to consider whether we have
that kind of knowledge of Christ which is necessary
both for our work at home and for our missions to
the heathen. Do we think it enough to know Christ
after the flesh?

During the last thirty or forty years there has been

a remarkable re-awakening of interest in the earthly history of our Lord and in all the investigations which contribute to illustrate the conditions of His human life and His relations to the people about Him. Partly as the result of increased facilities for Eastern travel, and partly as the result of the patient and laborious studies of a succession of scholars, we are able, I suppose, to form a more accurate and a more vivid conception of what manner of life our Lord lived than has been possible to the Church since the end or perhaps even the middle of the second century. M. Renan was the first to make use of these materials in a popular form. The charm of his style—though perhaps there was less of grace and fascination in the style of his " Vie de Jesus " than in that of his earlier works—and the freshness of his conception of the unique and wonderful history, achieved for his book immense success. It went over all Europe. Then came a succession of Lives of Christ in English, some of which have been extraordinarily attractive. There are tens of thousands of persons who had been reading the four Gospels from their childhood who feel as if they had come to know Jesus of Nazareth for the first time. He no longer floats in the air, detached from the common world. They have been able to *place* Him—to place Him in His true relations to His age and to His country. The whole story has become real and solid to them. It is almost as if they had been with the shepherds when the angels appeared and announced His birth, and as if they had gone to

Bethlehem and found Joseph and Mary in the stable with the Babe lying in the manger; as if they had lived with Him when He was a young man, and had walked with Him over the limestone hills which lie round Nazareth; and as if they had seen Him in Jerusalem teaching in the courts of the Temple. They know how He was dressed, and in what kind of a house He lived. They know His friends; they can re-construct the life of Peter and John and the rest of the apostles before they became our Lord's disciples—and afterwards. The Pharisees and Sadducees and Herodians are as well known to them as the political and religious parties of our own time. They know the kind of impression which our Lord made on different descriptions of people; on His fellow-townsmen; on the people of Galilee; on the Samaritans; on the crowds that filled Jerusalem during the great feasts; on religious men, on men that were not religious; on rich men, and on fishermen, carpenters, peasants. They see how His teaching was affected by the varying relations in which He stood to the faith and life of His contemporaries, and this gives definiteness and freshness to many familiar words. They know Him almost as well as the men and women knew Him who actually saw His miracles and actually heard His parables. Yes, they know Him—as these men and women knew Him—" after the flesh"; know Him in His place in the earthly order.

There is a real value in knowledge of this kind;

but if our strongest and most effective conception of Him is a mere historical conception—if we think of Him most vividly and most frequently in the place that He held in the visible order of the world—then we know Christ after the flesh, and our knowledge is rudimentary and imperfect.

Pass on—see Him descend into the mystery of death ; wait and watch for His emergence from the abysses of darkness ; join in the songs with which the Church hails His resurrection ; see Him ascending to the throne of God. Rejoice that He belongs not merely to the distant past, but that He is the contemporary of all generations. Rejoice that He is *here*, not under the limitations of His earthly life—as when He was in the house of Mary and Martha at Bethany—as when He was in the boat on the Lake of Galilee—as when He was in the upper room at Jerusalem ; but in the glorious fulness of Divine power ; here, and yet controlling the winds and the storms, and guiding the stars in their courses ; here, and yet maintaining the majestic order of all created things ; here, and yet surrounded with the splendours of God's eternal kingdom.

It was one of the immeasurable evils which the Roman Catholic Church inflicted on Christendom, that it held constantly before the eyes of the Church the exhausted, suffering, agonized form of Christ on the Cross—fastened the thought and imagination of Christian men on the extremity of His mortal weakness—and so deprived them of the animation and the courage inspired by the knowledge that He is now on the throne of the Eternal. A similar loss may be inflicted on ourselves if our thoughts are imprisoned within the limits of the earthly life of Christ, and if we do not exult in His resurrection and in His constant presence in the Church. The historic Christ is the Object of Memory; the present, the living Christ is the Object of Faith, the Source of Power, the Inspiration of Love, the Author of Salvation.

Are we, then, to forget His earthly history? Is that gracious, pathetic, entrancing vision to be lost and forgotten in the mists and clouds which gather swiftly and silently over the past? Ah, no! To us who see the Divine heights from which Christ descended when He became man, who see the Divine heights on which He now reigns—who know that even in His temptations and sorrows and death He did not cease to be the Eternal Son of the Father— all the incidents of His earthly history have a new and wonderful pathos and power. We know Him even during His earthly life not as His contemporaries knew Him—but with a larger and deeper knowledge. That poverty, that homelessness, that physical exhaustion, that agony—behind them all we see the Divine glory. His relations to His disciples, to His friends, to His enemies, to Pilate, Caiaphas, Judas— all these are present to us; but they are included in wider, more enduring, more essential relations—His relations to all men, His relations to the universe, His relations to the Eternal Father. For us the Transfiguration does not last for a brief hour merely; it begins with His birth; it extends to His burial; in Christ—even during His earthly years—we look not at the things which are seen and temporal, but at the things which are unseen and eternal. "Even though we have known Christ after the flesh, yet now we know Him so no more." We know Him for ourselves in His present and eternal glory.

There are times when, if the story of the historic Christ is to command confidence in its trustworthiness, it must be sustained by the testimony of living men who have been delivered by the living Christ from the consciousness of guilt, from evil passions and evil habits, and from eternal death. Indeed, according to the ordinary methods of the Divine mercy and power, it is this personal testimony that moves the hearts of men to repent, and inspires them with faith.

I appeal to the traditions and early triumphs of the great religious society which is represented in this congregation. The leaders of Methodism in the last century taught that something more was possible to a Christian man than a faltering hope that his sins were forgiven; they taught that he should never rest until he knew for himself that Christ had delivered him from this present evil world, and had translated him into the kingdom of God. The early Methodists received their teaching—believed that, as a rule, what they called "full assurance" was obtainable, and that it would contribute greatly to the energy and perfection as well as to the joy of their Christian life. They prayed for it earnestly and persistently; they prayed for it till they had it. And so there rose up a great army of preachers—many of them rough and unlearned men—men who knew very little else, but who knew enough to be *witnesses*—they knew their facts; and they were hot and eager to bear testimony to the power and grace of the living Christ. And it was not the preachers only that bore testimony. In your class-meetings, in your love-feasts, in your band-meetings, every man, every woman that had found God through Christ was sure of it, and was also hot and eager to bear testimony to the glory from the upper heavens which had fallen on the most cheerless and most desolate paths of human life. And not only in religious meetings, but everywhere, was the testimony borne. Brother spoke to brother, sister to sister, parent to child, friend to friend. A divine fire was kindled, and the fire spread; soon a great part of England, then of Wales and Scotland, then of America was aflame. It was an age in which the fortunes of the Christian Faith seemed desperate. Cool, speculative, learned men believed that they had wholly discredited the testimony of the four Evangelists to the power and glory of Christ; but instead of the four, here were hundreds of fresh witnesses to deal with—original witnesses; and the hundreds grew to thousands, and the thousands to tens of thousands; and Faith, which seemed beaten to the ground, rose exulting and won most splendid victories.

Even in this country, where it is possible for cultivated men to travel back along the lines of the Christian historic tradition until they reach the first Christian age, and by careful research to qualify themselves to form their own judgment on the trustworthiness of the original Christian records, it is the testimony of those who, in the most literal sense of the words, never knew Christ after the flesh, but who know Him after a diviner manner, that commonly secures belief in the Christian Gospel. In heathen nations, which stand out of the line of the Christian tradition, are unfamiliar with Christian literature, and undisciplined to the criticism of its varying value, it is of supreme importance that those who preach Christ should be able to speak of Him on the strength of their own knowledge of His present glory and of His power to redeem mankind. It is not enough that they can tell the story they have read in sacred books of His earthly life, of His death and His resurrection; to command faith, they must be original witnesses. They must know Christ for themselves as the Lord and Saviour of the human race. And the missionaries of the Church in heathen countries will not have this knowledge unless it is the common possession of the Church at home. To discharge our trust, we must be able to say, " Even though we have known Christ after the flesh, yet now we know Him so no more."

IV.

Nor is it enough that we cease to know *Christ*

after the flesh. The fires of missionary enthusiasm will burn low, and the courage which is necessary for this enterprise will be broken, unless we are also able to say, " We henceforth know no man after the flesh." Paul knew men as masters and slaves, kings and beggars; but he saw the infinite glories and infinite perils which surrounded the narrow area of their earthly life ; and for him the external conditions of men were controlled by their relations to the eternal kingdom. He knew their earthly life, he was touched by its sorrows and rejoiced in its joy. Wealth, poverty, greatness, obscurity, happiness, misery—he saw them all; but for him all these outward conditions were secondary and transient ; they would soon fall away, and the unseen glory or the unseen shame of their true life would be manifested.

We too must see men, not merely in their place in the visible and temporal order, but environed with all that is glorious and all that is terrible in the invisible and eternal order. This man has immense wealth ; but has he risen with Christ and made sure of the everlasting inheritance? If not, how poor! That man is poor, ill-clad, ill-fed, lives a hard and cheerless life ; but is he in Christ? Yes? Then how rich! for he is the heir of God's eternal righteousness and glory. This man is a prince; but has he taken his place in God's eternal kingdom? If not, he has failed to achieve the dignity to which the eternal purpose of God destines even the obscurest of mankind. That man is a slave; but is he one with

Christ? If he is, eternal glories sit already on his brow, and he may stand at last among the principalities and powers of the kingdom of heaven. This man has learning, a keen and vigorous intellect, genius which will give him fame through many generations; but does he know the Eternal? If not, he has missed the knowledge which it supremely concerns him to possess. That man, as men dream, knows nothing; his mind is dull and uninstructed; he has never mastered even the elements of the sciences; the songs of great poets have never kindled his imagination; he has never heard even the names of the great teachers of the race; but does he know Christ? Yes? Then he has been taught of God, and received the illumination of the Holy Ghost, and he has a wisdom transcending all the wisdom of the schools. This man has inherited from an honourable ancestry a gracious temperament; has lived with truthful, upright, gentle, and kindly people; has been disciplined to all the personal and social virtues which command the affection and confidence of mankind. Yes; but he belongs to the eternal order; he has relations to God; is he obedient to the Supreme Will? If not, his virtues are of the earth earthly, and contain no promise of eternal righteousness. That man, with the blood of vicious parents in his veins, was born with a temperament corrupted by their vices; he lived from childhood among men whose language was profane and unclean—coarse, brutal, violent, reckless men; and though now he means to do well, his conscience is imperfectly instructed, he has no delicate sense of honour, and the evil habits of evil days are hard to break. Yes; but he has caught sight of the awful majesty and glorious righteousness and infinite love of God; and with unmeasured abhorrence for all that he knows to be foul and base in his own life he has sought with an agony of earnestness—not only for the pardon of what he has done, and for the pardon of what he has been, and for the pardon of what he is—but for a life nobler than his own, and he has received it. Not yet has the power of the life which he has found in God subdued completely his grosser passions, not yet has it enabled him to achieve perfectly even those common virtues which are natural to men of happier birth and happier conditions; but in the very centre of his being he is loyal to the authority of God, and he has in him the roots of an eternal perfection.

In the presence of ancient heathen civilizations, which would have perished but for the virtues which they have disciplined, we must not suppose that our Gospel is unnecessary. This is the supreme question concerning every man—does he know God? In the absence of that knowledge the ethical traditions which have preserved through centuries the life of the earthly State fail to secure eternal life for the individual citizen. And in the presence of races brutalized and degraded through a long succession of generations, we must not despair, for they are living in a redeemed world; every man is dear to God, and by the power of the Spirit of God may rise to unknown heights of righteousness and glory. We must know no man "after the flesh."

Nor must we know ourselves after the flesh, if we are to have the strength and the fortitude which the great tasks to which we are called demand. Who are we that we should hope to change the religious faith of hundreds of millions of men of different blood from our own, of different manners, speaking other tongues, living under distant skies? What resources have we for so immense a work? We should lose all heart and courage if we measured ourselves against the difficulties, against the impossibilities, of our enterprise. But we are greater than we seem. We are one with Christ, who descended from the heights of God to seek and to save the lost, and who, now that He has returned to His glory, is seeking and saving them still. And it is He that is seeking, He that is saving them, through *us*. His power sustains our weakness, and in our very weakness is perfected. Our pity for the miseries of men, and our eager longing for their redemption are His, not ours. Through our hands it is He who is raising the fallen; through our lips it is He who is speaking words of consolation to the wretched, and words of immortal hope to the despairing. Is Christ, the Eternal Son of God, equal to saving the world for which He died? If He is, let us be of good courage; all things are possible to us, for we are one with Him.

III.

THE CHRISTIAN GOSPEL AND THE SPIRIT OF GOD.[1]

"Concerning which salvation the prophets sought and searched diligently, who prophesied of the grace that should come unto you : Searching what time or what manner of time the Spirit of Christ which was in them did point unto, when it testified beforehand the sufferings of Christ, and the glories that should follow them. To whom it was revealed, that not unto themselves, but unto you, did they minister these things, which now have been announced unto you through them that preached the gospel unto you by the Holy Ghost sent forth from heaven ; which things angels desire to look into."—1 *Pet.* i. 10-12.

THE closing words of the passage which I have just read remind us of the unvarying conditions of success in that great enterprise which should fill our thoughts and our hearts this morning. If through our preaching, men are to become Christian men, we must preach the Gospel to them ; and even this is not enough. We may preach the Gospel clearly and

---

[1] The Annual Sermon preached on behalf of the Baptist Missionary Society, in Bloomsbury Chapel, on Wednesday morning, May 1st, 1889.

earnestly, and heathen men may remain heathen still ; Mahometans may remain Mahometans; and nominal Christians may remain strangers to the power of the Christian redemption. Apart from the presence and power of the Holy Spirit, we shall preach to no purpose.

These truths are among the commonplaces of our faith ; on an occasion like this it would be presumptuous for a person like myself to ask you to adventure into regions of speculation, foreign and unfamiliar to the thought and life of the Church. Here we are sure of our ground. Here we stand where those have stood who in every land have achieved great victories in the name of Christ over the sins and miseries of the human race. Here we, in these last days, are of one mind with the original apostles of the Christian faith, the first leaders of the human race out of the ancient darkness into the light of God. Here, we can claim the sanction of a still more sacred and august authority. For our Lord, after He had risen from the dead, gave to those whom He elected to lay the strong foundations of the Christian Church a double charge: they were to preach the Gospel to all nations, and yet they were not to begin to preach at once. They were to wait in Jerusalem " for the promise of the Father," for they were "to receive power" to fulfil their mission when the Holy Ghost came upon them. We, too, are to preach the Gospel, and we are to preach it in the power of the Holy Ghost.

I.

It was a true instinct which led the Early Church to name the four narratives which contain the story of our Lord's early life—the four Gospels. For in Christ the Word of God became flesh, was translated into a human life, a human character, a human history, and found expression in human deeds and human sufferings. He Himself is the Gospel—the merciful and the mighty Word of the Eternal to the human race, "full of grace and truth." And if in a recent generation devout and earnest Christian men regarded the narratives of the four Evangelists with comparative indifference, as though for the most part they contained no Gospel, or contained it only in a few isolated passages, and if they supposed that even in most of these the Gospel was expressed inadequately and obscurely, this was surely a grave error The error, as we are accustomed to say, rested upon a narrow conception of the infinite variety and wealth of the revelation of God's grace. In the Sermon on the Mount there is a Gospel concerning the ideal perfection which is possible to us through Christ. In the miracles of Christ there is a Gospel which should encourage faith and hope in God, in the presence of the awful mysteries of disease and pain. The tears of Christ—the Son of God, whom to have seen is to have seen the Father—the tears of Christ at the grave of Lazarus are a Gospel of Divine sympathy to every sad company standing round the open grave

and mourning for their dead. The deep affection
of Christ for His nearer earthly friends, His pa
tience with their errors, limitations, and imperfections, His generous confidence in them, His hunger
for their sympathy, are a Gospel for the friends of
Christ in every generation—a Gospel for ourselves;
this is what Christ is to us. And so, if there have
been any who disparaged the narratives of the four
Evangelists, and supposed that the Christian Gospel
was to be found exclusively in the doctrinal contents
of the epistles, or in those parts of the four narratives
in which the doctrinal contents of the epistles are anti-
cipated—this, I repeat, was a grave error, and those
who committed it impoverished the great inheritance
of the Church. It is an error which, if one were disposed to treat it hardly and roughly, and without any
anxiety to be just, might be compared to the impossible folly of a man who should attach greater value
to the writings of Newton and Laplace than to the
solar system, or to the lectures of Sir Roderick
Murchison and Lyell, in which there may be found
an explanation of how the coal measures were
formed, than to the coal measures themselves. For
Christ Himself, whom we find in the Evangelists,
is the Saviour of men, and apostolic doctrine does
but illustrate the nature and method and greatness
of His salvation. In the Gospels we find the facts of
which the epistles are the explanation; and the explanation is incomplete, for the revelation contained
in the facts is inexhaustible.

But if those whom we are accustomed to reproach could speak for themselves, they might have much to say in their own defence, that we should find it difficult to answer. And perhaps they would begin by telling us that they insisted as we do not insist upon certain parts of the four gospels themselves ; that while we dwell on the ethical precepts of our Lord and on His teaching concerning the Father, *they* dwelt on the last hours of His earthly history, to which the Evangelists plainly attributed a greater importance than to all the preceding months and years. They would say, perhaps, that the first three gospels tell the story of our Lord's last sufferings and death with extraordinary fulness and with exceptional minuteness of detail ; but that John, who omitted nearly all that his three predecessors had written, thought it necessary to tell over again the whole story of the last four-and-twenty hours of our Lord's history, though it had been told so fully before.

They might, perhaps, maintain that if they had failed to see as we see the glory of the preceding ministry of Christ, it was because they saw as we do not see "the glory that excelleth," the glory of the supreme manifestation of His love. They might argue that for Christ to die, the Righteous for the unrighteous, was surely a diviner act of grace, and an act fruitful in larger and more enduring blessings for mankind, than to heal the diseases of a few hundreds of His contemporaries, or even to declare in words that can never pass from the memory of mankind the infinite mercy of the Father. Prophets and apostles might receive power to work miracles of pity as great as His own; and in the power of the Holy Spirit they, too, if not with the clearness of vision and with the personal authority of the Son of God, might make known to sinful men that God had not forsaken them, and that His heart was set on recovering them from eternal death. But Christ—and Christ alone—could say that His blood was shed for the remission of sins.

They might also appeal to the example of Paul, who is surely no inconsiderable authority, and who was the first and greatest of Christian missionaries to the heathen. Paul, as Dean Stanley says, "begins the account of his 'Gospel,' not with the birth or infancy of Christ, but with His death." "I delivered to you, *first of all*, that which I also received, how that Christ died for our sins according to the Scriptures." And Peter, in this passage, writing to those who had recently received the Christian Gospel, says that the ancient prophets sought and searched diligently concerning the salvation which was to come to the men of a later age—"searching what time or what manner of time the Spirit of Christ which was in them did point unto, when it testified beforehand the *sufferings* of Christ and the *glories* that should follow them. To whom it was revealed that not unto themselves, but unto you did they minister these things, which now have been announced unto you through them that preached the Gospel unto you, through the Holy Ghost sent forth from heaven." Prophets had seen clearly that a great salvation was to come to men through sufferings, and through the glories that were to follow the sufferings; and now the things which had been seen afar off by devout men illuminated by the Spirit of Christ, were announced by those that preached the Gospel in the power of the same Spirit. The "sufferings" and the "glories" appear to be the principal substance of the Christian Gospel.

It is true, indeed, that the Incarnation itself is a Gospel, and a Gospel of infinite power and glory. I suppose that the eternal Son of God would have become man if man had never sinned, and had needed no redemption; a theologian, therefore, who is constructing a theory of the ideal relations between God and the human race—I might say between God and the universe—will begin with the Incarnation; and the sufferings and death of Christ will appear in such a theory to be among those incidents of the Incarnation which have resulted from the actual moral condition of mankind. But the Christian Gospel is not a theory of God's ideal relations either to the universe or to the human race, though it discloses the foundations on which such a theory may be constructed. It finds man where he is. It is not a philosophy, but a Divine appeal to man in his guilt, weakness, and misery. And, therefore, as I have said, Paul's Gospel began with the sufferings and death of Christ; and Peter found the very substance of the

Gospel in the declaration of the sufferings of Christ and the glories which followed them. Whether we are preaching the Christian Gospel in foreign lands, or to our own countrymen who have not yet received it, we shall do well to be faithful to the apostolic tradition. We should tell them that Christ died for all men, and died for the sins of all men; and that His sufferings and death are the ground of the actual relations between all men and God.

We are born—not into a lost world—but into a world that has been redeemed by the death of the Son of man, who is also the Son of God. We are not under Law, but under Grace. The theology which teaches that men are in peril of eternal death because they have not perfectly obeyed the eternal law of righteousness is a theology which in its initial thesis ignores the Christian redemption, however loyally it may endeavour to acknowledge that redemption afterwards. It is not true that men are in danger of eternal condemnation because they have committed sin; Christ, apart from their choice, is the propitiation for their sin; and they are elect in Christ to eternal righteousness and glory; it is for them, in the power of God's grace, to make their calling and election sure. This is our message to heathen men—not that they are living in a lost world, and that till we came to them God's infinite mercy had left them to drift, unpitied and uncared for, into eternal darkness and death,—but that in His infinite love the Son of God has died for them, and that they were born, though they knew it not, to glory, honour, and immortality; that the fault was ours that they did not know it before. This is a Gospel worth telling men. It is a veritable Gospel—good news from Heaven to earth: *news*—for never in the loftiest reach of thought had man caught any glimpse of the transcendent glory. Listening to it, the hearts of men are filled with an infinite hope. The past, with its sins, has gone; there is a new force and a constraining motive rendering a diviner life possible. "One died for all, therefore all died; and He died for all, that they who live should no longer live for themselves, but unto Him who for their sakes died and rose again."

II.

But the Gospel includes the "glories" which were to follow the "sufferings"—the return of the Son of God who had become Son of man, and who for ever remains Son of man, to the heights from which He descended to save us; the expansion of all the powers of His human nature and the enlargement of all its capacities for wisdom and blessedness; the ascent of humanity in Him to other regions and conditions of life—an ascent in which all are to have part that consent to receive eternal redemption through Him; the revelation of the true dignity and greatness of human nature, of which in this world there are the faintest and obscurest premonitions; the revelation of the Divine idea of human perfection. But these splendours, if we suffered them to take possession of our thought this morning, would exhaust our time and strength ; and we should leave unconsidered the glory which lies nearest to the missions of the Church.

Christ died for men—for all men. Christ is now the Lord of men—of all men. It was apart from any consent of ours that God laid on Him the iniquity of us all. No consent of ours is necessary to give Him authority over us all. The authority was given to Him by the Father—" all authority . . . in heaven and on earth." It does not lie within a man's choice whether he will live under a law austerely just, which condemns men to death for every transgression, or under a Divine Prince who has died for the sins of His subjects. Christ reigns, not by popular election, but by Divine right. And so we do not send missionaries to found the kingdom of God in heathen lands, but to tell heathen men that God Himself has already founded it, and that, according to His thought and purpose, they all belong to it.

Our Gospel, therefore, is something more than the history of the appearance of the Son of God among men in a remote age ; something more than the recitation and exposition of His teaching ; something more than the repetition of the story of His miracles of pity ; something more, even, than an account of His sufferings and death for the sins of the human race. We tell men that He is living still—the very Christ that was born at Bethlehem, that walked through the cornfields of Samaria and Galilee, healed the sick, forgave the sinful, died on the cross ; that they need not look back with inconsolable regret upon those distant years, or wish that they had seen His gracious form and listened to His gracious voice, and been able to appeal to His mercy and His power; for He is living still, and His power is unspent—it is immeasurably augmented; His compassions fail not, His mercy endureth for ever. When He was here men knew Him in the weakness of the flesh; now they may know Him in the power of God. Then, He appeared in the form of a servant, and He lived among the people of one inconsiderable country; now He is King of men in all lands.

And if they ask us—as they have sometimes asked us—why God permitted generation after generation of their fathers to live and die without the knowledge of this great salvation, we must confess with sorrow and shame that God had charged *us* and *our* fathers to make the salvation known to them; that in the generosity of His trust in us He had called us to share with Himself the blessedness and glory of filling the whole world with the light of the Christian Gospel; but that we and our fathers had betrayed His confidence. But we must tell them, too, that the infinite mercy was not to be wholly baffled and defeated by our unfaithfulness.

It was an evil thing that whole generations should have been born and should have passed away without knowing that the Son of the Eternal had died for them, and that He was their Saviour and Lord; but for their sins, too, though they knew it not, Christ died ; they, too, though they knew it not, were born under the authority and shelter of His kingdom. The condemnation for their want of faith in Him rests, not upon them, but upon us, and upon all those who in past ages have not cared for the nations living and dying in the great darkness. But even in that darkness there was light, and the light came from Him who lighteth every man. *We* had forgotten them—Christ had not. The light was dim : it had to struggle through dense clouds stretching from horizon to horizon, with hardly a rift through which a glimpse could be caught of distant stars ; but for those in every land who love the light, and come to it, there is infinite hope ; for Christ died for all men —heathen, Mahometan, and Christian—and He is the Propitiation for the sins of the whole world. "This is the condemnation," not that men lived in darkness and died in darkness, but that when the light reached them, however dim the light may have been, they " loved the darkness rather than the light, for their works were evil." It may be—who can tell ? —that among these successive generations on whom the awful gloom has rested, there were many by whom the light which reached them was received with joy, and with deep affection. It is not safe to infer from their outward conformity to the traditions and manners of their countrymen that they had not discovered the rude elements of a diviner faith, and endeavoured to obey a diviner rule of life. Among ourselves outward conformity to nobler traditions is no sure evidence that a man is really living in God. He may inwardly resent the restraints of Christian morality while he submits to them; and while hotly zealous for the form of sound words which is accepted by his Church and his party, and which he has inherited from his fathers, the great truths of a lofty creed may for him be corrupted and degraded into the worst falsehoods by the power of an evil heart. And, on the other hand, it may be—God only knows—but it may be that there have been some, it may be that there have been many, for whom the coarsest and the most brutal forms of faith have been touched by light from the upper heavens; some, perhaps many, who have loved and practised gracious and gentle virtues, which the temper of their countrymen permitted, though it did not encourage. When God's lost children, for whom Christ died, are feeling after their Father in the darkness, if haply they may find Him, He knows it; and, for my part, I believe that, while they are yet "afar off," He will run to meet them, and will bring them safely home. But these are speculations. Our duty is clear. It is for us who have the larger knowledge to make it the common and actual possession of all nations. We are faithless to God and cruel to men if the duty is neglected.

III.

The methods by which a living Church will endeavour to discharge this duty must vary from age to age. In the same age they will be different in different countries and among different classes of people in the same country. If we are wise, we shall not disregard tradition, for tradition is the growth of the actual experience of a past time ; and yet we shall not be enslaved by it, for a new experience may correct the results of the old. We shall review and criticize our work in the light of principles and laws suggested by the substance of the Gospel itself and by the life of man ; but we shall not hastily assume that those of us who have only a distant and superficial knowledge of the conditions of life in other countries are the best able to determine how these principles and laws are to be most effectively applied. We should attach great and almost decisive authority to the general conclusions which have been reached by devout, able and earnest men who have had long experience of missionary work, and should hesitate to reject their judgment even when they insist on forms of work which achieve no apparent and immediate success. We should rejoice in spontaneity and welcome variety. We should regard uniformity with distrust. Those kinds of work which "seem to be feeble" may also " be necessary."

And in all discussions of methods we should remember first of all that the methods in which we preach the Gospel are of secondary importance compared with the power in which we preach it. Methods the wisest and most admirable will not secure success unless we preach the Gospel " in the

Holy Ghost sent forth from heaven." For we fail, unless the men to whom we preach discover for themselves that Christ is the Son of God and the Saviour of the human race; and this discovery is not an inference—more or less certain—drawn from considerations addressed to the logical understanding; it is an intuition; and if the discovery is to be made through listening to our words, we ourselves must have a clear vision of Christ, and an immediate personal knowledge of the greatness of His redemption. Such a vision and such a knowledge are possible to us only through the Holy Ghost. If He dwells in us we are not in the flesh but in the spirit; and we can speak, at first hand, of things invisible, eternal, and divine.

That is one of the great Christian commonplaces which we all believe, but the transcendent importance of which, both in relation to thought and work, we are in danger of forgetting. For example, it is sometimes assumed by those who are hostile to what is described as the extreme Protestant position, that our faith in Christ rests on an antecedent faith in the infallibility of the Holy Scriptures; and some of us do not appear to resent the assumption. But when a missionary connected with any of those Evangelical Churches in which the Protestant spirit and the Protestant traditions are most energetic—with your own Churches, for instance—begins to preach to heathen men, does he imagine that his first duty is to demonstrate the genuineness and authenticity of the several books of the Old Testament and the New, and the infallibility of the whole collection? Can he do nothing until he has laid this foundation? Must he arm himself with the erudition of a long line of Christian scholars? Must he attempt, among the people of New Guinea, or even among the people of India and China, a course of criticism and apologetics? To races—civilized or uncivilized—which stand out of the line of the historic and literary traditions of Christendom, must he quote a succession of authors whose names they never heard, of whose trustworthiness they cannot judge, whose testimonies they can submit to no critical examination, in order to prove that the sacred books were written by the men to whom they are attributed? And must he then demonstrate that these men were inspired of God? Can he say nothing of the authority of Christ until he has vindicated the authority of Moses? Or —if that seems to press the theory too far—must he be silent concerning the love of God, the death and resurrection of our Lord, the remission of sins, the gift of eternal life, until he has proved the infallibility of the four Gospels and the Divine commission of the Apostle Paul?

We know that it is not in this manner that the Christian missionary attempts to inspire heathen men with faith in Christ. The love of God—God's love for him and for all men—has been shed abroad in his own heart through the Holy Ghost; and he speaks of that love on the strength of his own knowledge. For himself Christ is the Way to the Father; and he tells men on the strength of his own experience that through Christ they too may find God. He has been oppressed by a sense of guilt, and a terrible darkness has descended on him ; he has confessed his sins to God, has asked for the remission of sins through Christ, and the heavy burden has fallen away from him and the light of God has shone round him ; and he tells men that if they confess their sins and ask for remission through Christ, they may be sure that the same blessedness will be theirs. There are wonderful hours in which he is conscious of the nearer presence of Christ ; and even when the splendours have passed away, the power of Christ is still with him to give vigour and constancy to righteousness. He has his own story to tell of miracles of mercy which Christ has wrought, and of Mounts of Transfiguration on which Christ has been glorified. Men listen, and they feel that his words have an accent of truth and reality ; that he speaks as a man who has seen and known these wonderful things. It is when we in England speak thus that the hearts of those who hear us are moved, that they become dimly conscious that they, also, were created to find their life and blessedness in the Eternal ; and then through the power of the Spirit of God the light breaks upon them ; they see for themselves that they may find God in Christ, and they trust in Christ for eternal salvation.

But if we are to speak thus we must be filled with the Spirit. This, I say, is the ultimate secret of our power in England, and in other nations which inherit the Christian traditions, as well as among heathen races. Christian scholars and apologists have an honourable—a necessary—function, but a living faith is generated among the masses of mankind by men whose preaching derives force from their immediate knowledge of Christ. It is this which, under God, gives a power that sometimes seems almost irresistible, to the words of a great evangelist. His earnestness counts for something; but earnestness often fails. The strength of his conviction counts for something; but strength of conviction often leaves other men unconvinced. What tells most is neither his earnestness nor his perfect certainty of the truth of the Christian Gospel, but the fact—apparent to those who listen to him—that his certainty rests on his own direct and personal knowledge of those eternal realities of which he is speaking. And when a revival has once begun it is the converts that have the larger share in converting the unconverted. Every man that breaks away from his old irreligious life and begins to live for God, brings home to other men the reality of God's authority—the authority has been actually revealed to him; and the power and the glory of the redemption achieved by Christ—for he has been actually redeemed.

"The Church of the living God" is "the pillar and ground"—or stay—"of the truth"; not the infallibility of the Church, but its life and experience. It was the faith of the past generation which, under

God, created the faith of the present; and the faith of the present generation must, under God, create the faith of the next. And when, after we have found Christ, cruel storms of doubt are beating upon us, and our intellectual heaven is darkened, and our perception of the august realities of the divine and eternal order becomes uncertain, and we begin to wonder whether, after all, the kingdom of God, into which we thought we had passed, may not be an illusion, we find relief in listening to the testimony of those whom the storms have never visited, or have left in peace. We learn from them that the eternal glories are not extinguished, but that for a time our own powers of vision have been enfeebled; for they can still see the sun shining in his strength, and for them the earth and the heavens are bright with his glory.

Nor is it from our contemporaries alone that our faith may receive support. The revelation of God in Christ, in its substance and power, has been subjected to every practical test, under an infinite variety of conditions. It has been verified in the life of countless millions of men, belonging to different races, living in different lands, speaking different tongues; of every variety of temperament and every variety of intellectual cultivation and power; men of every social condition, living under different forms of government, disciplined by different forms of civilization. They received the Christian Gospel from tradition; but they became, in turn, original witnesses to the redemption which was achieved for men by the sufferings of Christ and to the glories which have followed.

IV.

For the solution of our doubts we have not to make a tremendous leap over the gulf of eighteen hundred years which separates us from the earthly ministry of Christ, and to discover whether the evidence that they had received a message from God to which the Apostles were able to appeal in their own time was adequate and final; the evidence extends over all the intervening centuries. We need regard with no anxiety or alarm the investigations of criticism, nor suppose that the fortunes of the Christian faith depend upon the dates and authorship of sacred books: there are limits to the ultimate modification of the traditional opinion on these questions; and no possible results of Biblical criticism can shake the foundations of that Eternal City, of which we may say with greater confidence in our own time than in any preceding age, that its Builder and Maker is God.

We are craven-hearted if we have any fear of the criticism which is re-investigating questions which former generations had supposed to be settled concerning the early records of our faith. We shall be false to truth and to Christ if we endeavour to limit the freedom of that criticism. But shall I cease to believe that Christ is the Son of God, Creator of the heavens and the earth, the Propitiation for the sins of the world, Lord and Saviour of the human race—shall I hold my belief in suspense—till these critical questions are finally determined by the universal consent of scholars? God forbid. I am grateful to the critics who are endeavouring to assist me to determine the authorship of some of these ancient books, and the precise dates at which they were written; but I know already that they contain a revelation from God. The astronomer may correct my errors as to the precise minute and the precise point in the heavens at which the sun rose this morning; he may show that I am several minutes and several degrees wrong; but I do not ask him to tell me whether the sun rose at all. I know it. I see his glory. Nor is this a personal illusion; what I see others see. Their vision corroborates my own. It was the Puritan theory—and it is mine—that the Scriptures shine in their own light, and that those who have received the Spirit of God find God for themselves in the writings of apostles and prophets. The books derive their chief authority, not from any external source, but from their own contents; and if I want any confirmation of my faith, I appeal to sixty generations of saints, who, in the power of what these books contain, have lived in the very life of God.

The permanence of the Christian faith in Christian lands is secured, under God, by that immediate knowledge of Christ and that personal experience of the reality of the Christian redemption which are given to Christian men by the power and grace of the

Holy Ghost. This same knowledge and this same experience are plainly indispensable to the success of Christian missions in lands which are not Christian. Missionaries who are to speak with any effect to heathen men and to Mahometans must know for themselves the truth of the Christian Gospel. This personal and immediate knowledge is, indeed, more apparently, though not more really, necessary to the Christian missionary in heathen lands than to the Christian minister in our own country. *Our* words derive a certain measure of support from tradition; they receive a certain measure of corroboration from the faith and life of Christian Churches. The missionary, for a time at least, stands alone. He is powerless unless he has a clear vision of Christ and a vivid experience of the reality and blessedness of his restoration to God. He should be full of the Holy Ghost.

V.

But even with this vision and this experience, a man may not be an effective preacher of the Gospel. His testimony, resting on personal knowledge of the grace and glory of Christ, will have a certain force; but he may not have that special form of power which, under God, reaches the heart of the impenitent, creates a deep longing for God, inspires fear and hope, and, at last, perfect faith in Christ as the Saviour of men. A man may be a great saint and yet not have this power; his life may be lived on spiritual heights which enable him to apprehend the truths which are necessary to discipline the strength and to perfect the joy of the Church; but he may have forgotten, or may never have learnt, the secret of speaking with effect to those who do not know God. It is not every man who, like Paul, can become, in more senses than one, all things to all men, can speak wisdom among them that are perfect, and draw crowds of heathen men, guilty of the grossest vices, to the feet of Christ. A man may be intensely earnest, not only in his own religious life, but in his desire to seek and to save the lost, and yet may not have this power. It is not a natural gift—an earnest Christian man may have a genius for eloquence, and have no power to preach the Gospel. It is not to be acquired by discipline, though I suppose that where it exists discipline may add to its effectiveness. It is a gift of the Holy Ghost. The gift is sometimes —perhaps most frequently—conferred upon men who possess the corresponding natural faculty; the man who preaches the Gospel in the power of the Holy Ghost often speaks persuasively and impressively on whatever else interests him. But sometimes it is conferred on men who when they speak on any other subject are obscure, confused, wearisome, and ineffective. It is conferred upon men who have large intellectual powers, and who are enriched with various learning; it is also conferred upon men whose intellectual powers are very limited, and whose only learning is that which they have received from the teaching of the Spirit of God. It assumes many forms. Some men who have received the gift speak with passion; others speak calmly. Some appeal to conscience and the higher reason; some to the emotions. Some speak with a terrible severity; they pour out, as if in streams of burning lava, fierce denunciations of sin. They grip men with an iron hand, and drag them in terror as convicted criminals to the feet of God, to receive pardon and to be delivered from eternal death. Others speak with a winning graciousness, and lead God's lost children home by ways of pleasantness and paths of peace. The gift enables one man to work in one way, and another in another way. One man who has received it speaks to great crowds, and hundreds discover in an hour their sore need of God; another is powerless in the presence of a crowd, but speaks to men one by one with an irresistible charm and persuasiveness. Sometimes the gift is conferred after long and painful search and in answer to earnest prayer; sometimes it comes to men who have never asked for it. But even when it comes to a man who has never sought it for himself, it may, perhaps, come in answer to the intercessions of those who have sought it for him, and then the honour and joy of his work are theirs as much as his.

VI.

These, as I have said, are the commonplaces of the Christian faith; but I wonder whether with all of us they have passed into life. There is a kind of atheism of which Churches are in peril. Those Churches are in peril of it, as we think, which attribute sacerdotal prerogatives to the ministry and supernatural efficacy to sacraments. God may be forgotten because the priest and the sacrament are charged with grace. But we ourselves are in peril of it. For we may have such confidence in the Gospel as to forget that even the Gospel can never reveal the fulness of its power unless it is preached in the Holy Ghost, and unless to those who hear it it is revealed by the Holy Ghost. It is a great and wonderful force—this Gospel of the righteousness and love of God, this Gospel of salvation, this Gospel of eternal life; and we are in danger of coming to think that we have only to use it with earnestness in order to achieve the regeneration of mankind. We kindle as we think of the truths which we have to preach; the glory of them fills our imagination; we glow with passion; we think that with such a Gospel to make known to men it will be impossible for them to resist us. We know the miracles which it has wrought in other ages and in our own. We think that it will have the same power on our lips that it had on the lips of other men. And we have suffered —some of us—miserable disappointment and cruel defeat. *Cruel* defeat?—ah no! kindly defeat. For we had forgotten God in the power and glory of His truth, as other men forget Him in the power and glory of His material works. We, too, were drifting into atheism ; and but for our failures might have been swept into the dark abyss.

I venture to speak to my younger brethren in this congregation. Some of you have an exceptional reverence for the austere sovereignty of truth ; and have resolved, with a deep and serious earnestness, to discover the very thought of God concerning the life and destiny of man, and concerning the Christian redemption. For you the claims of truth are supreme. May God be with you, and may the Spirit of God illuminate you that you may discover all that you are seeking! But remember that a Gospel rudely conceived and coarsely expressed, eternal truth held in combination with the grossest errors, has through age after age proved the power of God unto the salvation of men when it has been preached in the Holy Ghost sent forth from heaven ; and that unless your purer and nobler faith is preached in the power of the same Spirit it will work no wonders. Some of you, while not disloyal to truth, care supremely for men. Your hearts are full of pity for all God's children who do not know as yet how dear they are to the heart of their Father, and it is the glory of your life to tell them of His love and of what He has done for their eternal redemption. You think that your pity must be contagious, and that while you speak, men will surely begin to pity themselves, and that in the flames of your own joy in the Christian Gospel the hearts of other men must catch fire. But there is only one force which can break into the centre of the life of men; your pity will not reach so deep, nor your joy in the Gospel of Christ. You will do nothing unless you preach in the Holy Ghost sent forth from heaven.

Some of us have but few years to live, and fewer years to work for God and men. The evening star is in the darkening sky. The autumn leaves are falling around us. We seem to be walking through fields of stubble from which the poor harvests of our past toil have been already gathered. Wintry days are coming on, and for us, in this world, there cannot be another spring. But you—you have your years before you. Receive the testimony of those of us who have the greater part of our life behind us. I speak in their name as well as in my own. Your generous impulses, your strenuous and exhausting labours, your eagerness to bless men, your natural powers, your learning, will achieve nothing—nothing in those higher regions of human life in which alone the enduring results of our work are to be found—unless you have received the gift of the Holy Spirit. Seek it—seek it reverently, persistently, in the name of Christ whose servant you are and whose Gospel you cannot preach effectively unless the gift is yours; seek it until you have it.

And at this time, when we are all keenly interested in discussions concerning the methods adopted by ourselves and our fathers for making known to heathen nations the blessedness and glory of Christ's eternal kingdom, permit me to appeal to all of you, and through you to the congregations throughout the country which you represent, not to allow these discussions to turn you aside from deeper considerations by which this great work is much more vitally affected. The gifts of the Holy Ghost for all forms of service sometimes come to those who do not seek them; to those who seek them I believe they always come. To me, to you, the special gift we care for most and pray for most earnestly may not be granted, but some power will be conferred on us that will enable us to discharge the function to which we are destined in the body of Christ. And our chief concern should not be that the greater gifts should be bestowed upon ourselves, but that they should be bestowed on those who will use them most faithfully.

If we are elected to obscurer forms of service which require only humbler forms of power, it is a blessedness and honour beyond all our deserts that we should be allowed to serve Christ at all. But if we and the Churches to which we belong entreat God to grant that a large number of men in our own time may, through His grace, preach the Gospel both at home and to other nations in the Holy Ghost and with great power, He will not refuse to answer the prayer. Let us thank Him for those who so preach the Gospel already; but let us entreat Him to increase their number greatly—and He will do it. This is our first—this our supreme concern. The money which we can give should be given as proof that we are in earnest in our prayers; but after our largest gifts are made, this should be our confession, that our gifts are powerless, and our wisest methods powerless, that the truth we have inherited from past generations of saints is powerless, and the truth which God Himself has revealed to us powerless, unless in our times God raises up devout men filled with the Holy Ghost and calls them—He must call them as He must qualify them—to preach the Gospel in the Holy Ghost sent forth from heaven.

The Christian Gospel—this is the truth on which I want to insist with an earnestness and energy of conviction which I do not know how to express— the Christian Gospel, in its purity, is as powerless to restore men to God as the most corrupt forms of heathen superstition, apart from the power of the Holy Ghost. If we lost Christ, what should we have to say to men? Ah! but if we have lost the Spirit, it matters little what we say to them concerning Christ. Not only is it true that one man filled with the Holy Ghost, and possessing the special power for preaching the Gospel which the Holy Ghost confers, will do more than a thousand men, whatever their gifts and whatever their earnestness, in whom the Holy Ghost does not dwell,—the thousand will do nothing, and the one man will, through God, draw a great multitude to Christ. In my very heart I believe that this is the critical question for ourselves in this country, and for all that represent us in heathen, Mahometan, and Roman Catholic countries.

And the relations between ourselves and our brethren in those foreign lands are not only intimate, they are vital. Sometimes God in His infinite mercy confers upon individual men great and remarkable spiritual power when the Christian Church generally has no vigour of faith and no depth of life; but that does not seem to be the law of His kingdom. Or if such exceptional power is conferred upon individuals, it is that the Church generally may discover what transcendent grace, in manifold forms, is possible to all that are in Christ; and if that revelation is not received with faith and joy, if there is not a general and eager desire and prayer for the manifestation of the presence and power of the Holy Ghost throughout the whole Church, when the individual fires sink and their splendours are quenched, there comes a more wintry darkness, a more deathly cold.

We live in each other's life. If the visions and prayers of saints are to be fulfilled, and if the final victories of the Divine love and the Divine righteousness are to be achieved, this is our first duty, to begin ourselves to pray as we never prayed before for the fuller manifestation of the power of the Spirit Who already dwells in us, and to appeal to our brethren throughout the country, rich and poor, learned and untaught, in scattered hamlets, in great cities, to unite in one penitent confession that we have never yet acknowledged or felt as we should that *we* are powerless and the Gospel powerless, apart from the Holy Ghost sent forth from heaven, and in one persistent, earnest, hopeful prayer that in these last days, through us and through our brethren in all lands, the exceeding greatness of His power may be gloriously revealed.

IV.

THE FAITH ONCE FOR ALL DELIVERED TO THE SAINTS.[1]

"Contend earnestly for the faith which was once for all delivered unto the saints."—*Jude* 3.

WHILE men were still living who had received the Christian Gospel from Apostles, the faith which was once for all delivered to the saints was in peril. Even in those early days, as Jude tells us, there were some who turned the grace of God into lasciviousness and denied our only Master and Lord, Jesus Christ. Nor was it their creed only that was corrupt. They were guilty of the foulest sensual sins, and they sheltered their immoralities under perverted conceptions of the Gospel of Christ, and, perhaps, under such theories of the relations between the flesh and the spirit as assumed a more definite and elaborate form during the first fifty years of the second century.

In the Churches to which this epistle was written,

---

[1] Preached in Mansfield College Chapel, Oxford, on Monday evening, October 14th, 1889, at the opening of the College Buildings.

it is implied that the Christian faith had to rely for its preservation and defence on the fidelity of the Christian commonalty. Jude makes no appeal to any of the books which now constitute the New Testament in condemnation of these heresies; indeed it is probable that at this time very few of these books were written, and that those which were written were not generally known. Nor does he impose any special responsibility on elders or bishops to preserve the Christian tradition from corruption. His appeal, I say, is to the commonalty of the Church.

Those to whom he was writing had listened to the teaching of the Apostles. He reminds them that the Apostles had warned them that in the last time there would be mockers walking after their own ungodly lusts; already the warning was being fulfilled. By the same Apostles they had been instructed in the Christian Gospel. They were to hold fast what they had received. They were to build up their thought and life on that holy foundation, praying in the Holy Spirit, keeping themselves in the light and blessedness and security of God's love for them, looking for the mercy of our Lord Jesus Christ unto eternal life. And they were to "contend earnestly for the faith once for all delivered to the saints."

With all the Churches of Christendom, we who have erected these buildings for the worship of God, for the discipline of the Christian life, and for the cultivation of Christian learning, are the heirs and the trustees of this great faith. It has descended to us through sixty generations of saints. In the power of it we, too, have received the remission of sins and the gift of eternal life, have seen the glory of God, have passed into His eternal kingdom. We, too, have to contend earnestly for the faith in the presence of all the perils with which it is menaced in our own times. On us, too, rests the awful, the glorious responsibility of transmitting it uncorrupted and unimpaired to the generations that are to come. In the humble endeavour to fulfil our trust we have built this College. We give God hearty thanks for the noble generosity—not of the rich alone, but also of some of the poorest members of the Congregational Churches of this country—which has enabled us to build it; generosity so munificent that the whole cost has been already provided, and we open it to-night with hearts untroubled by even the lightest debt. These buildings are the visible proof, and we trust that they will remain through centuries to come the monument and the memorial, of the gratitude of many hearts for God's infinite mercy in the redemption of the world through the incarnation, death, resurrection, and ascension of His Eternal Son; of a zeal for His glory, whose fires sometimes burn low but are not wholly quenched; and of an earnest desire to maintain the purity and assert the immortal power of the faith which was once for all delivered to the saints. And now we entreat God to bless our work beyond the measure of our largest hopes.

I.

The Revelation of God in Christ—whose contents are the object of Christian faith, and are therefore described as the faith which was once for all delivered to the saints, does not consist merely— I might say, does not consist primarily—in additional knowledge concerning God. Christ is the Saviour as well as the Teacher of men. A large part, the larger part, of the revelation of God which has come to the race through Christ, consists in the actual redemption of men from sin and eternal death. Ancient prophets had spoken of the great mercy of God, and had declared that if the wicked would forsake his way and the unrighteous man his thoughts, and if he would return to the Lord, the Lord would have mercy upon him, and would abundantly pardon. But the Lord Jesus Christ died for the remission of sin. He bore our sins in His own body on the tree; He is the propitiation for the sin of the world; His death is the ground of the forgiveness of sins.

To the devout of earlier ages there had come wonderful visions of the justice, the mercy, the graciousness, the fidelity, the holiness of the Eternal; visions which filled their hearts with awe and reverence, with love and faith and joy. And in the righteousness of God they had discovered that they were called to a perfection far transcending all that could be demanded in the letter of definite laws.

They meditated on that ideal righteousness; they longed to reach it; and they found that it was above their strength. Christ came not merely to reveal a still loftier ideal, but in new and mysterious ways to raise the life of man to a higher plane, to re-enforce it with nobler powers, to make man one with Himself, that in Him man might share the life of God. As the Spirit of God dwelt in Christ, so He dwells in all that share the Divine life through union with Christ. And as Christ, even during His earthly life, lived in God, they too are conscious that even during their earthly life they are environed by an invisible, eternal, and Divine order which is their true home.

Christ, I say, did not come merely to give us additional knowledge concerning God. He did not come merely to found a school that should be the permanent home of the great tradition of His larger teaching. His incarnation, His righteousness—tried and disciplined by temptation and suffering—His resurrection, His ascension—in which He carried Humanity with Him to the glory which He had with the Father before the foundation of the world—were great redemptive acts; they have had a direct effect, apart altogether from the moral consent of individual men, on the whole order of the world. He remains through age after age the living Lord of the human race, in whom men are to find God, and to receive the life of God, and to become one with God. Those who receive the Christian Gospel are not only brought under the power of great and pathetic and animating religious truths; they enter into the actual possession of a redemption which God has achieved for the race. To them the faith was once for all delivered.

II.

That is—the revelation of God in Christ, the Christian Gospel, which is the object of the faith of all Christians, and which is here described as "the faith," is committed to the trust of all who have been actually redeemed and restored to God by Christ. *They* are responsible for its purity and integrity.

There are other provisions for perpetuating it and for restoring it when it has been corrupted or wholly lost. The written narratives of the earthly life and ministry of the Lord Jesus Christ, and the authoritative teaching of the Apostles in those of their writings which have been preserved till our times, have a great and unique place of their own, which we, the descendants and heirs of Reformers and Puritans, are of all men least likely to dishonour. But those sacred books were written by elect saints in discharge of the same trust that has been inherited by ourselves. They stand apart. They have an exceptional authority. But they illustrate the fidelity which is required of the saints of all succeeding generations; and in our age, as in all past ages, the effective defence of the faith lies, under God, with living men and women who through Christ have received the remission of sins and the supernatural life and the grace and light of the Holy Ghost. To the saints was the faith delivered once for all ; the saints of every age are responsible for defending it in times of peril, and asserting its power.

For they, and they alone, have an independent, personal, and immediate knowledge of the divine objects of faith. It is unnecessary to quote isolated texts in order to prove that the "natural man receiveth not the things of the Spirit of God"; that "they are foolishness to him"; that he cannot know them because they are spiritually discerned." It is part of the very substance of the Gospel that the knowledge of God as He has revealed Himself in Christ and the knowledge of His eternal kingdom is given to those, and those only, who have received the supernatural life and the illumination of the Holy Spirit.

There are no doubt, certain outlying departments of theological science in which considerable results may be achieved without these diviner resources. With industry and learning, a clear intellect and a sound judgment, men may write histories of the external fortunes of the Church, histories of the growth of ecclesiastical institutions, and of the various forms of ecclesiastical polity, histories of doctrine, histories of controversies ; they may make substantial contributions to our knowledge of the languages in which the Holy Scriptures are written ; they may assist in forming a trustworthy text. Even in these departments, the absence of a direct knowledge of the great objects of faith, and the absence of the life which renders the knowledge possible and is sustained by it, will show itself in conspicuous defects and failures. In higher regions—as, for example, the interpretation of Holy Scripture—the defects and failures will be more conspicuous still. Some kinship with a poet's genius is necessary for a true understanding of his verse ; and spiritual kinship with the writers of the Old Testament and the New is necessary to catch their real thought.

To take the New Testament alone—it deals with that Divine order which is revealed only to those who are in Christ, and with sorrows, fears, conflicts, hopes, joys, and triumphs, which are unknown except to those who have received the life of God. Its great and characteristic words are found elsewhere, but with an inferior meaning. In the New Testament they are charged with new powers ; filled with a new wealth ; they are transfigured by their new uses. They are not exact terms of science, as some of them became in a later age, and it is hard to fix the definite outlines of their meaning. A new life is in them, and they are growing under the very hands of the writers. To know what they stand for, we must look at them from within,—not from without ; we must see for ourselves what the writers saw, or we shall impose upon them an inadequate sense. Who can tell what is meant by Christ's being the propitiation for the sins of the world, except the man who has been filled with desolation and dread by the discovery of his guilt, and who knows the wonder and the joy, the large freedom, the buoyancy of spirit, the glad and secure trust in God which come from the consciousness that he has received the Divine forgiveness through Christ? Who can tell what is meant by being "in Christ," except the man who is conscious that he himself is "in Christ"? Who can have any clear perception of the great truth—the paradox of the Christian Gospel—that we are justified, not by our own righteousness, but in Christ, except the man who, out of the fulness of his own happy experience, can join in the exulting triumph of saints and say, "Being justified by faith, we have peace with God through our Lord Jesus Christ; through whom also we have had our access by faith into this grace wherein we stand; and we rejoice in hope of the glory of God."

III.

Christian Theology has been described as being nothing more than the result of the application of the lexicon and the grammar to the New Testament Scriptures; but this is a wholly inadequate account of the true task and method of even what is called Biblical theology. And if it were in any sense true in relation to that department of theological inquiry, the question would have to be asked, Who is to make the lexicon which is to be finally authoritative? For, as I have said, some of the great words on which the meaning of the New Testament largely depends, are words which the Christian faith has regenerated and disciplined to new uses ; and there would be hardly any exaggeration in the contention that instead of finding Paul's thought or John's thought in the words which they use to express it, we must find the thought before we can know the power of the words. The lexicon is the result rather than the condition precedent of Biblical theology. The substance of apostolic faith governs the meaning of the terms in which apostolic doctrine is defined. No man, I will venture to say, is an adequate expositor of Paul's doctrine of justification until Paul's doctrine has been verified in his own experience, so that his faith in it has become independent of Paul's authority.

In relation to theology in its stricter sense—that is, in relation to dogmatic theology—the description of the task and method of theological investigation as consisting in the application of the lexicon and the grammar to the New Testament, is not only defective —it is erroneous and misleading. The work of the dogmatic theologian begins where the work of the Biblical theologian ends. For the work of the Biblical theologian is historical; the work of the dogmatic theologian is creative and constructive. The Biblical theologian has to discover the forms in which the contents of the Christian Gospel were apprehended by the original apostles. A revelation direct from Heaven came to them all. They saw God in the light of God ; and in that same light they saw the Lord Jesus Christ, and man, and the thoughts of God concerning man, and the redemption which

God had achieved for man in Christ. But the revelation was too immense for all its heights and depths to come within the vision of any one of the apostles —even the greatest of them. They knew in part; they prophesied in part. There are many mansions of thought as well as of rest and blessedness in the Father's house. Paul lived in one; John in another; they might sometimes be each other's guests; but the home of John was not the home of Paul.

They knew in part. Even Peter found in Paul's epistles some things hard to be understood. And what they knew in common they conceived and stated differently. For their intellectual methods were different. Their minds did not work alike either in seizing the great objects of faith which were revealed to them by the Holy Spirit, or in giving an account to others of the revelation which had come to them. The differences were the result, in part, of differences in the original make of their intellect; in part, of differences of intellectual training and discipline. And further, each of them had his characteristic temperament; and each of them lived his own ethical and spiritual life, and had his own separate experience of the power of God's manifold grace. The heart of each knew its own bitterness; neither could a stranger intermeddle with its joy. Their apprehension of the supernatural revelation was conditioned by these differences in their personal powers, their personal history, and their personal spiritual life; it was still further conditioned by the nature and circumstances of the separate service and work to which they were severally destined. They shine—every one of them—with a divine splendour ; but "one star differeth from another star in glory."

These differences appear even in the four Evangelists. They tell the story of the same Christ ; but they do not tell the same story. Matthew, Mark, Luke, John, each had his own conception of the life of our Lord ; each conception is true ; no conception is adequate ; His life, like His love, passeth knowledge.

The office of the Biblical theologian is to discover and define the several conceptions of Christ and of the contents of the Christian Gospel characteristic of the several writers of the New Testament ; and I say that he cannot do this with any success unless there is some spiritual kinship between him and them, and unless he, too, has had a direct vision of the objects of Christian faith.

The office of the dogmatic theologian is more arduous, more adventurous, more perilous. He has to construct for himself an intellectual conception of those Divine and eternal things on which the faith of the Church through all generations has rested. The accounts which Apostles gave of the Revelation, and which remain authoritative for the Church of all ages, were determined by their own personal and intellectual characteristics, by the intellectual methods of their own time, and by the controversies which agitated the first days of the Christian Gospel.

They thought—as they wrote and spoke—in the idiom of their own race and their own generation. And similar conditions have determined the thought of the great though unauthoritative theologians of later days. The intellectual methods of the Middle Ages governed the speculations of the schoolmen concerning the invisible and spiritual universe as they governed the speculations of their contemporaries concerning the visible and material universe.

We, in our turn, have to give our own account of the great objects of faith. We have to construct our own conception of them. We have to conceive of them according to our own intellectual methods, and under our own forms of thought—as we have to speak of them in the language of our own age and of our own countrymen. We have to ascertain the relations between the separate objects of faith and to organize our separate conceptions of them, if we can, into a coherent system. We have to learn how they have been obscured by the errors of earlier generations and of our own; and how they have been misapprehended through that defective vision which is largely the result of defective spiritual life. We have to consider whether hostility to any of the contents of the Christian Gospel has been created by the eternal truths themselves, or by the imperfect account of them which has been given by the Church. We dare not modify any traditional Christian doctrine in order to conciliate hostility; but it will be our duty to modify whatever tradition misrepresents the eternal fact. We have to learn whether the thought of the Church has forsaken any of the great truths which are of the substance of the Christian revelation; and whether, as the result of this aberration of thought, the strength and joy of the Church, its righteousness and sanctity, have been impaired. This is the office of the dogmatic theologian—arduous, adventurous, perilous, demanding for its largest success a rich and varied learning, a keen, patient, cautious, and courageous intellect, genius in one of its highest and rarest forms; but demanding, first of all, a clear vision, a direct knowledge of the unseen and the eternal.

A true and noble dogmatic theology, like a true and noble science of the material universe, must be founded on observation and experience. Things must be known at first hand. Conclusions and theories must be subjected to constant verification. In theology, as in natural science, enormous errors have resulted from trusting methods which did not insist on a perpetual recurrence to facts. In both it is unsafe to rely on long-drawn deductions, beginning, perhaps, with certainties, but untested and unsupported from point to point by actual observation and experience.

The theologian, therefore, must, first of all, be a saint. It is not enough that he has mastered conflicting theories concerning the Christian atonement, the forgiveness of sins, justification, the new life which is given to the race in Christ, judgment to come. He must know for himself the greatness of the Christian redemption. His own consciousness that in Christ, and through the death of Christ, he has received the remission of sins, must find explanation in his theory of the Atonement. His joy in the discovery that Christ's relations to God determine his own relations to God must be explained in his theory of Justification, and of the Divine sonship of all that are in Christ. He must be vividly conscious that in the power of a new life he has passed into a new world, if he is to be able to give any true account of that Divine regenerative act in which the new life is imparted. He must have trembled at the judgment to come, if he is to speculate to any purpose on the principles and issues of the judgment.

His science is the science of God. He must have a large and varied knowledge of God—not merely of the speculations of other men about God. His faith in Christ as the Eternal Word who has become flesh, must rest, not on proof texts, but on a direct vision of Christ's glory; and his faith in the Holy Spirit on his own consciousness that that august and gracious Presence dwells in him as in a temple. For his thought to move with any certainty in the great mysteries which surround the Being of the Eternal, he must be able to say with other saintly souls—"Through Christ we have access in one Spirit unto the Father."

To *all* Christian men the great objects of faith are

revealed by the Spirit of God. No man can really say that Jesus is the Lord but in the Holy Spirit. The *theologian*, who is called of God to be the teacher of the Church, must receive in larger measure than his brethren "the spirit of wisdom and revelation" in the knowledge of God; and fuller light must come to him, that he may know what is included in the hope of the Divine calling, and what are the riches of the glory of God's inheritance in the saints, and what is the exceeding greatness of that Divine power which raised Christ from the dead, and from earth to the heights of heaven, and is now working in us, that we too may ascend to a perfection and a blessedness transcending all hope and all thought.

It is not given indeed to one man to know in this direct way all the wonders of the Divine Kingdom; and the theologian, like the discoverers in other sciences, must sometimes rely on the observation and experience of other men. The great things he should know for himself. Where his own vision is defective, and his own experience at fault, he will try to learn what other men have seen, and what other men have experienced. He will distinguish between their speculations and the facts which they have actually verified and which have been verified by ordinary Christian men in different ages and under different conditions. In this investigation he will probably attribute more authority to books of devotion than to the decrees of Councils, and to the actual lives of saintly men than to their most laboured discussions of Christian dogma. He will maintain spiritual fellowship with the living as well as with the dead; with the simple and unlearned as well as with scholars. He will remember that to the meek God teaches His way. But if he himself has no direct knowledge of eternal things, he will be unable to use wisely the knowledge of other men.

He has to give an intellectual account of the faith once for all delivered to the saints. He will therefore attribute supreme value to that central substance of Christian truth which has been the life and strength of Christian men in all generations. The spirit of intellectual adventure will not be uncontrolled. He will not imagine that after nineteen centuries of Christian history the saints have yet to learn what are "the first principles of Christ." Believing that the light of God has come to himself, he will also believe that it came to devout men of past generations.

We who have erected this College have broken with the polities of the great Churches of Christendom, and are unable to accept their confessions, creeds, articles, and canons of doctrine. But we listen with reverence to the saints of all Churches when they speak concerning those great things which may be actually verified in the saintly life. They are authorities, not indeed for the soundness of theological theories, but for those supreme objects of faith of which theological theories should give an intellectual explanation. We differ from many of them concerning the human methods and discipline by which the spiritual life is to be perfected; but our own faith is re-invigorated when they tell us of the eternal springs of life which they found in God, and of their blessedness in the vision of His glory. We think that they missed the true conception of the external organization of the Church; but we, too, believe in the communion of saints, and are conscious of kinship with all who have found God in Christ, living and dead, in every country, and in every age. Yes; we rejoice in the sacred traditions of Christendom; we claim our part in the great inheritance. The fathers and martyrs of the Early Church are ours; and the doctors and saints of the East and of the West; and the mystics and the Reformers; devout Anglicans and devout Puritans; the leaders of the Evangelical Revival—Calvinistic and Arminian; and those who in later times have renewed the faith and rekindled the sinking fires of zeal in our own and other lands. They are our elder brethren in Christ. We, too, have seen the eternal things that were revealed to them. We, too, have breathed the diviner air. Through Christ we, too, have received the remission of sins and the gift of eternal life. In Christ we, too, have found God. Theologies are in conflict, but the faith of the Church is one.

IV.

There are some who say, that since the faith once for all delivered to the saints has been preserved in substance by Churches whose theologies are mutually antagonistic, it would be well for the peace of Christendom and for the power of the Christian gospel over the life of Christian nations, if we were satisfied with contemplating the great objects of faith, and abandoned the attempt to construct theories of them. The suggestion is an impracticable one. We might as well be told to be satisfied with contemplating the great objects of sense, and to abandon the attempt to construct a science of material things. There is a generous curiosity which cannot be suppressed. There is a passion for knowledge—for definite knowledge—of God and the thoughts of God, as well as for righteousness; and between the two there are intimate and vital relations.

For ourselves in this place we assert the duties and the rights of the intellect in religion. We assert them against those devout and timid persons who regard the intellect with a vague terror, as though it were some vast and awful power, untamed and untamable, the reckless and irreconcilable foe of the authority of the Supreme, a power that must be fettered, manacled, and imprisoned, if it is to be prevented from tearing up the very foundations of the City of God. We assert them against the adherents of a philosophy by which the intellect is disparaged and declared to be incompetent to the task of reaching any sure results in its attempts to know the truth concerning man's relations to the invisible, the eternal, the Divine.

Man was made for God, and he is all of a piece. The faith of Christ gives no sanction to the Manicheeism which regards the *flesh* as the necessary foe of the Diviner life, and incapable of reconciliation to righteousness. The flesh was created to be the organ of the spirit, and the body of the Christian man is the temple of the Holy Ghost. In Christ, the Word, that was in the beginning with God, and was God, became flesh.

And the faith of Christ gives no sanction to the subtler Manicheeism which regards the *intellect* as the necessary foe of faith, and as incapable of receiving and comprehending after its manner the very truth concerning the thoughts and acts of God. Between the intellect and God there is no impassable gulf. It can reach the thoughts of God, as revealed in the structure and laws of the material universe; and for us every fresh discovery of science is an addition to our knowledge of God's methods and God's ways in one vast province of His activity. It can reach the thoughts of God in ethics; and for us ethical science is an attempt, not wholly unsuccessful, to give an intellectual expression to the laws of God for the guidance of human conduct. The thoughts of the Infinite and the Eternal are not in themselves inaccessible to the human intellect, or incapable of being translated into intellectual forms which may be subjected to verification; for a science of ethics is possible, and a science of material things is possible. Why should *we*—we who believe and know that God and the eternal universe are revealed to the spirit— suppose that in that loftier region the intellect is guilty of presumption if it attempts to organize, after its own manner, the contents of the revelation? If the material universe were unrevealed to us through the senses, physical science would be impossible. If duty were unrevealed to us through the conscience, ethical science would be impossible. Those who deny that God is directly revealed to the spirit may consistently maintain that theology is impossible; but for us to whom that revelation has come, theology is the most necessary as well as the noblest form of intellectual activity.

More than once in the history of the Church it has been seen that a Pietism—lofty, as well as devout in its origin—by disparaging intellectual activity in relation to faith, has encouraged a feeble religious sentimentalism, has been fatal to masculine robustness of Christian character, has made Christian men ineffective in the practical duties of the Christian calling, and has enfeebled and impoverished their whole spiritual life. From these evils, those who have founded this College humbly hope to do their part in saving the Congregational Churches of this country.

We claim for the intellect the largest freedom. It can render no worthy service to the Church or to Truth if it is fettered. We claim for it in religion a freedom as large as is conceded to it in science. In science it cannot change the facts; its function is to ascertain and to interpret them. In faith it cannot change the facts; its function is to ascertain and to interpret them. In both departments the facts are supreme. Wherever facts are known, the speculative intellect is under limitations and restraints; it is absolutely free, only where it is absolutely ignorant.

The methods of the intellect in the investigation of religious truth differ from its methods in the investigation of scientific truth, as the methods of the historian differ from the methods of the chemist. But the claim for intellectual freedom in theology needs no other qualification than that which is imposed upon it in every other province of intellectual activity—facts, through whatever channels the certain knowledge of them may come, and by whatever methods they are discovered or verified—facts are its only limitation.

Freedom to criticize and reconstruct the text of Holy Scripture; freedom to re-investigate traditional opinions concerning the dates and the authorship of the sacred books of the Old and the New Testament; freedom to revise and amend the traditional interpretation of their contents; freedom to revise and amend definitions of great Christian doctrines by whatever venerable authorities the definitions may be sanctioned; this must be conceded, conceded frankly, not under compulsion, but with the full consent of the judgment, the conscience, and the heart. The public opinion of the Church should be friendly to intellectual integrity in its theological scholars. It is better that they should reach a false conclusion by fair means than a true one by foul. Truth itself is not the truth to the man who has been disloyal to his intellectual conscience in the formation of his belief.

To encourage this intellectual integrity in its theologians, the Church should keep an open mind to their discoveries, should not assume that after the developments and vicissitudes of its theological thought, extending over eighteen hundred years, it has nothing more to learn. We have learnt much from the saintly theologians of past generations ; we may learn much from the saintly theologians of our own time ; and we must be willing to learn, or God will give us no new teachers.

But the Church, too, must hold fast its liberty in Christ, and must discharge its trust as keeper and defender of the faith which was once for all delivered to the saints. The fathers were not infallible ; and modern theologians are but men. We have it on excellent authority, that even General Councils "may err, and sometimes have erred, even in things pertaining to God ; " nor can exemption from error be claimed for great critical schools brilliant with genius and learning; they must consent to have what they confidently proclaim as "the final results" of criticism, examined, tested, controverted, and sometimes rejected by their successors. We, who have vindicated our freedom from authorities which have commanded the reverence of a long succession of generations, should be false to our principles and our history if we accepted with blind and unquestioning submission the conclusions of any critical school which has suddenly achieved splendour and fame. We must prove all things, and hold fast that which is good.

V.

It is our duty to keep an open mind to the discoveries of theologians and scholars; but this does not mean that we should consent to regard all the articles of the Christian faith as open questions. On the great subjects our mind is made up. The facts we know, and under God we have to assert and defend them.

We are willing, if necessary, to revise definitions; but can accept no definition which obscures the Divine glory of the Lord Jesus Christ, Son of God, Son of Man, Creator, Brother, Lord, Redeemer of the human race. We are prepared to discuss theories of the Atonement; but can accept no theory which would dislodge our hearts from their sure confidence in Christ, in whom we have redemption through His blood, even the remission of sins according to the riches of God's grace. Theories of Justification may be reconstructed; but we can receive no theory which does not rest on the fact that we are in Christ, and that His relations to the Father determine our own. We are not irrevocably committed to any theory of what theologians have called the depravity or corruption of human nature; but any theory which does not explicitly and fully acknowledge the awful reality of sin, and maintain that only in the power of the supernatural life can man escape from spiritual ruin, is for us an impossible theory; we know that the facts are against it. We confess that the mystery of the eternal life of God transcends our science; that the terms of the creeds must be inexact; that they point towards august truths, but do not reach them; and yet with reverence and awe we worship Father, Son, and Holy Spirit—one God, blessed for evermore; and in the knowledge of God we have eternal life. We are ready to revise and correct, when adequate cause is shown, the traditional belief of the Church concerning the dates at which the books of the Old Testament and the New were written, concerning the kind of relation between the books and the authors to whom they are attributed; we are ready to revise theories of Inspiration; but in these books we ourselves have found the record of the supreme revelation to mankind of the righteousness, the mercy, the grace, and the will of God; what we ourselves have found in them has been found by millions of men of many races, many tongues, and many forms of civilization; by simple and unlearned men, by men of noble genius; by humble penitents, by glorious saints; and whatever conclusions and theories assume that this discovery is an illusion we vehemently reject.

The substance of the faith delivered once for all to the saints of the first age has been verified in the experience of the saints of every succeeding generation, and has, in these last days, been verified in our own. Theologians have not to create new heavens and a new earth, but to give a more exact account of that spiritual universe whose mysteries and glories have environed the saints from the beginning. A theology which quenches the fires of the sun and the splendour of the stars—whatever temporary triumphs it may win—is destined to failure. It is an account of another universe than that in which the saints are living, and the faith of the Church has authority to reject it.

VI.

The largest intellectual freedom in theological inquiry, a passionate loyalty to Christ, and an incorruptible fidelity in the maintenance and defence of the faith which was once for all delivered to the saints—these are not irreconcilable. And if I know the mind of those who have founded this College, it is their earnest desire that in Mansfield the reconciliation may be illustrated. It is their prayer and their hope that, through God's infinite mercy, students and teachers may be filled with the Holy Spirit, that they may be the true brethren and successors of those saintly men who in all Churches and in all ages have known for themselves the power and glory of Christ. We pray and we hope that among those who teach and those who are taught in this place there may be, through generation after generation, men of intellectual force and patience, adventure and courage, keenness and subtlety, disciplined by manly studies, enriched with varied learning, and who, having received themselves that Divine illumination, apart from which God cannot be truly known, shall be elect of God to lead the Church into a deeper and fuller knowledge of Himself and of all His merciful thoughts and purposes concerning our race. We pray and we hope that in our own times, and in coming generations, the class-rooms of this building may be filled with men who, with awe and with a great joy that trembled into a devout fear, have heard the voice of God calling them into the ministry of the Christian Gospel; and that within these walls, where we are met to-night, the fire of God may descend upon them, kindling into passion their longing for the salvation of all mankind. We pray and we hope that from their lips a great multitude of their own countrymen may learn the freedom of the Divine mercy and the glory of that inheritance of wisdom, righteousness, peace, and blessedness which God has conferred upon man in Christ. We trust that God will give them courage and tenderness to rebuke sin; the very pity of Christ to console sorrow; the infinite hopefulness of Christ to recover the wretched and the sinful from despair; and that under their ministry, Churches in every part of the land will learn the secret of the perfect life. We trust that many of them will be called to the still nobler task of preaching Christ to heathen races; and that in coming centuries, when countries now covered with a great darkness are filled with the light of Him who is the Light of the world, famous Churches, of which they were the founders, will cherish with veneration the traditions of their labours and their sufferings, their sanctity and their zeal.

With these hopes and these prayers, we commit

this College to the love and keeping and defence of Him who is able to do exceeding abundantly above all that we ask or think, "and unto Him be the glory in the Church and in Christ Jesus unto all generations for ever and ever. Amen."

V.

GOD'S GREATNESS AND CONDESCENSION.[1]

"What is man, that Thou art mindful of him? and the son of man, that Thou visitest him?"—*Psalm* viii. 4.

IF God has not been mindful of us, and is not mindful of us still—if He has not visited man in past ages, and if He does not continue to visit man in our own days—this building is the monument of a ruined hope, and the enduring memorial of a glorious but tragic illusion. The illusion, indeed, has been shared through generation after generation by the noblest of mankind. The hope may be described by those who do not share it as originating in the immense ambition of the human heart; but in its very presumption there is a moral grandeur so august, and in its appeal to the infinite love and wisdom and power of God there is so pathetic a consciousness of weakness, ignorance, and sorrow, that even those who think it vain and audacious may well regard it with sympathy and wonder rather than with scorn, and

---

[1] Preached at the opening of Union Chapel, Islington (Rev. Dr. Allon's), on Wednesday morning, Dec. 5th, 1877.

may look upon its extinction with pity rather than with exultation.

How are we to learn whether the ancient faith of our race is an illusion or not? How are we to verify the hope that it is possible for man to have access to God?

I.

Paul declares that ever since the creation of the world the invisible glories of God, even His eternal power and Godhead, have been revealed in the material universe. But the influence on religious faith and hope of what we call Nature,—of the sun, the moon, the stars, the mountains, and the seas,—varies with different men, and it varies with the varying temper and mood of the same man at different times. It is not always that Nature makes it easier for us to believe that God is near. There are aspects of Nature which sometimes make it difficult for us to believe that there can be any real communion between the Creator and ourselves. Those of us who usually live in great cities are perhaps especially sensitive to the austere influence of the material universe. Its vastness and grandeur oppress us. Lying among the ferns and the blossoming heather, with the foundations of granite mountains beneath us, and their jagged peaks rising into the clouds above; or standing alone on the shore of a desolate sea unwhitened by a solitary sail; or lifting our eyes to the heavens at night, and knowing what David did not know about the immense magnitude of the stars, about their numbers, about the enormous distances which separate them from each other and from ourselves— we are crushed by the sense of our insignificance. The sense of our insignificance is strengthened by the permanence of God's material works. If we perished, what difference would it make in this stupendous creation? The "everlasting hills" would stand firm; the tides would continue to ebb and flow; the stars would rise and set; the heather would still blossom; the bracken would become brown on the hill-sides in the autumn; the wild flowers would fill the glens with beauty in the spring; the mountain-streams would continue to make their pleasant music just as before. What is man, that God should be mindful of him? what is man, that God should visit him?

All our deepest thoughts have been expressed for us ages ago. David felt the insignificance of man when compared with the greatness of the heavens and the earth, and expressed what he felt in the words of the text; and the writer of the book of Ecclesiastes felt the solemnity and pathos of the contrast between the brief life of man and the endurance of the material universe, which is man's temporary home: "One generation," he said, "passeth away and another generation cometh, but the earth abideth for ever."

It is true, indeed, that the earth itself has had its changes. The elements have already melted with fervent heat; the igneous rocks, rising into mountain-ranges, are the gigantic castings which came out of that vast and awful furnace; and as the metal ran off, it broke its fiery way, in veins and dykes, through rocks of other orders. We live above a great cemetery, in which the bones are still preserved of millions upon millions of creatures that lived and perished millions upon millions of years ago. Water and fire have again and again changed the face of the globe. The earth's surface has fallen in, and the depression has been filled with the ocean; the ocean-bed has been heaved up, and islands and continents have risen from the depths of the sea. Even in more recent times, and in our own days, changes, though less startling, have been continually going on. Here and there, cliffs have been rent, and have broken down in gigantic ruins under the disintegrating influence of frost and rain; the coast has advanced on the sea, the sea has advanced on the coast. But yet how firm, how strong, how enduring the great forms of Nature appear when compared with ourselves!

The changes—the apparent changes, at least—which are passing in the remoter regions of space are slower still. The sun may be consuming away in its own fires; the stars may be moving less swiftly in their orbits; the forces which find their expression in the life and motion of the universe may be gradually approaching equilibrium, and millions of years hence the music of the spheres may be silent; but how gradual is the approach of the mighty procession to its close! The years by which we measure the life of man, the centuries, the millenniums by which we measure the life of nations, roll by, and there is no sign of change or decay. The sun burns with a heat and splendour apparently undiminished since the tribes of Asia first worshipped his glory as Divine; the stars will look down from their shining thrones on London to-night with a calmness as majestic as that with which they gazed on Athens when Pericles was clothing the fair city with imperishable beauty, and on Memphis and Thebes when the ancient Pharaohs were erecting the monuments which have been the perplexity and wonder of mankind for more than two thousand years. The most gigantic, the most enduring of the triumphs of human pride and power, are but of yesterday compared with the wonderful works of God. What is man that God should be mindful of him? or the son of man that God should visit him?

Nor, again, is it merely the vastness and the permanence of the great objects of the material universe, by which we are sunk into abysses of humiliation in which we begin to be incredible that God should care for us. The humiliation is deepened by the discovery that our own life is akin to the inferior forms of life around us—akin, not only to the life of those animals in whose structure there are the closest analogies to our own, but akin to forms of life which look most remote from ourselves. I came from the dust,—the book of Genesis had told me so before science had discovered it,—and in the very lowest types of living creatures there are prophecies of the life by which I am animated. The gradations which separate rank from rank in this living hierarchy are so fine, so subtle, that there seems to be no clear break in the ascending series; and in the very highest there still survive affinities to the lowest. What right have I to separate myself from the creatures to which I am so closely related? What right have I to claim a different rank and a different destiny from the deer which browse in the glens, from the fish which flash in the burns, from the very grass and heather which cover the hills?

I do not wonder that men whose whole strength is given to the investigation of the phenomena and laws of the material universe refuse to believe that man can be the object of any special interest on the part of God.

And still farther, when we consider those imperial laws which govern with steadfast and relentless authority the whole range of material existence with which we are acquainted, what presumption there seems to be in supposing that He, from whom those laws derive all their authority, will think of us and care for us one by one? The Most High, as a great philosopher has said, does not seem to manifest Himself in particular volitions, but by universal and unchangeable laws. He appears to take no heed of the moral qualities of men, or of their weakness and helplessness. He sends His rain on the evil and the good, and causes His sun to rise on the just and on the unjust. He destroys in the same storm the ships of an aggressive and tyrannical empire and the fishing-boats of an obscure, harmless, and industrious village ; smites with the same lightning the churches erected to His own honour and the temples of false gods ; permits drought and famine and pestilence to desolate whole nations, so that the virtuous and the wicked perish in a common misery. What right, it may be urged, have we to claim any special remembrance from Him? What is man, that God should be mindful of him ? or the son of man, that God should visit him ?

This is the gospel of science—a gospel harder, sterner, more appalling than the law which came from the thunders and lightnings of Sinai. Is it true, or is it false? If true, then the most radiant hopes of man are extinguished, his dearest consolations are dried up ; he is stripped of those regal prerogatives which have been his chief glory and the inspiration of his noblest virtues. Is it true or false ?

II.

Of the truth which is in it David had a glimpse. To him, as to many of us, the material universe in its majesty seemed to make it hard to believe that man could be a special object of the Divine thought and care ; but, instead of yielding to the dreadful doubt, David triumphed over it, and clung fast with exulting confidence to his assurance that, after all, God *is* mindful of us and does visit us.

Let us see whether we, too, cannot escape from the gigantic and oppressive shadows which the material universe throws upon us, and recover our faith in the animating truth that for *us* God is a God nigh at hand. Even apart from Revelation, there are some answers to be given to this dreary and desolating creed. What are the pleas urged on its behalf? What are they worth?

The whole world in which we live is a mere speck in the universe ; and it is said to be incredible that God should have any special care for it, or for those who inhabit it. There are times when this plea seems to have a terrible force. But when I come to myself, and recover from the power which the vast spaces of the material universe exert over my imagination, there seems to be a certain moral and intellectual vulgarity in attaching such importance to mere material magnitude. Jerusalem in its glory was a mere hamlet compared with Babylon ; Florence, when it was brilliant with the genius which shines only the brighter as the ages pass by, was a mere village compared with Pekin ; but who is so gross as to estimate the importance and dignity of a city by its magnitude? A sonnet of Milton's, an essay of Bacon's, a dialogue of Plato's, a volume of Newton's, could be less easily spared than whole tons of lumber that load the shelves of libraries. On a few square inches of canvas there is sometimes more costly work than in a picture which would cover the side of a house. No doubt the world is very small, but it does not follow that it contains nothing for which the great Father of us all can think it worth while to care. In a palace it may happen that there are rooms hardly noticed by those who are confounded with the splendour and stateliness and space of its great apartments—rooms hidden away in one of the wings, plainly furnished, insignificant in size, but which are more in the thought and heart of the king than all the rooms in the palace besides. They are the rooms in which his children play by day and sleep at night. Yes, the world is very small; but what then? If it is large enough to hold the children of God, God may be mindful of us; God may visit us, and God may bless us. In this controversy, the appeal to material magnitude is irrelevant.

The second plea is, that the life of man is brief and momentary compared with the ages during which the universe has existed. No doubt; but science itself suggests a reply to this argument. If the most recent and most fascinating theories of science are ultimately established, it will appear that all these ages have been necessary in order to render it possible for a creature like man to come into existence. Let the doctrine of Evolution on its purely scientific side be true, and instead of being overawed and humbled by the long succession of ages which have preceded me, I find in them a new testimony to the greatness of my nature and the dignity of my position. They were necessary, those enormous stretches of time which even the boldest have not dared to measure, during which the original matter of the universe was consolidating into innumerable worlds; they were necessary, those vast geologic periods of fire and of flood, of volcanic fury, of awful convulsion, of slow subsidence, of slow upheaval; they were necessary, those dark, mysterious epochs of conflict between inferior types of life;—they were all necessary, in order that at last I might have a clear heaven above my head and a firm earth beneath my feet, that I might have an atmosphere to breathe, that I might have rivers to fish and fields to plough, that I might have wood and iron for use, and flowers and pearls and precious stones for beauty; that I myself might have the brain which is the organ of my thought, the hand which is the instrument of my will. I, a man, am the consummate result, the ripe fruit, of those immense and awful ages. Do you appeal to them in order to sink me into insignificance? The more immense, the more awful they are, the stronger is their testimony to my dignity; for they were all working for me; for me they spent their strength; for me they suffered; they bring their wealth to my feet; I am the heir of all; they confess that I am their lord. It is still possible that God may be mindful of me and may visit me.

The third plea is, that we are encompassed by laws which take no heed of the personal differences of men, of the varieties of their character, of the vicissitudes of their condition. These laws determine our outward destiny; they control our very frame. To ask God to deal with us separately and apart, to deal with us as individuals, is to forget that He governs the whole universe by laws which are fixed, irreversible, and inexorable.

But when this universal reign of law is asserted, one supreme fact—the essential fact in relation to ourselves—is altogether ignored. Let it be granted, that in the physical universe, including in it my own physical nature, there are no signs or traces of what Malebranche calls particular divine volitions. Let it be granted that the magnitudes and motions of the stars, the structure and form of mountains, the courses of rivers, the outlines of continents, the varying depths of the ocean, the tint of every flower, the veining of every leaf, have all been determined by fixed laws; that the colour of my hair, the quality of my blood, the form of my limbs, the weight of my brain, are all the final effects of the complex working of forces which have never felt the hand of the Creator since the origin of the universe. But Science asserts the authority of facts; let us, then, have all the facts. It remains true that I am conscious of the power of choice, of moral freedom; my acts of virtue, my acts of vice, are my own. You tell me that law and the effects of law enter even into my moral nature; for the energy of my resolution, my susceptibility to special temptations, my capacity for special forms of goodness, are affected to some extent—to a large extent—by my physical nature which law has contributed to mould. But in the heart of all there is a mysterious freedom. I am not absolutely bound by the chain of necessity. In my moral life I am not like the tree or the flower which has no choice whether it shall blossom and bear fruit or not ; I am not like the star which must move in the orbit to which it is bound ; I am involved in the universal system of necessity, and yet in the centre and heart of my being I am free.

Demonstrate, therefore, if you please,—I listen with tranquillity to your demonstration,—that as far back as the faintest records of the existence of the world extend, there are traces of the steadfastness and invariableness of the natural order ; that the rain and the winds and all the forces of the universe which seem most wayward and restless are as absolutely under its control as the rising and setting of the sun ; let science take the words of the ancient saint addressed to the living God, and show that there is no extravagance in using them of the mighty, the universal, the irresistible power of law—" Thou hast beset me behind and before, and laid Thine hand upon me. If I ascend up into heaven Thou art there; if I make my bed in hell Thou art there. If I take the wings of the morning and dwell in the uttermost parts of the sea even there shall Thy hand lead me, and Thy right hand hold me." All this, instead of destroying my faith in the nearness of God and the possibility of intercourse between myself and Him, banishes the fear, annihilates the doubt, which the discovery of the vastness of the universe had suggested ; for this demonstration is the assurance that in the midst of these tremendous and awful forces, in the midst of the almost infinitely varied phenomena of beauty, majesty, glory, and terror by which you have endeavoured to confound and humiliate me, I stand alone ; alone, because I am invested with the unique and Divine prerogative of freedom. The whole universe is subjugated to the authority of natural law ; but for me there is reserved an inviolable liberty. You have demonstrated that I am separated from Nature. I may be akin to God. It is possible, after all, that God may be mindful of me, and may visit me.

As for those modern thinkers who are renewing the old controversy concerning the moral freedom of man, they are engaged in a hopeless struggle. Their controversy is not with a philosophy or with a religion, but with the human race. The whole history of mankind is the proof of man's consciousness of freedom. The proof appears in the literature, the language, and the laws of every nation in the ancient and the modern world.

We acknowledge that law reigns all around us —stretches from our feet to the farthest limit, not only of our vision, but of our thought ; and yet, so long as in our moral life we know that we are free, we can look up into the face of the living God with the hope that He will deal with us one by one, that He will care for us, and that there may be direct communion between us and Him.

With the *hope*—yes; but with the hope and nothing more, so long as we have only Nature and the consciousness of our moral freedom to assist us.

III.

Where did the Psalmist, where did the Jewish race discover that heaven is so near to earth, and that God has so keen an interest in the life of man? David, when he looked on the shining heavens, asked, "What is man, that Thou art mindful of him? and the son of man, that Thou visitest him?" Nature came between him and God, until Nature was transfigured by the power of a victorious faith; and then the splendour of the heavens became the symbol of a diviner glory, and the thunder the echo of a mightier voice, and all the wealth of earthly harvests the expression of a celestial love.

But where did this faith come from? Where did David learn that the Lord is nigh unto all them that call on Him? The answer is to be found in that long series of supernatural revelations, of which we have the record in the Jewish Scriptures.

The most ancient traditions of his race—traditions preserved in the earliest pages of the Jewish sacred books—had taught the Psalmist that the most glorious and terrible forces of the material world, all its awfulness and all its beauty, the light and the darkness, the sun, the moon, and the stars, the mountains and the sea, and all living things, came into being at the word of God, and that God was apart from them all and above them all. These same traditions had taught him that although man is akin to the basest forms of life, and sprang from the earth which had brought forth cattle and creeping things and the beasts of the earth after their kind, he had received a diviner breath, which made him akin to the Creator of all things. Whence these traditions came —on whom the revelation first dawned that one living God created all things, and made man in His own image, who it was that gave this revelation the noble and poetic form in which it appears in the earliest pages of the book of Genesis—we do not know. But these thoughts concerning God and His relations to the universe and to man lay at the very root of the whole life of the Jewish race.

The rest of the sacred story was in harmony with the august beginning. Of a creature having such an origin, God could not but be mindful. If in the infancy of the world there was sin against Himself, God came to man, even in his sin, punished him for it, and yet originated the hope of redemption. If there was murder, human life was so sacred that the blood of the victim cried to heaven, and the terrible crime was terribly avenged. If wickedness spread through the whole race it grieved God at His heart, and He repented that He had made man on the earth. Do you tell me that repentance is impossible to God, that with the Absolute there can be no change, that with Him who foresaw all things from the beginning there can be no surprises ; I answer, that in this rude and rugged language the faith of ancient saints has uttered a deeper moral truth than the plummet of the profoundest speculation has ever touched, and that it would be one of the noblest triumphs of philosophy to give this truth a fit expression.

But still the story runs on ; and David saw that God had watched over the tents of Abraham and Isaac and Jacob, was mindful of them when their children were born, and when they buried their dead. They multiplied and grew into a nation, and endured great sufferings ; God was mindful of them still ; " I have surely seen the affliction of My people which are in Egypt, and have heard their cry by reason of their taskmasters ; for I know their sorrows, and I am come down to deliver them." Plague after plague descended upon their oppressors—it was because God was mindful of the oppressed. When they were delivered, He gave them laws, and, through His servant Moses, He organized their national life. The tabernacle was His home. The pillar of cloud and of fire was the visible assurance to the people that God was with them. The priests were the ministers through whom the nation might draw near to Him. The sacrifices were the ceremonial with which they were to enter His presence.

These were the facts, these the institutions, on which the devout man, whose delight was in the law of the Lord, meditated day and night ; and out of this meditation came the tranquil trust in the Divine goodness and care of the 23rd Psalm, the clear vision in the 19th Psalm of the glory of God shining through the radiant heavens, the bright thanksgivings of the 103rd Psalm, and all the keen and deep sense of God's close and free relations to mankind which invests the devotional poetry of the Jewish people with an imperishable value. These Old Testament Scriptures, we cling to them with an invincible affection,— they contain the earliest answers to the cry of the human heart after God.

IV.

But *we* have received a fuller and richer revelation, anticipating—perhaps augmenting as well as anticipating—the moral difficulties of a more complex civilization, and a more varied intellectual life. For, if in these Christian times the light is more intense than it was, the shadows are deeper. I suppose that some men have lost their faith in the very existence of God, who but for the influence on their moral and spiritual life of a Christian civilization would have looked almost unmoved on the confusion and sorrow which have driven them into unbelief. But I repeat that we have a fuller and richer revelation than that which was the strength of David's faith; and in this pulpit, week after week, as we trust, through many generations, this revelation, assuring us that God has not forgotten or forsaken our race, will be illustrated, and these walls will resound with songs of thanksgiving that the Eternal Word, the brightness of the Father's glory, and the express image of His Person, was made flesh and dwelt among men.

The Incarnation is the central truth of the Christian faith; and is the final answer of God to the natural fear of the human heart that God must be too great and high to have any close and permanent relations to our race. For this truth the Church had to maintain a fight which was protracted through many centuries against Gnostic and Arian and Nestorian heresies; and we in these last days should remember with devout and hearty gratitude the theologians who defended it with incorruptible fidelity and heroic courage, as well as with extraordinary intellectual subtlety and force.

It is the habit of our times to speak contemptuously of the great doctrinal controversies of the Church, and to depreciate the spiritual importance of dogma. I wish to remind you that in the greatest of these controversies those truths and facts have been imperilled which assure us that God is very near to our race. Nothing is easier than to provoke unintelligent laughter by poor jests about the fanatical enthusiasm which was kindled in Alexandria and Constantinople between the partisans of the *Homoousion* and the partisans of the *Homoiousion* theory of our Lord's person. Nothing is easier than to assume a tone of impressive solemnity in rebuking the orthodox theologians of those days for their profane presumption in venturing with their logic and their metaphysics into the mysterious depths of the Divine nature, and for endeavouring to frame definitions when they ought to have fallen prostrate in adoration and awe. But let it never be forgotten that it is not the orthodox that are ultimately responsible for the presumption with which they alone are charged; they only pursued with the logic of orthodoxy the logic of heresy. The attempt was made so to define the relation of the Son of God to the Father as to rob the Church of the great truth that Christ was God Incarnate; and the Athanasian theology was a metaphysical protection of the fundamental truth of the Christian revelation against a metaphysical theory in which that truth was evaded or suppressed. The weapons by which the faith was defended were necessarily of the same kind as the weapons by which it was attacked. Both may have become as obsolete as the ships and the guns of the Armada, and the ships and the guns of the gallant sailors who fought for England against the power of Spain; but the freedom and independence of England, and the very existence of Protestantism on the continent of Europe, were at stake when our fathers went out to fight the fleets of Philip. I for my part am not disposed to speak of their rude vessels and their ruder guns with contempt; and I see in the metaphysics and logic of Athanasius and his comrades the best weapons which the Church in those centuries could command for the defence and the security of the most precious truth contained in the Gospel of Christ. The controversy between the Homoousians and the Homoiousians, was a controversy between those who affirmed and those who denied that Christ is God manifest in the flesh. That is a controversy of infinite significance. In the metaphysics—the unintelligible metaphysics, if you will—which formed so large a part of the theology of the early Church and which is perpetuated in ancient creeds, the real struggle was not for a theory of the Divine nature, but for that perfect faith in God's nearness to man which the truth of the Incarnation inspires, and of which it is the sure and enduring defence.

One form of heresy arose after another, and the struggle had to be maintained through century after century. It was successful at last. For a thousand years Eastern and Western Christendom, notwithstanding transient and local divisions, have confessed with St. Ambrose, "Thou art the King of glory, O Christ. Thou art the everlasting Son of the Father. When Thou tookest upon Thee to deliver man Thou didst not abhor the Virgin's womb. When Thou hadst overcome the sharpness of death, Thou didst open the kingdom of heaven to all believers. Thou sittest at the right hand of God, in the glory of the Father." God helping us, we are resolved that the results of the triumphs of the ancient Church shall not be lost.

They *would* be lost if we so preached about the earthly life of Christ, His humiliation, His sufferings, His death, as to accustom men to think only of His mortal weakness. "The Word was made flesh and dwelt among us;" but while we tell men of His hunger and thirst and pain, His human affections, His accessibility to temptation, and His nights of prayer, we must also enable them to recognise His glory—"the glory as of the only begotten of the Father, full of grace and truth." I think I have sometimes seen, in the writings even of those who would claim for themselves exceptional fidelity to the orthodox and Evangelical creed, the unambiguous proof that they have a most inadequate sense of the majesty of the Son of God. They speak of Him with a fondling affection which is inconsistent with true reverence. Their faith in His sympathy with them in their sorrows is real; but there is no such awe as must come from a deep and living sense of His moral authority. They are always lying on His breast; they never fall at His feet with wonder and fear. There is a similar failure to recognise Him as "the brightness of the Father's glory and the express image of His person," in theologians of a very different school—theologians who acknowledge in their creed the true Deity of our Lord, but who are so interested in His human development, so fascinated with the ethical perfection of His character, with His tenderness to the infirmities of men, His merciful words to those who had grievously sinned, and the charm of His human friendships, so touched with the pathetic story of the tears which He shed over Jerusalem, and the agony which came upon Him in the garden, that they ignore the manifestations of that supernatural and Divine glory which again and again broke through the clouds in which it was for a time concealed.

It is true that in His love for us sinners and in His eagerness for our salvation, He descended from the throne of God to the low levels of our human life; but while we are telling the story of His voluntary poverty, it becomes us to remember that it *was* voluntary, and to speak of His infinite wealth. While He wears for us the form of a servant, it is for us to confess that He is Lord of all. While we look upon Him in the likeness of men, it is profane presumption for us to forget that He is Divine. And when He humbles Himself and becomes obedient unto death, even the death of the cross, we who are watching His sufferings and shame should remember the glory which He had with the Father before the world was. It is not for us to prolong His humiliation, to keep Him uncrowned, to withhold in these the days of His triumph the homage which He voluntarily surrendered during the years that He was visibly present among men. If we do, we shall wrong *Him;* we shall also wrong ourselves, and shall impair the force of the Gospel which is entrusted to us. The power of the Christian Gospel as an assurance that God has been mindful of man and has visited him, depends upon the earnestness and the vigour with which we are able to assert the great truth that Christ Jesus our Lord was God manifest in the flesh.

V.

The ultimate—the spiritual—question at issue in the controversies of the early Church concerning the

Person of Christ and the Trinity was, whether God is a God nigh at hand; the same question was at issue in the controversies of the Reformation.

Those who have built this Church claim to be the true heirs and representatives of the Reformers. We are not, indeed, so presumptuous and arrogant as to assert that we Congregationalists, and we alone of all English Christians, are true to the genius of the great movement which gave inspiration and freedom to the religious, the social, the intellectual, and the political life of the northern nations of Europe in the sixteenth century, and which renewed the energy and arrested the corruption even of those nations which resisted it. We recognise and honour the fidelity of those clergy and laymen of the Anglican Church who, under adverse conditions, harassed by great difficulties and perplexities, are endeavouring to protect the Protestantism of the Establishment. We rejoice in the vigour of the great communities outside the Establishment in which the fires of a generous Protestant zeal are burning with all their ancient ardour—the Methodists, the Baptists, the Presbyterians of England. But we claim our place in the ranks of those who are most faithful to the traditions of the Reformation, and we accept the responsibilities which the claim implies.

The struggle of the Reformation did not begin with Luther, and Luther did not carry it to its final issue; and we shall fight with more courage and energy for the victory, which still lies perhaps in the remote future, if we see clearly that Protestantism is a testimony, on the one hand, to the infinite condescension and mercy of God, and, on the other, a vindication of the noblest prerogatives which God's goodness has conferred upon man.

It is not merely the vastness and the permanence of the material universe, contrasted with his own apparent insignificance and the brief limits of his mortal life, which sometimes make it hard and almost impossible for a thoughtful man to believe that there can be any free intercourse between himself and God. The consciousness of guilt and of moral infirmity oppresses him. How can we hope that God will come near to us in our sin? How can we dare, while our sin is upon us, to draw near to God? If it is possible for us by bitter penitence, by self-inflicted pains, by successful conflict with our inferior passions, by a lavish charity, to atone in some sense for our past offences and to show the sincerity of our amendment, then perhaps, after long and weary years of suffering and of austere living, it may be that the light of the Divine presence will shine round about us, and we may have the perfect rest which comes from the assurance that God is at peace with us. Luther said, No—God is mindful of you already, and already He is eager to visit you. He does not condemn you to pass cheerless years in austere self-discipline and incessant conflict with temptation before He is willing to make you glad with the assurance of His forgiveness and His love.

At the best, there is pain before you and severe effort, and battle and storm; but He comes to your side at the beginning of it all, instead of at the end. You are to be justified, not by works, which it may take years to get through, but by faith, which may be the act of an hour, the act of a moment. As soon as you confess His authority and trust in His love, He will absolve you for Christ's sake from all your sins— absolve you without qualification and without reserve; He will reveal His absolution, that the knowledge of it may make you happy and strong; He will be your ally in the great battle with sin, will fight by your side from the very first, instead of leaving you to fight alone and only receiving you into His favour when the battle is almost over and the victory almost won.

This was what Luther meant, this was what all the Reformers meant, by the great doctrine of Justification by Faith. The doctrine is the answer to man's natural fear that while he is conscious of sin God will not come near to him. The doctrine may have been expressed in forms which to some of us are incredible and intolerable; but half Europe knew what Luther and the Reformers meant, saw in it a Divine message, and hailed it with rapturous joy. Rome had been compromising with the natural fears suggested by the consciousness of sin; Luther declared war against the fears as well as against the sin, and told the world that Christ had died, the Just for the unjust, to bring, not saints, but sinners to God.

The whole of the Protestant controversy in the sixteenth century was a struggle for the truth involved in the controversy on the doctrine of Justification by Faith; and from this truth the controversy in our own times derives all its dignity and interest. The question at issue is, whether God is a God nigh at hand.

The secular life appears to many men common and unclean. They think that God may be with the monk or the nun whose nights and days are spent in seclusion and prayer, but not with the mother in her family, not with the manufacturer in his works, not with the tradesman in his shop, not with the lawyer in his office, not with the physician in the sick room, not with the artist in his studio, not with the statesman in the agitation and excitement of political conflict. Rome makes a shameful concession to this distrust by drawing a distinction between the secular and the religious life, and she invites those who would live in the light of God to devote themselves to celibacy and to forsake the world. The majesty of the Divine throne fills men with awe and dread, and they ask, Who are we that we should venture to draw near to God? Rome takes sides with their fears, and tells them that they may have the intercession of the Virgin and the saints, when, conscious of guilt, they shrink from the immediate presence of Him whose law they have broken. And Rome permits the confession of sin to be made to a priest; and the lips of a priest pronounce absolution from sin. The devout soul is troubled and perplexed by questions concerning the ways and the will of God to which it can find no answer; it despairs of discovering the truth ; and Rome, instead of asserting that those who listen for themselves to the words of Christ, and who invoke the illumination of the Holy Ghost, will receive Divine teaching—all the teaching necessary for faith and holy living—confirms the despair and tells all Christendom to wait for the decisions of Councils and Popes.

Against all these compromises with a faltering faith, these concessions to unbelief, we protest. These are not speculative errors ; they touch the very centre and heart of the Christian faith. They strip the commonalty of the Church of the prerogatives which God has conferred. They close up the direct access to God which has been opened for all men by Him who is the "Way" to the Father.

VI.

We protest ; but let us not forget, in the vehemence of our protest, that the God who, as we contend, is so near, is a living God. He is near, and yet He may surround Himself with clouds and darkness, and may be altogether hidden from us. The old Calvinistic doctrine of the Divine sovereignty was sometimes defined in terms which revolt our moral sense ; but it was a hard and stern method of expressing a truth which is essential to a just conception of God and of our relations to Him. He is a living Person—not an unconscious force, or "a power not ourselves working for righteousness." The free access of one person to another depends on the voluntary action of both. It is not enough that *we* draw nigh unto Him—He must draw nigh to us.

It is possible to think of God as though He were like the air and the sunlight, so that, when we throw back the shutters and open the windows of the soul, we shall, as a matter of course, be filled with the fresh wind and with the glory of heaven. The dogma of the Divine sovereignty was, in its essence, a formal denial of this degradation of the conception of God. It affirmed that He, too, has a will, and that all His acts in relation to mankind are controlled and directed by it. In the material universe His will may manifest itself in forces which are constant and invariable; and those who search after God in that inferior region of His activity may find no trace of His free personality. In the spiritual universe He is a Person in relation with persons, and *our* freedom is an imperfect symbol of His.

There is nothing arbitrary in His volitions, but it remains true that His volitions are free. No blind necessity constrains Him. The blessings which He confers are not like the harvest which is yielded by the unconscious earth; they are the voluntary gifts of an infinite love. If the brightness of His presence shines upon us, the brightness does not come like the splendour of the rising sun, but as the effect of His own voluntary revelation of His glory.

There is an atheism of which the Church may be guilty which is not less fatal, and which, in many respects, is infinitely more tragic, than the atheism of speculative unbelief. Against that atheism I warn you this morning. It is not enough that when you assemble within these walls your hearts should be melted and penetrated with awe, by the reverence and pathos of the prayers in which you confess your sin, and invoke the Divine pity and acknowledge the Divine goodness; or that you should be excited by the vehemence and passion of sacred song. Do you believe that the living God listens to your prayers? Do you expect Him to accept your worship and your praise? It is not enough that the preacher should illustrate the Divine law. Do you expect God Himself to reveal His authority and incline your hearts to obey His commandments? It is not enough that your sorrow should be soothed by listening to tender words concerning the Divine consolation. Does God Himself console? It is not enough that you should hear eloquent and impassioned declamations on the Divine mercy. Is God present to forgive? You can find no enduring courage and strength in noble and trustful declarations that God is near to you in your weakness and peril. Is God mindful of you, and does He visit you?

If a Church relies for all moral and spiritual good on the reflex influence upon its moral and spiritual life of its own spiritual acts, it is a Church which has renounced its faith in the living God.

VII.

This stately and beautiful building is set apart to-day to sacred uses. No mystic glory symbolizes the permanent presence of God within its walls; nor do we believe that there is any sense in which God dwells in this place in which He does not dwell in a Christian home, or in a house of business where His authority is supreme, or in the halls where statesmen meet to legislate for the secular affairs of nations, if only they confess that He is King of Kings and Lord of Lords, and discharge the duties of government in the eye of God and for His glory. But God will be here whenever you meet together in the name of Christ. His presence is assured, not to consecrated buildings, but to consecrated persons; and this church is erected that those who believe that God is mindful of men, and is nigh to all them that call upon Him, may meet together to invoke and to rejoice in His presence.

On this ground I appeal to you to contribute generously to the cost of its erection. I ask you to think of those who will come here distracted with care and worn with grief, and who will find in God rest and consolation; of those who will come with their hearts burdened with sin, to whom God will mercifully grant absolution. Your own children may sit in future years on the very seats which you are now occupying, and may sit there when they are in the very crisis of a struggle with fierce temptation, and from the lips of the preacher they may hear words of warning or of hope which will move them to implore the defence of God ; they will receive it and be saved from shameful sin. How many thousands of men will learn within these walls to fear God and to hate iniquity ; will receive strength to master the world, the flesh, and the devil ; will be inspired by Christ Himself with a universal charity ; will see the glory of heaven breaking through the clouds which gather about the grave ; will anticipate, in the joy of present communion with God, the eternal blessedness which is the inheritance of the saints on the other side of death. Here, through generation after generation, the Good Shepherd who came to seek and to save the lost will lay His strong and gentle hand on thousands of His sheep that have erred and strayed from the flock and the fold, and bring them back to the green pastures and the still waters which they have forsaken. Here, through Him who is the Way to the Father, innumerable devout souls will have access to God. It is a noble and sacred work which has been undertaken by this congregation, and of which we now witness the completion ; and I ask you by the generosity of your contributions to show, not your sympathy with them merely, but the vigour of your faith in God's nearness to man, and the depth of your gratitude for His condescension and His grace.

VI.

SOCIAL SCIENCE AND THE CHRISTIAN FAITH.[1]

"What shall a man be profited, if he sha'l gain the whole world, and forfeit his life? Or what shall a man give in exchange for his life."—*Matt.* xvi. 26.

THESE words seem to me an admirable motto for a Social Science Congress. They express the real spirit which originated assemblies of this kind nearly thirty years ago. They define the principle which should govern the discussion of all the questions which the Congress has met to consider. They give unity to the inquiries of all its sections. For although Lord Brougham, the first president of the Association described its aim to be "the scientific study of the laws which govern men's habits as members of a community, and of the principles of human nature, upon which the structure of Society and its movements depend," its real work has not been speculative. It has contributed very little to

---

[1] Delivered in Carr's Lane Meeting House, Birmingham, on Sunday morning, September 21st, 1884, during the meetings in Birmingham of the National Association for the Promotion of Social Science.

the science of Sociology, but has promoted many practical reforms.

I.

According to the traditions of these annual congresses, the province of social science is to discover how social conditions may be made more favourable to the perfection of human life. Other definitions of the science might be given,—definitions which would attribute to it quite a different function. But the proceedings of these meetings have shown that their promoters have desired to consider the relations of the whole social environment to the whole nature of man, and to investigate these relations with a definitely practical aim. As treated at these Congresses, the science has really been, not a science, but an art.

Consider for a moment how this distinguishes what has been described as Social Science from the science of Political Economy as expounded by the great English economists. Political economy has a very definite and a comparatively narrow problem. It deals with the laws which determine the production and distribution of wealth; and because the true limits of the science have been misapprehended, it has been attacked with extraordinary violence, as though it were inspired with some malignant spirit, unfriendly to the highest interests of the human race. It has been called the dismal science. Those who cultivate it have been denounced as men without pity for the miseries of the poor, indifferent to human rights, careless about all that contributes to the happiness and honour of individual men, and to the true strength and glory of nations. Great legislative measures, founded on justice, and intended to redress enormous wrongs which have inflicted misery on millions of men, and shaken the foundations of national security, have been described—with a certain exultation—as violations of the principles of political economy.

All this vehemence is unreasonable: it is the result of a misapprehension. Political economy does not profess to give rules of conduct to statesmen. It claims no authority to guide public legislation and policy. It holds a merely subordinate and ministerial position.

Take, for example, the question of Free Trade. A political economist will prove that protective duties diminish national wealth. But if an American statesman says, Wealth is not the supreme object of national existence; we care for wealth, but we care still more for the rich and varied development of our national life; we do not want America to become a nation of farmers; we want a variety of occupations for the sake of developing variety of personal character, and for the sake of stimulating different kinds of intellectual activity; we want cotton-spinners, cloth-weavers, workers in iron, workers in silver and gold, as well as ploughmen, reapers, shepherds, herdsmen, and therefore we protect our manufactures against European competition—if an American statesman says this—the political economist answers, Very good: questions of that kind lie beyond my province: they belong to the science of politics, not to political economy: all that I have to say is, that to get this variety of national life by a policy of protective duties, you must sacrifice some portion of your national wealth: you may be rich enough to do it: for the sake of the "variety of national life" the farmers of the West may be willing to subsidize the manufacturers of New England and Pennsylvania: it may be worth their while to do it: that is not my concern: my only business is, to show you what you are doing, and to make it quite clear that protective duties cannot increase national wealth, but must lessen it.

You have no right to find fault with an economist because he refuses—as an economist—to deal with subjects lying outside the limits of political economy. It is his duty, as an economist, to explain to you the laws which affect wealth—the production of wealth—the distribution of wealth. Wealth may be a dismal subject; and the science of wealth may, therefore, be a dismal science. But it is just as necessary to investigate questions relating to wealth, however dismal they may be, as to investigate questions relating to sewage, which is also very far from being an exhilarating subject of inquiry. And I say, again, that when the investigations of the political economist are ended, the results have absolutely no authority to guide the conduct of nations and statesmen; all that the economist professes to do is to discover how legislation, how different forms of industrial and social organization, affect the production and distribution of wealth. By one policy a nation will get more wealth—by another, less; but no economist that understands the true nature and position of his science presumes to say which of these two policies a nation ought to pursue. For nations, as for individuals, wealth is not the end of life; it is only one of the means of living. What shall a nation be profited if it shall gain the whole world and forfeit its life—physical health, intellectual activity, manly vigour, womanly gentleness, the joy of childhood, the calm repose of old age, honesty, courage, truthfulness, kindness, the purity of the home, public spirit, the virtue and the happiness to which wealth ought to contribute? The statesman ought to care for the development of all the strength, and grace, and nobleness, and joy of the national life; the increase of national wealth, and its wiser and more equitable distribution are only means subordinate to this.

Social science has a much wider province than political economy. It deals not merely with questions about wealth, but with questions about man. It does not consider the organization of society merely in relation to the production of things which can be bought and sold, nor merely in relation to the distribution of these things, but in relation to human life.

The Congress, therefore, divides itself into sections

—investigates, for example, questions relating to public health. In the long run, the increase of public health may contribute to the increase of wealth; but the true sanitary reformer does not ask whether an improvement in the water supply of a town, or the increase of its open spaces, or a change for the better in the homes of the people, will add to our exports and imports, increase our turn-out of cotton goods and hardware, make the income-tax more productive; it is not his business to show how the community is to become richer; his business is to show how it is to become healthier. Other sections discuss questions of education and art, not primarily, much less exclusively, with the purpose of learning how to increase the productive power of the nation, but of learning how to enrich and discipline its intellectual life. The education section, the art section, decline to be considered as merely subordinate to the section for economy and trade. It is not their duty to consider merely how boys and girls can be made more effective "hands" in a manufactory, but how their whole life—including their life in the manufactory, but also including their life in hours of leisure—can be made more vigorous, more varied, more delightful. It is not their business to consider by what artistic cultivation the products of their industry can be made so beautiful as to command the markets of the world, but by what artistic cultivation the people themselves may come to find delight—and something more precious than delight—refinement of thought, delicacy of sympathy, grace and gentleness of manner —in those realms of beauty which should be the common possession of all ranks and orders in the State.

We might therefore claim for social science what the Greeks would have called architectonic rank; except that the statesman would maintain, and maintain justly, that social science is only one department of politics; and the moralist, in his turn, would assert, and assert justly, that even politics are only a section of morals; and I should add, that the province of morals is included under the still wider sovereignty of religion.

II.

In discussing the relations of the Christian faith to such questions as those which come under the consideration of the Social Science Congress, it is natural for a Christian preacher to recall the influence which has been already exerted by the Christian Church on European Society. That subject is a very interesting one. The history is full of attractive and brilliant incidents. To illustrate it fully would require an estimate of the change produced in the general spirit and temper of Christian nations by the honour which the Christian faith attributes to charity and all the gentler virtues; we should have to consider the immense effect of the story of the Christian miracles which have taught Christian men of all lands and of all ages that in the imitation of

Christ works of mercy for mankind have as large a place as prayer and the worship of Almighty God; it would also be necessary to inquire to what extent the Christian revelation of judgment to come, even when it has been degraded and corrupted by a mechanical and legal theology, has compelled men to believe that to be clothed in purple and fine linen, and to fare sumptuously every day is an offence against the infinite charity of God, while the sorrows of the wretched are unconsoled and the wants of the poor are unrelieved.

We should have to tell the story of slaves redeemed from slavery by the sale of the silver and golden vessels used in the celebration of the Holy Communion; of the administrative power of bishops who built workshops for the destitute, and organized relief for cities and provinces suffering from famine. We should have to remember the times when a great hospital for the sick, the aged, the poor, was a part of the organization of nearly every great Church, and when learning found its only shelter and encouragement in the schools and colleges established and taught by the Christian priesthood.

But this review of what has already been achieved by the power of the Christian Gospel has a certain danger in it. The splendid achievements of remote centuries may so master the imagination as to prevent us from discovering the new and unfamiliar ways in which the Christian Gospel should exert its force in our own times. It is not only in theological belief that tradition may be too strong for us; and both in practical life and in speculation originality is the characteristic of a real and vigorous faith. If we are to render any great service to our own age, we must derive our chief inspiration, not from the remembrance of the services which the Church rendered to countries, to centuries, to populations, very unlike our own, but from the Christan revelation itself, which is not a tradition, but a fresh and living word from God our Father in heaven to His children in every age.

III.

I have said that the province of social science is to investigate the relation of the social environment to the whole life of man. We shall be indifferent to this investigation or shall regard it with supreme interest according to our estimate of the worth and dignity of the life of man. The loftier is our conception of what man is—the individual man—the more earnest, the more laborious, will be our endeavour to discover how man is affected by his social condition and what changes in the social order would contribute to his perfection.

There are many ways in which the Christian revelation may contribute both guidance and inspiration, light and enthusiasm, to those who are engaged in the various sections of this congress, the section of jurisprudence, the section of economy and trade, the health section, the section of education, the section of art—but this morning I ask you to consider the Christian account of man himself, in relation to whose life all these separate inquiries are being conducted.

Our conception of man lies at the foundation of our theory of social duties and of a just organization of society. Before we can determine what are the obligations of society to individual men and to classes of men, before we can discover the obligations of individual men and of classes of men to society, we have to arrive at some conclusion concerning the powers and capacities, the real contents and possibilities of human life. How does man differ—does he differ at all—from the inferior races which we enslave, which we compel to live for *us*, not for themselves, which we train to do our work, which we kill for food? Our whole theory of the social order will depend upon our answer to that question.

The Christian revelation answers it in a very surprising manner. The answer is not worn out. It has not spent its force. It is of a kind that must make it full of inspiration to the latest ages of human history. But there is another reason for its freshness and vigour; it has never yet been fully expressed, either in the institutions of society or in the organization of the Church. It contains an immense reserve of unexhausted energy.

The Christian account of man has indeed never secured its true place even in the confessions of the great Churches of Christendom. Theologians have

never adequately defined it. About the Christian
idea of God there have been prolonged controversies which have left conspicuous monuments in
famous creeds; but the controversies about the
Christian idea of man have been much less thorough;
they have rarely passed beyond the limits of the
questions at issue more than fourteen hundred years
ago between Augustine and Pelagius; they have
approached the subject on only one side, and have
left large provinces of truth wholly unexplored.

And yet about the *substance* of the Christian doctrine of man there can be no doubt; and though it
has been so imperfectly apprehended by scientific
theology, it has exerted an immense influence on
Christian life and conduct. For the Christian doctrine of man is really a part of the Christian doctrine
of God. The two are not only inseparable; the one
is largely included in the other. I suppose that to
most men, and perhaps to most orthodox Christians,
the discussions which were carried on in the Council
of Nicæa and the doctrines which are defined in the
creed inaccurately attributed to Athanasius, lie far
remote from Christian practice. Very many of those
who believe in the doctrine of the Trinity regard it
as a mystery, to be received on authority, but rather
a strain on faith than a support to practical righteousness. That there is any real and direct relation between that supreme truth and Christian morals or
the Christian ideal of the social order, never occurs
to them. And this is one reason why Christian

morality is wanting in energy, originality, dignity, and grace, and why the Christian ideal of society has not become infinitely nobler. The Christian doctrine of man is implicated in the Christian doctrine of God, or, to speak more exactly, in the Christian doctrine of the Trinity; and the Christian doctrine of man determines the Christian theory of morals and the Christian theory of society.

Let me explain this as briefly as I can. The faith of Christendom, its ethics and its worship, rest on the Lord Jesus Christ, in whom the Church has recognised the eternal life and the eternal glory of God. That it should be possible for God to be manifested under the forms and conditions of a human history, in the character and the life of man, is a wonderful illustration of the greatness of human nature. A certain kinship between man and God is implied in the Incarnation.

And, according to the faith of the Christian Church, this alliance between God and humanity in the person of the Lord Jesus Christ was not transient. In Him the eternal Son of God *became* Man, and in Him the eternal Son of God *remains* Man. The human nature of the Lord Jesus Christ, exalted and transfigured, its powers enlarged beyond the limits of our thought, is the permanent manifestation and organ of the life of God. The awful personal supremacy which we attribute to God belongs to the Lord Jesus Christ. We never know the immeasurable possibilities of development belonging to human nature, its possibilities of power, its possibilities of wisdom, its possibilities of moral perfection, until we receive the revelation of these amazing facts.

Nor was the Incarnation of our Lord Jesus Christ an isolated and abnormal wonder. It was God's witness to the true and ideal relation of all men to God. Man, according to the earliest representation of him in the books which preserve and illustrate in various forms, in history and in song, in prophecy and in myth, in proverb and in prayer,—man, I say, according to the earliest representation of him in the books which preserve and illustrate the successive movements of the chief divine revelations to our race, belongs on the one hand to the material universe; he sprang from the dust; he shares the physical life of the inferior races; but he belongs on the other hand to an invisible and eternal order; he was made in the image of God and received the inspiration of the Divine life. According to the fuller and clearer discoveries of a later age, his higher life has its springs in the eternal life of the Son of God. A Divine word, said some of the ancient Stoics, is at the root of the life of every man—a noble conception of human nature, carrying with it the inference that every man's history is to be the translation into character and conduct of a Divine thought and purpose. Men were created, according to a Christian apostle, in Christ, the eternal Son of God, the eternal Word of God, and they were created in Him that they might share His eternal relations to the Father. We are branches of Christ, the eternal Vine—branches which began to grow out of the eternal roots but yesterday, but destined, if we are loyal to Him, to remain in Him for ever. And as the branches are necessary to the vine, so the human race and its relations to Christ, and to the Father through Him, were in a very true sense necessary to the fulfilment of the law of Christ's own relations to the Father.

Christian theology finds the ultimate explanation of man, the transcendent ideal of the life of man, the prophecy of the perfection of man, in the very life of God. Our faith is not a Deism, which affirms an infinite distance between man and God; nor a Pantheism, which merges the personality of man in the personality of God. It finds in God Himself distinctions which, for want of a better term, we must call personal, and in union with the eternal Son of God we share His Divine nature and His eternal blessedness in the Father.

For this every man was created, and only as this is actually realized does man reach the perfection to which God has destined him. Christ's prayer for His disciples expresses the Christian ideal of the relations of all men to each other and to God. "Neither for these only do I pray, but for them also that believe on Me through their word; that they may all be one, as Thou, Father, art in Me and I in Thee, that they also may be in us: . . . and the glory which Thou hast given Me I have given unto them, that they may be perfected into one."

To us, therefore, there is in every man—no matter how mean and wretched may be his external condition—no matter how feeble his intellectual powers —no matter how narrow the limits of his knowledge —no matter how coarse his habits—no matter how gross his vices—to us there is in every man the possibility of realizing this wonderful relationship to God. In his perception, however obscure, of the authority of duty, and of the infinite difference between right and wrong, we recognise the presence and activity of Christ, who is the Light that lighteth every man; in his capacity for religious faith and worship we recognise his relationship, not merely to the invisible and eternal *world*, but to the invisible and eternal God— his Father and ours. His moral freedom leaves it to his own choice whether he will fulfil the Divine ideal or not. Divine purposes may be thwarted. It is God's purpose that men should be truthful, and many men are liars; it is God's purpose that men should be temperate, industrious, kindly, and many men are self-indulgent, indolent, malicious; man was created for virtue, he may live in vice. And as God's purpose may be defeated in the region of man's moral life, it may also be defeated in the highest region of all—in the region of man's direct relations to God Himself. By perverse resistance to conscience, by hostility to the gracious and beneficent and ennobling restraints of moral law, by a refusal to submit to the personal supremacy of God, and to find all perfection and honour and blessedness in Him, man may defeat the Divine purpose for which he was created in Christ; but he was created that he might share the Divine life in Christ, and be eternally one with God in Him.

That great conception of man, which, as I have said, is implicated in our conception of God, lies at the root of Christian morals, and determines the Christian ideal of the social order. Every man has in Him the capacity—not only for knowing God, obeying God, worshipping God—but for eternal union with God. All our duties to other men—in the family, in business, in general society, as members of the same municipality, as citizens of the same, commonwealth,—are to be modified and controlled by this conception. Christian morals, a Christian social order, must be based on the Christian conception of the greatness of individual men.

IV.

But it may be objected that the Christian conception of the grandeur of man's relation to God and to eternity, if it really takes possession of the faith and of the imagination of great communities, must encourage indifference to social injustice, to physical misery, and to all the evils of man's present condition. What is there in the most cruel sufferings of this transient earthly life to touch the pity of those who believe that the human race was created for an infinite and eternal inheritance in God?

The objection, however plausible it may look, and

whatever strength it may derive from abnormal and fanatical developments of the Christian life, finds no support in the general *history of the Christian Church.* The fresh enthusiasm of the first converts to the Christian faith led to what a cool criticism may pronounce to have been a reckless and pernicious provision for the poor. The early Church—the Church of the first chapters of the Acts of the Apostles—took the form of a great philanthropic association; Christian men became suddenly indifferent to wealth, and those who had lands and houses sold them to feed the hungry and to clothe the naked. They ceased to care about comfort and luxury for themselves, but they cared a great deal for the relief of the wants of other men. And throughout the history of the Church, whenever Christian faith in the eternal glories by which we are environed has been most vigorous, Christian men have shown the most passionate earnestness in the endeavour to lessen the temporal miseries of mankind. Secular charities have derived their inspiration from religious zeal.

The objection finds no support in the *teaching of the Lord Jesus Christ.* Nothing is more characteristic of that teaching than its perfect sanity. He did not, like the Stoics, teach that hunger and thirst and nakedness are not real evils; but while He told men to seek first God's kingdom and God's righteousness, and not to be anxious about what they should eat and what they should drink, and wherewithal they should be clothed, He added, "your heavenly Father knoweth that ye have need of all these things." The eternal God recognises the reality of the physical wants of men. Christian men, if they accept the authority of Christ, must recognise it too.

The objection finds no support in the *history and example of the Lord Jesus Christ.* He who came to reveal to men their present kinship to God, their capacity for union with God and for immortal blessedness in Him, was moved with compassion by every form of human suffering ; and His miracles, which to the men of His own time were among the proofs that He came from heaven, have perhaps their chief value in our age, as striking, startling, and most impressive illustrations of the duty that rests upon us to relieve the physical miseries of the race—to feed the hungry, not merely by acts of charity, but by a national policy which will give encouragement to industry by increasing its productive power and securing the most equitable distribution of the wealth which it creates ; to lessen pain and disease, not merely by care for the sick, but by sanitary legislation, which will prevent sickness ; to conquer death itself, not by restoring the dead to life again, which is beyond our power, but by social reforms, which will prolong the duration of human life, and delay the sad hour of bereavement.

The objection finds no support in the *Christian conception of human nature.* For, according to that conception, which, however, it would take too much time to illustrate fully, man is not a spiritual being, subjected to an accidental and transient connection with a physical organization ; his body is as real a part of him as that which has been called his soul, and is as necessary to the integrity of his nature. His life is a unity, though it touches the earth on one side and God on the other. Manicheeism, which surrenders this visible world to the devil and regards the flesh with hatred and contempt, was one of the heresies which the Church had to fight in very early centuries, and which it sternly condemned. Our whole life, including the intellect, the social affections and the physical organization, is one ; touch any part of it, and you touch the whole ; injure any part, and the whole may suffer harm. That is the Christian theory.

The physical condition of large masses of men is unfriendly to common morality ; and whatever is unfriendly to common morality, is hostile to the achievement of union with God. When we raise the physical life of men—give them purer air, better water, more wholesome food—we contribute to their chances of moral improvement, and by contributing to their chances of moral improvement we contribute to the possibility of their Christian perfection. It is a good thing, whatever may be our conception of man, to improve his physical condition. The discovery of man's relations to the eternal Son of God, creates new motives for doing it. The sanitary section of the Social Science Association is the fast ally of the Christian Church.

The intellect, which is disciplined in schools and

universities, is worth cultivating for its own sake; but when it is cultivated, men are less likely to be mastered by superstitions which conceal the glory of God—they are less likely to be governed by prejudices which impair the clearness of their moral perceptions—they are capable of a wider and exacter knowledge of the Christian revelation; and by the discipline of the intellect you increase a man's chances of knowing God and Jesus Christ whom He hath sent, whom to know is eternal life. The education section is the fast ally of the Christian Church.

The poverty of large classes in the community, a general want of employment, conflicts between labour and capital, mutual suspicion, distrust, and antagonism between landlord and tenant, any uncertainty in the rewards of industry, are fatal to the nobler moral qualities of a nation, and are therefore perilous to religious faith. The section of economy and trade is the fast ally of the Christian Church.

Art, whatever may be its direct relations to the more robust moral virtues, refines the coarseness of the fibre of men and may contribute to the grace and beauty of the moral ideal, and to the delicacy of the moral perceptions. It cultivates and enriches that region of sentiment which lies near the region of the religious affections. It may find expression for Christian faith and hope, and by finding expression for them may add to their fervour and their strength. The art section is the fast ally of the Christian Church.

Equitable laws are demanded by that eternal law of righteousness which is one with the will of God. They are good in themselves. They are good in their beneficent effect on the material condition of men. But they are also good for other reasons. Unjust laws confuse the moral sense of a nation, and encourage private injustice. Just laws are a discipline of morality, and a noble morality is friendly to faith. The section of jurisprudence is the fast ally of the Christian Church.

V.

But, to recur before closing to the main position which I have endeavoured to assert, I may be asked whether it is possible for those mysteries of the divine life—mysteries which cannot be explored by the boldest, hardiest, most adventurous thought, and which may seem to be inaccessible to the common mind,—I may be asked whether it is reasonable to suppose that these can have a real relation to the morals and the social order of Christian nations. But surely there is nothing to surprise us in the fact that truths which lie far beyond the reach of the great masses of mankind should have the most powerful influence on their lives and fortunes. Scientific discoveries, which are intelligible only to experts, change the organization of great industries, impoverish or enrich millions of men to whom they are wholly unintelligible. Not one in a hundred thousand of the people who use the telegraph have any apprehension of the scientific truths of which it is the application. The mastery of the principles of every science is possible to comparatively few; the applications of those principles improve the condition and lessen the labours of the commonalty of the race. Philosophical speculations, which in their principles and methods were beyond the comprehension of most men, have been the origin of political and social revolutions.

If the Christian revelation concerning the life of God were as remote from the minds of common men as the question implies, it might still be true that that revelation had the power to produce the most stupendous changes in the morality of nations, and in their social order. But however intricate, however perplexing, however confounding, may be the speculations of theologians on this great mystery, the substance of the revelation is received by millions of untaught men, for whom the commonest technical terms necessary to define it have no meaning. And the mystery is verified in their personal experience. They know that their life is a life in the eternal Son of God, and therefore a life in union with the Father; they know that it was for this life that all men were created.

And it is only by a return to those transcendent facts which have given to the Christian faith in past ages its power over the social life of Christendom that its power will be renewed and enlarged in our own times. Here lies the secret of that freshness and originality of moral thought, which is necessary to the Christian Church if it is to retain the moral leadership of Europe. Here lies the secret of that inspiration and vigour which alone can enable the Church to translate its new and loftier moral ideals into practice.

For the elevation of the social order we need a deeper reverence for man—for the individual man, and it is to be found in the relation of every man to the eternal Son of God. This gives sanctity to the outcast, and confers a more than royal dignity on the meanest of the human race. It is no metaphor that Christ uses in His account of the judgment of the nations. " I was an hungered, and ye gave Me meat ; I was thirsty, and ye gave Me drink ; I was a stranger, and ye took Me in ; naked, and ye clothed Me ; I was sick, and ye visited Me ; I was in prison, and ye came unto Me." No metaphor ; for between Christ and the hungry, the starving, the naked, the desolate, the sick, the oppressed, there are relations so intimate that the service we render to them is rendered to Him ; they are His brethren and more than His brethren. They were created to share His eternal life and blessedness, to be one with Him as He is one with the Father. " Inasmuch as ye did it to one of these least, ye did it unto Me."

In a sense far deeper than perhaps we have supposed, the two great commandments are akin to each other : " Thou shalt love the Lord thy God with all thy heart and with all thy soul, and with all thy mind and with all thy strength." This is the first and great commandment. But the second is *like* unto it : "Thou shalt love thy neighbour as thyself." Like—yes—because between man and God there are relations so close, so vital, that to love God perfectly is impossible without loving man. The first commandment requires us to love God; the second is like unto it, for it requires us to love man, who was made in the image of God. He that honoureth the Son, said Christ, honoureth the Father; and in truly honouring, loving, and serving men, who were created to share the eternal life of the eternal Son of God, we also honour, love, and serve God. The central mysteries of the Christian faith are the inspiration of a lofty morality, and the foundation of a noble social order.

NOTE.—Some parts of this discourse were used in an Introductory Essay written for a translation by my friend Mrs. Thorpe, of M. Schmidt's admirable treatise on the Influence of the Christian Faith on the Moral and Social Condition of the Roman Empire.

VII.

FAITH AND PHYSICAL SCIENCE.[1]

"No one knoweth the Son, save the Father; neither doth any know the Father, save the Son, and he to whomsoever the Son willeth to reveal Him."—*Matt.* xi. 27.

"NEITHER doth any know the Father, save the Son, and he to whomsoever the Son willeth to reveal Him"—that is an august and unique claim; the Lord Jesus Christ declares that only through Himself can any man come to know God. The august and unique claim has been followed by an august and unique history.

I.

During the eighteen hundred years which have passed since the earthly life of our Lord ended in the crucifixion, it is apparent that His influence on the thought of the human race has been immense. It has guided and governed the highest forms of intellectual energy. For more than a thousand years

---

[1] Delivered in Carr's Lane Meeting House on Sunday morning, September 5th, 1886, during the meeting in Birmingham of the British Association for the Advancement of Science.

after the meeting of the Council of Nicæa, early in the fourth century, it is hardly possible to mention the name of a single man of great speculative power in Europe, in Northern Africa, in Western Asia, who was not a Christian theologian; the only striking exceptions are to be found among the scholars who illustrated the brief but brilliant period of Saracenic civilization. The great poets, the great painters, the great orators, the great architects also did homage to the supremacy of Christ. It was confessed that He stood alone and apart, and that in Him man had found God.

And even since the great revolution in European thought which originated, partly in the recovery of the splendid creations of the genius of ancient Greece partly in the early triumphs of modern physical science, a long succession of men of the keenest, most vigorous, and most courageous intellect have found a more intense and more stimulating speculative interest in the Christian revelation than in any of those new fields of inquiry which have yielded to the patience and genius of recent times such dazzling and exciting results.

The influence which Christ has exerted on the thought of the commonalty of those nations which have accepted the Christian faith is not less remarkable. He has made the loftiest and sublimest conceptions of God, of the Universe, of the dignity and destiny of mankind, the common possession, through age after age, of uncounted millions of men who knew nothing of the learning of the schools and were familiar with only the rudest forms of secular literature —peasants whose strength was worn by their labour in the fields in the summer's heat and the winter's storm, shepherds who kept their flocks on lonely hills, workmen at the bench and at the forge.

But the influence of the Lord Jesus Christ has extended far beyond the limits of the intellectual life of man. The central elements of the Christian faith have vital relations to conduct. They imply and form a specific type of character. They contain a law of perfection. All the mysteries of the Christian revelation — the Trinity, the Incarnation, the Death of Christ for the redemption of the human race, the remission of sins, the gift of eternal life, the discovery of that city of God of which all Christian men are citizens, Judgment to come, the glory, honour, and immortality to which God has destined us in Christ,—all these are directly related to the Christian virtues which are commanded in the Sermon on the Mount. In the teaching of Christ doctrine and duty, promise and precept, go together. Christian mysteries which transcend the most adventurous speculation affect the humblest and obscurest forms of Christian practice. The fires of the sun in the distant heavens are not more necessary to ripen the wheat or to perfect the grace of the wild-flower than are the great revelations of Christ concerning God to create and sustain the characteristic Christian virtues. The religion of Christ regulates, inspires, and sustains the morals of Christ. The morals are a part of the religion.

II.

But it may be contended—it has been contended—that Art is also a religion, and that delight in beauty, and the study of beauty, may also create gracious and noble forms of morality; that Science—the patient, laborious investigation of the structure and laws of the physical universe—may render the same service. Dismissing the first of these contentions—the contention for the religious and ethical functions of Art—I propose, before considering more closely the great claim of Christ in the text, to say something about the contention for the religious and ethical functions of Science.

It is maintained that Science may answer some of the great ends which have hitherto been answered by Religion—may, in fact, have many of the attributes of Religion, may contribute similar, if not the same, elements to human life—may exert a similar, if not the same, influence on human character.

The discussion of this question may, perhaps, recall to some of you a book of great interest,[1] published a few years ago by a very eminent living author; and it is necessary, therefore, that I should say that I am not attributing to the writer of that book the claims on behalf of the religion of Science

---

[1] *Natural Religion*, by the Author of *Ecce Homo*.

which I propose to examine, although he has stated these claims with a clearness and force which I cannot find elsewhere. The argument of his book was missed by some of his readers; it was no part of his intention to maintain that what he described as Natural Religion could, without grave loss to mankind, take the place of the Christian faith.

But it is contended, I say, that Science—the investigation of the physical universe—is a kind of religion; and that the scientific man, though he rejects the Christian Gospel, and rejects every form of belief commonly described as Theistic, still retains what may be properly called a religious faith.

(1) For—"That man believes in a God who feels himself in the presence of a Power which is not himself, and is immeasurably above himself, a Power in the contemplation of which he is absorbed, in the knowledge of which he finds safety and happiness. And such now is Nature to the scientific man."

"Immeasurably above himself,"—there, perhaps, lies one of the chief perils of a deep devotion to the study of the physical universe. We are in danger of being mastered by its immensity, by the awful energy of its forces, by the contrast between our own brief and uncertain years and the ages of its vast duration—ages stretching back beyond the reach of the most daring thought—lost in clouds which imagination cannot pierce. But this is to surrender our regal claims, and to consent to the suppression and paralysis of those very powers of our nature to which religion appeals. The universe—the universe which lies within the range of the physical sciences—"immeasurably above" ourselves! I refuse its title to supremacy. I decline to confess inferior rank. The universe above me!—it is not my equal; much less is it great enough to be in any sense my God.

Do the planets know the laws which constrain them to keep their orbits? The man who can calculate their path is greater than the planets. Is the sun conscious of the fierce heats of its secular fires? The man who, at the distance of nearly a hundred millions of miles, can tell us about the fuel which feeds them is greater than the sun. The painter, or the poet, whose imagination kindles at the vision of mountain and river, cloud and sky, and who reveals on canvas or in song a diviner beauty than was caught by the outward sense, is greater than the physical earth and the physical heavens, which are unconscious of their own loveliness and to which no dream of a greater glory has ever come.

Let us stand erect, and scorn ourselves for the baseness which would acknowledge the supremacy of the unintelligent and unconscious forces of physical nature. Reason, memory, speculation—these raise us to a nobler rank.

It is no answer to this protest on behalf of the greatness of humanity, that our intellectual activities, wonderful as they are, may be only functions of our physical organization, and that our physical organization is the felicitous growth and creation of those unconscious powers whose last secret will in future centuries be wrested from them by physical science ; if the case is so, the dignity of the race still remains, and we can but say that these mysterious powers have achieved something that transcends themselves. In the presence of mere physical phenomena, however glorious, and of mere physical forces, however immense, the superior rank of the intellectual life asserts itself. Its titles are not imperilled by any impeachment of its origin and ancestry. It needs no other vindication of its supremacy than its own intrinsic and apparent greatness.

(2) It is said that in the presence of the physical universe the man who has a large knowledge of the revelations of modern science may be filled with a wonder and awe that are too rarely present in popular religion. This may be true. Our sense of the infinite greatness of God has been impaired. Religious thought in recent times has deserted those mountain solitudes in which devout hearts learnt to fear and to reverence the Eternal as well as to trust and to love Him. And a sense of the awful majesty of God is necessary not only for reverential worship and for some of the deeper experiences of the spiritual life, but for many moral virtues. It is the discipline of humility ; it is the inspiration of fortitude ; it contributes to that vigilant self-command which is one of the guarantees of fidelity to the highest law. The very virtues of a man who is not conscious of living under the control of a power immeasurably above

himself will miss a certain refinement and a gracious dignity which are necessary to perfection. But we must take care that the power which we reverence is really above us. The servility of slaves who are held down by a stern and irresistible force is something different in quality from the loyal courtesy and the manly reverence with which a free people regard an august throne. Science may render a service to the religious life of our times by its illustration of the immensity and grandeur of God's works; for if the universe is great, God is infinitely greater. But our religious awe must be reserved for God Himself.

(3) It is said further that—"the true theist should recognise his Deity as giving him the law to which his life ought to be conformed," and that to the scientific man his science is a religion because he believes that all happiness depends upon the careful adaptation of human life to the laws of nature.

There is no doubt an admirable ethical temper encouraged by devotion to scientific pursuits; and the patience and accuracy which they demand are the discipline of certain excellent ethical habits; but when the claim is preferred that scientific discovery discloses the laws to which human life ought to be conformed, the claim must be challenged.

For in what province of physical investigation has the scientific man any occasion to use the word "ought" in announcing his discoveries? Where does he find the idea for which the word stands? It belongs to a region of inquiry in which his instruments and methods are altogether valueless. He is conversant with facts and with facts which are not of the highest order; with the idea of duty he has nothing to do. He has to tell us what is, what has been, what will be, in certain limited regions of observation and experience; he passes into another and a higher world when he begins to speak of what ought to be.

What are called the laws of Nature are in no proper sense laws of conduct. They give us no assistance in determining what are the true aims and obligations of human life; they can only inform us when the aims have been already determined, how some of them may be reached; when the obligations have been already accepted, how some of them may be discharged; they perform even this humbler service imperfectly at the best, and sometimes they fail us altogether. In relation to "the law to which human life ought to be conformed," the function of science is secondary and ministerial, not authoritative and supreme. We must derive the law from religion and ethics; science can only assist us to discover the methods by which in some cases the law is to be fulfilled.

Take one of the most obvious illustrations. The physician, with his scientific resources, may tell me the methods by which I may be able to maintain my health, or to check the growth of a disease by which my life is endangered. But are the directions of the physician final in relation to conduct? Clearly not.

They are submitted to another and higher tribunal. Some of them are approved, some dismissed, on the authority of laws which lie beyond the reach of physical science. The physician tells me to drink claret instead of sherry, and to eat less meat. I obey, for I can do it without violating any ethical or religious duty. But he tells me that I must live near the moors or the sea; that I must leave my books and my desk; must spend five or six hours every day in the open air; must ride, or drive, or fish, or shoot; that if I go on working I shall break down in a very few years, and, a year or two later, shall die. That may be all true, but it contains no law which I am under any obligation to obey. Even supposing that I have the resources necessary to carry out his directions, it may be perfectly clear that I am bound to disregard them. My work may be of a kind which I have no more right to desert for fear of breaking down in health and shortening my life than a soldier has to desert his post for fear of being shot. It is the clear duty of the soldier to run the risk of being shot—that is his vocation; and no scientific demonstration of the mischievous effects of a gun-shot wound in the chest can in any way affect his duty; it may be just as clearly my duty to keep to my work at the risk of ruining my health and of dying before my time; and no scientific demonstration of the mischievous effects of those habits of life which are incident to my work can relieve me from guilt and dishonour if I leave the work undone. Is it a man's first duty to preserve his health and to live as long as he can? Does this take precedence of the duty of a statesman and a soldier to defend the safety and honour and prosperity of their country? Does it take precedence of the duty of a poet, of an artist, to enrich mankind with the most perfect creations which can be achieved by their genius? Does it take precedence of the duty of a man who has received a great faculty for scientific discovery to extend the boundaries of human knowledge? To these questions physical science can give no answer; the answer must come from higher sources.

But this is only an example and illustration of the inability of science to give us a law to which human life should be conformed, and of the invalidity of the claim that man is to find his happiness in obeying the laws of Nature. The laws of Nature are not to be obeyed; the knowledge of them is to be used in obedience to the laws of another and diviner authority.

And where—in all the discoveries of physical science—can you learn the obligations of truthfulness, of justice, of pity, of showing mercy to those who have erred and gone astray from the paths of righteousness, of self-sacrifice, or devotion to the public good? The man who recognises Nature as his Deity, and who receives from her "the law to which his life should be conformed," will find in the sacred books which contain the revelations of her will, neither the Sermon on the Mount nor even the Ten Commandments.

(4) But further, it is alleged that the scientific man finds in the contemplation of the universe endless delight. Nature is not only a power immeasurably above us; she is infinitely interesting and infinitely beautiful, interesting and beautiful not only in those aspects which are open to the common eye, but in the regularity of her methods; in the fascinations of mysteries partially revealed; in the broken clouds which half disclose and half conceal the wide regions which have as yet been only imperfectly traversed and imperfectly surveyed by scientific thought. It is suggested that the delight of the scientific man in the vision and admiration of Nature has a certain analogy to the delight of the Theist and the Christian in the vision and worship of God.

But as the greatness of our intellectual life requires us to assert our superior rank in the presence of the unconscious forces which are revealed in the phenomena of the physical universe, so the still higher greatness of our moral life requires us to demand a diviner object of admiration and diviner fountains of delight than can be discovered in the infinite beauty and infinite interest of Nature and her laws.

Our deepest reverence and joy should be reserved for that which is really greatest; and if we are arrested by any subordinate and secondary glories, our own life must suffer harm. The order of Nature is majestic; but to the majesty of Eternal Righteousness is due a more devout and reverential homage.

We may be fascinated by the beauty of Nature; but the mercy of the living personal God,—

> "Mercy carried infinite degrees
> Beyond the tenderness of human hearts,"—

should inspire a far more passionate affection and a far intenser delight.

The moral virtues—justice, courage, generosity, truthfulness, kindness, pity, self-sacrifice—belong to a nobler order than the fairest and most brilliant discoveries that in recent times have filled the world with wonder; and whatever indications of the moral perfections of God may be found in Nature by the man who has discovered them elsewhere—these lie beyond the limits of the physical sciences, and what the scientific man admires in Nature by virtue of his science can have no moral element in it. It does not belong to him to inquire whether the laws which he investigates are just, or whether Nature is kind and pitiful: these are terms which belong to men of other pursuits; he has learnt their meaning from other teachers than those who have achieved their authority and fame in those provinces of discovery which he can claim as his own, and which are sometimes spoken of as if they included all human knowledge.

Nature as revealed to science is not great enough for us to worship. The courage and fidelity of martyrs are greater than anything that science has discovered in the heavens above or on the earth beneath. The purity of saints is greater. The pity of kindly hearts for human suffering is greater. The dear affections of home and kindred, the loyalty of friends, the cheerful patience of old age, the innocence of childhood, are greater. Nature, as revealed by science, has no love ; and—

> "The loving worm within its clod
> Were diviner than a loveless God
> Amid His worlds."

A famous Frenchman said, that in the great moments of life he was "stifled by the universe"; and if you ask me to worship Nature, I answer,— I have seen visions of something infinitely fairer and more wonderful; and in the worship of Nature my highest powers and my strongest affections are suppressed, pent in : they struggle for the freedom which they can find only in the presence of the Living and Personal God.

It would, indeed, be ungrateful for a Christian preacher not to remember, that in addition to the knowledge—precious for its own sake—with which physical discoveries have enriched the human race, and in addition to the new and wonderful command which they have given us over the power and resources of the material universe, they have rendered services of many kinds to the Christian faith. Of these services, one of the greatest may some day be attributed to that lofty scientific idea which, within our own memory, has secured such a rapid ascendency in every field of scientific inquiry. We have come to think of the work of creation as unfinished, and of ourselves as spectators of the mystery. The ages are as yet in the remote future in which the universe will reach that consummate perfection to which it was destined by the forces which have determined its development and history. Perhaps that perfection may never be actually achieved, but the mighty movement which in the past has struggled forward through storm and conflict and suffering, may some day pass into a peaceful progress towards an ideal glory, a progress to be prolonged through eternity.

This new scientific conception of the order of Nature will compel Christendom to revise some of its theological conceptions of the life of God,—conceptions which have been largely derived neither from the Jewish nor the Christian scriptures, but from a cold metaphysical philosophy. For some theological definitions of God which pass as Christian have come from deism rather than from Jewish prophets and psalmists, or Christian evangelists and apostles. We have been taught to think of Him as a necessary hypothesis to account for the origin of all things; but that ever since He created all things His power has been inactive except in miracle. That was not the faith of Jewish saints. They believed that God not only "laid the foundations of the earth, that it should not be moved for ever," but that through age after age, before their own eyes, He continued to work: "He causeth the grass to grow for the cattle, and herb for the service of man." To all His creatures He gave their meat in due season: "Thou openest Thine hand: they are satisfied with good." It was He who in the spring-time renewed the face of the ground; and in the winter fire and hail, snow and vapour fulfilled His word. "My Father," said Christ, "worketh hitherto"—worketh on holy days, set apart for the rest of man, as well as on days which man spends in common toil—"My Father worketh hitherto, and I work." It will be something if science enables us to recover a firmer hold of the ancient faith, and enables us to see for ourselves the present activity of God.

We have been taught to think of creation as if by a few successive exertions of the Divine power, God achieved and completed an ideal universe. That was not what Paul believed. Knowing nothing, suspecting nothing, of the tragic story of long millenniums of conflict and pain which preceded the appearance of man on the earth, the great Apostle, grasping the true conception of the manner in which the thoughts of God are fulfilled, used language which might have been taken as the motto and text of many a recent scientific treatise, and told the Christians at Rome that "the whole creation groaneth and travaileth in pain together until now," and that its blessedness and glory are still to come. God, too, has His unrealized ideals; He, too, is in pursuit of an unachieved perfection; He is thwarted, hindered, baffled by we know not what hostile powers; but "He fainteth not, neither is He weary;" and though age after age may pass, the golden years will come when the eternal purposes of His righteousness and His love will be fulfilled. In this perpetual effort of God to reach a perfection that still lies far before Him, we may find new grounds for faith in His sympathy with ourselves in the pursuit of an ideal righteousness.

Yes, Physical Science may render service to Religious Faith; but first of all Religious Faith must render a greater service to Science by teaching her that Nature is not God, and that although the Heavens declare His glory, and the earth is full of His goodness, in Nature God is not seen at His highest and best.

"Neither doth any know the Father save the Son, and he to whomsoever the Son willeth to reveal Him." I say again, as I said at starting, that this is an august and unique claim. The Lord Jesus Christ declares that it lies with Himself, depends upon His personal volition, whether any man shall have a true knowledge of God. In no age, in no country, in no Church, can any man discover God for himself, or learn from priest or theologian what is revealed concerning God by Christ. It is not enough to have the tradition of Christ's own teaching, or even the authoritative record of the discourses and parables in which He assured the men and women of His own time that they were the children of the Eternal. He deals with us one by one—not in crowds. "Neither doth any know the Father save the Son, and he to whomsoever the Son willeth to reveal Him."

Think what it means. He tells us of the ardours of love for the human race that glow in the Divine heart ; He tells us that we are God's children ; but that we cannot know our Father except He—Christ —wills to make the Father known to us. The claim is more daring—or more sublime—than if He had said that God's rain fell on no man's meadow, God's sun ripened no man's wheat, except by His will,— that He determined whose grass should be parched by drought and whose grass should receive the kindly showers ; whose fields should be green at harvest time, and whose should be rich with the golden wheat.

If He had said simply that only through His teaching could the men of His own time and country come to know the Father, and that in other lands and in later generations only those who were reached by the traditions or written record of His teaching could come to know the Father, this would have been wonderful. But He said infinitely more than this. In the crowds that heard the Sermon on the Mount and the Parable of the Prodigal Son, He determined whether this man or that should receive the revelation of God. Among the millions that have heard or read the sermon or the parable in after centuries He has determined whether to this man or that He would reveal the Father. Just as it was by His will, exerted in individual cases, that blind men received sight and dumb men recovered speech, so it is by His will, exerted in individual cases, that men reach the knowledge of God.

We must take Christ's teaching as it stands, and this unique claim is not separable from the rest of it. It affirms that you cannot learn what Christ reveals of God by reading any treatise of Christian theology as you learn Newton's theory by reading the *Principia;* that you cannot learn what Christ reveals of God by reading even the four gospels as you learn the thought of Socrates by reading Xenophon or Plato. It is as if you needed Newton himself to enable you to master the *Principia*, Socrates himself to enable you to understand the *Memorabilia* or the *Republic*. Do you care to know God—to know God, in your measure, as Christ knew Him—as Christ knows Him? You need Christ. You must appeal to the living Teacher, must be taught by Him who is the Eternal Word—the Eternal Revelation of God.

How He may answer that appeal He only knows. Not, perhaps, by sudden illumination, but after long and painful discipline may the knowledge come. He may see that to you, however it may be with others, a protracted search is necessary to make you capable of the final discovery. Who knows? It is not for us to make terms with the Giver of that supreme knowledge which is eternal life, or to be impatient if His methods perplex and trouble us. Of this, however, you may be sure, that He who descended from the heights of eternal blessedness and glory to reveal

God will not withhold the revelation from any man that desires to receive it, and will grant it as soon as the power to receive it is present.

The new light may begin to shine, the dawn may break, at unexpected points of the horizon. Christ may prepare you for the revelation of God by teaching you first to love and to care for men. He may remind you of forgotten duties. He may trouble your heart by reproving follies and sins which your conscience has ceased to rebuke. Whatever word of His comes to you, however simple, however elementary it may be, receive it with reverence, with devout fear; listen and obey; the path of righteousness is the path to God. It may be that for a long time whole regions of the truth He taught may be covered with dense clouds; but if as you read the gospels—remembering that He is at your side—a sentence here, a sentence there—not those perhaps which you desired to master—begins to brighten under a divine light, let your thought and heart dwell on what He is revealing, and wait patiently till in His own good time, and as you are able to bear it, the clouds break and reveal the rest.

And then life, throughout the whole range of its duties, its pleasures, its sorrows, will be drawn into close relations with the Eternal, and you will discover that you have passed into that fair city which is the home of the saints. The visible creation will be the symbol of a diviner order, and the common paths of thought will all end in God. You will become conscious of your kinship with the Creator; and the universe, with all its infinitely varied phenomena of glory and of terror, instead of being a power above you, will lie beneath your feet. You will not be humiliated by the awful procession of ages which moves before your imagination when you look back upon the history of Creation; you will look up to the Creator and say, "Before the mountains were brought forth or ever Thou hadst formed the earth or the world, from everlasting to everlasting thou art God; and as for me, I am more than Thy creature; I am Thy child; in Christ Thou hast made Thine eternal life my own." You will find God; God will find you: and in the blessednessof that meeting life will reach its consummate perfection and power.

VIII.

CHRIST AND THE STATE.[1]

"Jesus therefore perceiving that they were about to come and take Him by force, to make Him king, withdrew again into the mountain Himself alone."—JOHN vi. 15.

WERE not the people wholly in the right? Did not our Lord miss a great chance when He refused the position which they offered Him? If a nation has the good fortune to discover such a man as our Lord was—a man so upright, so fearless, with such pity for suffering, such hatred of injustice, and with resources so immense—what can it do better than place in his hands supreme political power, all legislative, judicial, and administrative authority? For a king, according to Jewish ideas and traditions, was not a constitutional sovereign, limited by a Parliament, but a real king, governing as well as reigning. The people might have said—to use our modern language—"If we make this man king, He will give us an ideal economic and social order, just

---

[1] The Annual Sermon preached on behalf of the Home Missions of the Baptist Union in Westbourne Park Chapel (Rev. Dr. Clifford's), on Friday evening, April 24th, 1891

judges, an equitable system of taxation, institutions which will relieve and diminish existing poverty and will gradually make poverty impossible; He will bring prosperity to the whole nation." According to Plato, the world will never be happy till its kings are philosophers, or its philosophers kings; and here was One whose wisdom transcended all the wisdom of mortal men. A great opportunity had come to the Jewish nation—an opportunity such as never came to any nation before, and could never come to any nation again. They tried to take Jesus by force and make Him king. Were they not wholly in the right?

And I ask again, Did not Jesus miss a great chance? Had He accepted the supreme authority, might He not have introduced into the Jewish State economic reforms, which would have lessened the hardships of large numbers of the people, changed the conditions which made it difficult for them to live an upright and devout life, brought home to them in the most effective way the power and the beauty of His teaching concerning God and God's relations to mankind, and the relations of men to each other? Might He not have made the Jewish State the illustration of an ideal political and social righteousness? Would not the visible realization of the principles and spirit of His teaching in the actual order and life of a nation, have invested His Gospel with an irresistible charm and been a decisive demonstration of its Divine origin? And our Lord Jesus Christ really claimed sovereignty over men; He was the king of ancient Jewish prophecy and hope—Why did He not consent to reign?

I.

Yes, He claimed to be King, but not a king of the kind that these people desired,—a political Ruler, a Prince mightier indeed than other earthly princes, but belonging to the same order, surrounded with similar splendour, the leader of armies, imposing laws to punish crime and to regulate agriculture and commerce, levying tribute on subject races. This was their conception of a king; it was not His.

Suppose that He had consented to reign. Imagine that He has driven out the Romans, that His armies are holding the roads into Palestine from the North the South and the East, that He has powerful fleets at Tyre and Sidon and riding off Joppa, so that the country is absolutely safe from invasion. Imagine Him in Jerusalem, accepted there, as well as in Galilee, as King of the Jewish nation. Now, what is He to do? He has to provide for the administration of justice all over the country; is it certain that He will be able to find just, sagacious, and courageous magistrates? Even among the men who had lived with Him during a great part of His earthly ministry there were conflicts for personal supremacy; and one of them robbed the common purse. After removing Caiaphas and the rest of the unscrupulous men who exercised under the Romans supreme authority in Jerusalem, where is He to look for men whom He can perfectly trust to fill their places?

What kind of laws can He establish? What social and economic order can He set up? Ideal laws and an ideal order are only for an ideal people. In constructing institutions it is necessary to take account of the capacity and the virtue of the people who have to work them. The best social and economic order for any particular nation is an order largely determined by its actual, material, intellectual, and moral condition. For example, representative institutions are admirable for a people on whom you can rely for public spirit, a willingness to undertake laborious and difficult duties in the public service, and a capacity for forming sound judgments on large questions of public policy. It may take time even for such a people to learn how to govern themselves wisely. They may make serious blunders, and may bring upon themselves great misfortunes; but the discipline of intelligence and of character which is secured by the discharge of grave public responsibilities will more than compensate for the transient sufferings which follow their political errors. If, however, those great qualities, which are necessary for the effective working of representative institutions, do not exist, if the germs of them do not exist, there will be such confusion and corruption in the conduct of public affairs, that by an imperious necessity these institutions will soon give place to another kind of government. Had Christ become King, He could not have organized the national life of the Jewish people on a noble model, for their national life itself was not noble.

Or take the department of criminal jurisprudence. Laws which are not supported by the moral convictions of the great mass of the people are always ineffective; they may do something, no doubt, to educate the national conscience, but they fail to do even that if they are far in advance of it. It would be useless for a Government to enact laws against theft, if the national conscience did not condemn theft; useless for a Government to enact laws protecting the sanctity of contracts, if the national conscience did not regard contracts as sacred. Take an illustration: the law of divorce which was given to the Jews was given to them, Christ says, because of the hardness of their hearts. In a social condition which allowed men to dismiss their wives at their own pleasure, it would have been useless to insist on the sacredness and permanence of the institution of marriage. Some check was imposed on this brutal licence when a man who divorced his wife was required to set down in writing the reasons why he divorced her. That was a very slight advance towards a better regulation of marriage, but it was an advance, and apparently it was all the advance that was possible. Your jurisprudence, I say, must take account of the actual moral condition of the people. Laws which punish as crimes acts which the national conscience allows, are powerless; if maintained at all, they must be maintained by a constant exertion of force. It may be necessary, in order to hold society together, and to lay the foundations of a better and nobler organization of the national life, for a Government to fight hard against practices which the moral sense of large masses of the people does not condemn; but while this struggle lasts the foundations of national order are shaken; there is civil war, though there may be no armies in the field.

If Christ Himself had become the King of the Jewish people, His legislation would necessarily have been lowered towards the level of the national morality. He would have had to tolerate many grave evils and to leave many grave offences unpunished. His laws could not have been the ideal laws of an ideal State.

There were other reasons which might well have prevented Him from accepting the power which the people wished to force upon Him. It was the miracle of the loaves and the fishes, of which you heard earlier in this service, that provoked the popular enthusiasm. No doubt the people thought that if He were their King all their material wants would be certain to receive satisfaction. Ah! but it is not Christ's first object to secure for men in this life outward conditions favourable to universal ease and comfort. That was clearly not His object in the creation of the material universe which He has built for our home. Men have to live by the sweat of their brow, and in most parts of the world they have to work hard in order to live. There are fogs and floods; harvests are blighted; there is intolerable heat; there is intolerable cold; men are disciplined to endurance by physical discomfort; their intellectual life is provoked to strenuous activity by the hardships and difficulties of their condition. The proverbial garden of the sluggard is not a reproach to Providence but to the sluggard. It was God's will that he should have not only a garden bright with flowers but that he should have the physical vigour, the industry, the intelligence that would come from cultivating it. God cares more for the man than for the garden. Nor is it Christ's first object to give us a social and political order that shall certainly secure for men universal physical happiness. Government is a Divine institution, but it is through human virtue, human self-sacrifice, human patience, human sagacity, that the material blessings which are possible through the social condition are to be actually won. And it is not God's will that we should have the material blessings apart from the virtues and intellectual labours which are necessary for the maintenance of a just social order. It was impossible that Christ should accept power on the terms upon which He knew that it was offered Him.

II.

The relations of Christ to the political, economic, and social order have exercised the thoughts of men ever since He returned to His glory. He declared before His ascension that all authority had been given to Him in heaven and on earth; the great words of the Psalmist had been fulfilled; not the elect race only, but all nations, had been given to Him as His inheritance, and the uttermost parts of the earth as His possession. During His earthly ministry He and His apostles had declared that the kingdom of heaven was at hand; after His resurrection that proclamation ceased; the kingdom was no longer at hand, it had actually come, for the King had come; and through the redemption which He had achieved the whole race stood in a new relation to God. He was King of kings and Lord of lords, King by Divine right, Lord by Divine appointment. There were no longer any aliens from the Divine commonwealth; every man was a subject of Christ by birth. Revolt was still possible, but revolt is a crime of which only subjects can be guilty. Men are the subjects of Christ by the Divine will, though it lies with their own will to determine whether they will be obedient to His laws and loyal to His throne.

His authority extends over every province of human life; over the business of men and their pleasures; over science, literature, art; over the family; over the State as well as over the Church. This is acknowledged, but the question, How is that authority to be asserted in relation to the State, and to the economic and social organization of the State? has received many answers. I am not clear that the final answer has yet been given. Perhaps the final answer can never be given. During the last thirty or forty years the question has been discussed with great seriousness and earnestness; it is being discussed now on all sides with vehemence and passion. The subject is so intimately related to the great work which has drawn us together this evening—the evangelization of England—by which I mean the realizing in our own country of the Christian ideal of personal, social, and national life—that I may be permitted, perhaps, to say something about it.

III.

I suppose that we should all agree that during the present generation there has been a gradual change among Evangelical Nonconformists in their conception of the State and of the functions of the State. Half a century ago there was a very general acceptance among us of the theory that the whole business of the secular Government is to repress force and fraud. The State was even regarded by many of us as founded on a kind of mutual contract for the purpose of protecting life and property—a Limited Liability Company, with its objects and powers strictly defined in the articles of association. To restrict its action within the narrowest possible area was supposed to be the first duty of a wise and liberal politician. Many of us, I suppose, owed our emancipation from that theory, partly to Mr. John Stuart Mill, whose authority was at its zenith in 1850; partly to Edmund Burke, who taught us that the State is a great historical growth, not an artificial creation, and that instead of having any analogy to a voluntary association with limited liability, it is a "partnership in all science, in all art, in every virtue, in all perfection."

To Mr. Frederick Denison Maurice, probably more than to any other man, many of us owe the original impulse which started us on another line of thought. I think that I am not in error when I say that many Evangelical Nonconformists had come to have a vague impression—it was not inherited from their greatest ecclesiastical ancestors—but they had come to have a vague impression that political activity lies beyond the true province of the Christian life. When I was a young man I believe that that impression was a very general one. Mr. Edward Miall had already done something to dissipate it, but it had not disappeared. The State, with all its affairs, was regarded by large numbers of Christian people as belonging in an evil sense to this world, and to be political was to be worldly. They went to the polling booth, many of them, no doubt; but they went, as many Christian people now go to the theatre, feeling that they were hardly in their right place. Mr. Maurice insisted that the State is a Divine institution—like the Family, like the Church; many of us, I say, probably owe to him more than to any other man the original impulse which started our thought in that direction. But as soon as we began to look seriously into the New Testament we found it there, and we were astonished that we had not found it before.

Paul had taught that the powers that be are ordained of God—"therefore he that resisteth the power withstandeth the ordinance of God: and they that withstand shall receive to themselves judgment." He was writing to the Romans when Nero was Emperor of Rome and master of the world—Nero, whose murders, whose brutal lusts, whose tyranny, whose insane follies have covered him with eternal infamy. Even then, according to Paul, rulers were "not a terror to the good work, but to the evil." Government, though administered by bad men, and administered badly, was still a Divine institution; as long as it held society together it was better than no government at all. And men were to "be in subjection,"—they were to acknowledge the Divine sanction of the authority even when the authority was wickedly used. They were to "be in subjection, not only because of the wrath," through fear of the penalties of disregarding the law, but also "for conscience' sake,"—their obedience was to be as unto the Lord, not unto men. At what point a nation may determine that the Government has become so bad that it is justifiable and necessary to resist it by force, and to transfer the authority which is exercised in the name of God to worthier hands, is a question which there was no occasion for Paul to discuss. When it emerges it is a question of appalling difficulty. That a nation may be driven to this awful extremity is, however, our assured belief.

But Paul's principle—and it is that about which I am speaking—is clear. The State is a Divine institution, the political ruler is the minister of God. Having learned this, most of us have been teaching for many years past, that in a country like our own, where the ultimate choice of those who are to administer both local and national government, lies with the great mass of the people, it is the duty of Christian men to use the franchise and to use their political influence so as to secure that rulers, who are the ministers of God, shall discharge their trust according to the will of God. In the State, as in the Church and in the family, the will of God is supreme.

Yes, in the State as in the Church and in the family, the will of God is supreme. But the State, the family, the Church, are different institutions, existing for different ends, and securing their ends by different methods. In each there is Authority, but in each the Authority is of a different kind, possesses different powers, and asserts those powers by different instruments. We want the will of God to be done in the State; we want the laws of the State and the policy of the State to be in harmony with the will of God; but what is the will of God in relation to the State?

It is our belief that the Church and the State, though both of them are Divine institutions, are Divine institutions of such a different description, and with such different immediate objects, that any organic alliance between them is certain in the long run to be injurious to both. The State is primarily the visible representative and defender of the Divine justice in the temporal order ; the Church is primarily the visible representative of the Divine mercy and the Divine redemption in the eternal order. The State has other functions ; the Church has other functions ; but there is that deep distinction between them. When listening to Christ in the Church, and learning His conception of what our life should be, we hear Him say, " Resist not him that is evil, but whosoever smiteth thee on thy right cheek turn to him the other also ; and if any man would go to law with thee and take away thy coat, let him have thy cloak also." But when we want to learn the Christian conception of the function of the civil ruler, we discover that if any man does evil he is not to expect the ruler to treat him after that manner ; and that it is not the will of God that the ruler should treat him after that manner. " If thou do that which is evil be afraid, for he beareth not the sword in vain ; for he is a minister of God, an avenger for wrath to him that doeth evil."

That is the ruler's function,—to assert in the visible order the principles of eternal justice. The ultimate ground of punishment is, that the criminal deserves to suffer. Apart from that, punishment is unjust and intolerable. You have no right to subject a man to suffering for the sake of doing him good, for the sake of reforming him, unless he deserves to suffer. You have no right to subject a man to suffering merely for the sake of giving a wholesome lesson to the community; unless he deserves to suffer, the man becomes a martyr for the public benefit, instead of a criminal.

What theologians call retributive justice is as real an element in the Divine life as compassion and grace, and the ruler is the minister of the retributive justice of God in the temporal order. This austere task is imposed upon him, and he cannot decline it without unfaithfulness to his trust. We on whom this heavy burden is not directly laid, are graciously called to kindlier duties. But in one memorable precept we are reminded that, if *we* are destined to be compassionate and merciful, it is not because the punishment of wrong-doing is contrary to the Divine will, but because God has provided for it without our aid:—"Avenge not yourselves, beloved, but give place unto the wrath,"—leave room for the anger of God against wrong-doing to do its own stern work, " for it is written, 'Vengeance belongeth unto Me; I will recompense, saith the Lord.'" Within limits, this work is to be done by the civil ruler,—"He is a minister of God, an avenger for wrath to him that doeth evil."

IV.

The State, the Church, both are Divine institutions; the State, the Church, in both the will of God is to be supreme; but the characteristic function of the State is to assert the authority of law; of the Church to reveal the infinite wealth of grace. The State is to secure to all men their due in the temporal order as far as its powers extend; to protect the peaceful, upright, industrious citizen in his person, property, and reputation; to punish the disorderly and the violent. The Church, on the other hand, by its very constitution and the ends for which it was founded, is not to deal with men after their sins, nor to reward them according to their iniquities. It is to declare to all men the remission of their sins in Christ. It is to shelter men from evils which they have deserved; to rescue them from miseries into which they have fallen by their own follies and crimes. This sharp contrast between the characteristic functions of the Church and the characteristic functions of the State cannot, as I believe, be obliterated without peril. When ecclesiastical authorities have become princes they have weakened the foundations of the political order, and they have paralysed the redemptive powers of the Church.

And yet the growth of the Church, by which I mean the gradual conquest of the people of any country by the spirit and truth of Christ, must have and ought to have a great and increasing effect on national laws and national policy. This will happen even under an absolute government; it will be illustrated on a greater and more impressive scale in a country which has achieved political freedom. The

State is a Divine institution, and some of its ends are definitely determined by its very nature; if these are not secured it will be broken up, and will have to be re-organized. But it is not a Divine institution of the same kind as the solar system, which is fast bound in the iron chains of necessity. It has to be realized by the concurrence of free agents, and its actual form and activity will vary with their sagacity and their folly, their public spirit, their courage, their unselfishness, their purity, their intellectual vigour and cultivation, their baseness, their cowardice, their covetousness, their sensuality, their intellectual feebleness and sluggishness. Change the people by the power of the Christian gospel, and you will change their laws. The State is still the representative of justice; but as a nation becomes increasingly penetrated with the spirit of Christ, its ideal of justice in that temporal order which is under the control of the civil ruler will be gradually elevated. The austere severities of government will not be weakly relaxed, but there will be eager questionings as to the possibility of effecting changes in the political and economic order which, without making justice less awful, shall contribute to the relief of misery, give to the unfortunate a chance of comfort and ease, and add to the brightness of the life of the whole community.

The material prosperity and physical happiness of the community can never be the exclusive or even the chief aim of those who desire to carry into the State the spirit they have received in the Church, for in the Church they have learned that these do not constitute the supreme good either of individuals or of nations. Personal righteousness, the discipline of both the robust and the gracious virtues, so far as they can be disciplined by political and economic institutions, will take precedence of mere physical ease and enjoyment ; and yet the compassionate words of Christ will be always remembered, who, after charging His disciples to seek first His kingdom and His righteousness, and not to be anxious about what they should eat or drink or wear, added, " Your Heavenly Father knoweth that ye have need of all these things."

In our own country during the present century the power of religious faith over the nation has been shown in great public acts of compassion. It was the new energy of the religious life created by the Evangelical revival which gave intensity and passion to the great movement against the slave trade, and which, at last, by a splendid act of generosity, abolished slavery throughout the possessions of the Crown. The justice of that achievement was as conspicuous as its mercy. It was not the triumph of a cheap philanthropy, which was willing to confer a great good if it could be conferred without great cost. Hateful, intolerable, iniquitous as was the system which gave to the master a property in his slave, the property had been sanctioned by national opinion and protected by national law, and the nation gave £20,000,000 in order to cancel the master's rights. Legislation of other kinds, and affecting our own population, has had its origin in that pity for the poor, that reverence for all men, which the Church has caught from Christ, and which the world has caught from the Church. Act after Act has been passed limiting the hours of labour of women and children employed in factories and workshops, and preventing them from working at all in mines. Acts have been passed for protecting the life and limbs of persons exposed to accidents from machinery. Attempts have been made, not I trust wholly unsuccessful, to prevent men from being sent to sea in ships that are unseaworthy. Local authorities have acquired new powers for compelling owners of houses to keep them in a sanitary condition. Here and there a great municipality has begun to build healthy homes for the less fortunate classes of the community. One great town after another has provided public baths, public gardens, public parks, free libraries, and art galleries. The Education Acts of 1870, 1876, and 1880 have secured a public elementary school for every child in the kingdom that needs it, and have provided that every child shall be sent to school and kept there until it has received a moderate measure of education. These are but examples of the social legislation of the present century, and they have come, not from a fierce and violent struggle of the poor for a larger share in the public wealth, but mainly from the sincere and earnest desire of the more prosperous classes in the State to secure for all classes of the people an easier and a happier life. We are but at the beginning of the tasks which must be undertaken if the miseries which still remain are to be lessened, and if a life of honourable industry, of comfort and dignity, is to be made possible to all our countrymen.

The precise forms of the social troubles which now perplex and confound us are new. They are largely the result of the breaking-up of the ancient order which in France was violently destroyed by the great Revolution, and which in this country has perished more peacefully as the result of the immense development of our manufacturing industry in the last half of the last century and the first half of this. To discover the solution of the new problems which have thus been forced upon us is not easy. Patience is necessary as well as zeal, or attempts at reform may issue only in worse confusion and worse suffering. A genuine love for man, and an intense desire that God's thought concerning our national life should be fulfilled —let these inspire and guide our policy, and then, though we may commit some great errors, we may be certain that, as time goes on, the real strength and happiness of the nation will be constantly augmented.

V.

But in the work which has drawn us together tonight we are sure to be wholly in the right. If the social order is to be just, men must be just; if the social order is to be kindly, men must be kindly.

We can only hope for great and enduring changes for the better in the social order, as the result of great and enduring changes for the better in the spirit and character of the whole people. The ethical quality of the organization of a State, political, economic, social, must, I suppose, be always more or less inferior to the general ethical life of the nation. Reforms which are far in advance of that life may be carried, as the result of transient enthusiasm, but they will not be effective, and they will not endure.

We ought to take our full share, we Christian people, in every movement for the practical amelioration of the condition of our fellow-countrymen. But speaking as one who for many years took an active part among the obscurer members of a great political party, I think that we must often be doubtful whether political and social schemes which are full of promise may not, from causes which human sagacity is unable to anticipate, turn out mischievous. In endeavouring to draw individual men to Christ—in disciplining to Christian intelligence, to righteousness and sanctity, those who already acknowledge His authority—we cannot go wrong. Every man that has received the Spirit of Christ, and is eager to do the will of Christ, is a new power for bringing in more just and more gracious conditions of economic and social life. John Wesley and George Whitefield did more for the social redemption of England than all the politicians of this century and the last, whose names are associated with great reforms; under God, they created those moral and spiritual forces which have rendered all reforms possible.

In this work, I say again, we cannot go wrong. We trust that future generations of men, inheriting our name, speaking our tongue, living on English soil, will achieve an organization of life so just and so beautiful, that the poverty, the crime, the ignorance, the social strife of our own days shall seem to them an evil dream. But the great harvests of the world ripen slowly. We rejoice that while they are ripening it is possible, through God's grace, for God's lost children to be found and brought home to their Father. Their life in this world is brief at the longest. They are destined by the thought and purpose of God to an endless life of righteousness and wisdom, of joy and glory. That thought and purpose are not to be defeated by the inequalities and confusions of their earthly condition. The Apostles did not wait till slavery was abolished before they preached the Christian Gospel to slaves; slaves received the Gospel, and, remaining slaves, became children of the Eternal and heirs of the glory of God. Nor need *we* wait till the social miseries of many of our own countrymen disappear before we endeavour to make clear to them that they are born to an inheritance in the infinite love of God, and in the redemption which has been achieved for the human race by Christ. To those who are suffering from these miseries in their intenser form we should carry material relief, which, thank God, the Church has always been eager to give to the wretched. But with the material relief we should also carry the animating and glorious hope of a larger, freer, and nobler life when their earthly troubles are over. But the immense majority of our people are not worn with anxiety, wasted with hunger, crushed by despair; and among these there are millions who know nothing of the power and blessedness of the Christian Redemption. To these we have free access; there is nothing in their circumstances and condition to prevent them from receiving the Gospel of Christ, and from living according to His will. Let *them* learn to acknowledge Him as the true King of men, and within a generation the whole life of the country would be changed. Have courage, have faith. In the power of Christ, and in the power of the truth of Christ, we may confidently hope to recover our country both from its sorrows and its sins.

And in this great work you are asked to take some part to-night. There are many in this congregation who could speak with a larger knowledge than I can of the work which is being carried on all over England by the Baptist Home Missionary Society, on behalf of which I have now to plead. But of this I am sure—you cannot tell what light, what consolation, what hope, what strength for righteousness, what endurance for suffering, are carried to lonely cottages by the colporteurs and evangelists associated with this society; you cannot tell how much of the best life of England in obscure places is sustained by the Churches and the pastors that you are asked to stand by to-night. Ah! Dr. Clifford, it is pleasant enough for you and me to preach the Gospel; but what courage is necessary, what faith, what zeal, by multitudes of our brethren in the country districts of England! You are asked to show by your contributions to-night that you have some sympathy with them in their heroic struggle.

You know, many of you, what they are doing, and you know it to their cost; for young men and women who in these country districts have been trained to faith in Christ and loyalty to the great ends for which the Free Evangelical Churches exist, come in crowds to the great towns and cities of England; and among our most effective workers in the Churches in the great towns and cities are those who have been disciplined and trained by the men and the Churches for whom I plead to-night. You need not go to your secretaries to learn what they are doing; look round your Sunday schools, look into your diaconate, look at those who are taking part in all the mission work connected with your own Churches, and you will learn the kind of work which—shall I say?—these men and these Churches turn out, and you may judge with what fidelity and earnestness they are discharging the trust which they have received from God.

I wonder when the imagination of our Churches will be touched by this Home Mission work as it has been touched from time to time by the great work of evangelizing the heathen. Do not misunderstand me. I have never found that the men who are most disposed to criticize the work that we are carrying on in remote countries are the men who either consecrate personal service or give large contributions to sustain evangelistic work at home. Let them earn the right to criticize our missions to the heathen by doing more for our missions to our own countrymen; if they distrust our foreign work, there is ample room for all they can give and all they can do in connection with our evangelistic work at home. But, I repeat, I wonder when our imagination will be touched, and when our passion will be stirred, by this work of evangelizing England, as they have sometimes been touched and stirred when a new nation has been thrown open to the Gospel of Christ. How is it that splendid gifts are not consecrated to this work, as splendid gifts are sometimes consecrated to the other? How is it that this work is not regarded as being just as heroic under many conditions as that? England for Christ is surely as lofty an aim as China for Christ, or India for Christ. I trust that there will be a change in the scale of contributions to our home missionary work among the Free Evangelical Churches of this country And I ask you to begin that change to-night.

IX.

THE THEOLOGY OF JOHN WESLEY.[1]

" When it was the good pleasure of God, who separated me, even from my mother's womb, and called me through His grace, to reveal His Son in me, that I might preach Him among the Gentiles ; immediately I conferred not with flesh and blood : neither went I up to Jerusalem to them which were Apostles before me."—*Gal.* i. 15-17.

THE faith of the Galatian Churches was being corrupted by Judaizing teachers, who assailed that large and spiritual interpretation of the Gospel of Christ which was given by Paul ; and they sustained their assault by insisting that he was not one of the original Apostles who had received their authority from our Lord, and that the original Apostles had given him no commission. He does not attempt to qualify his independence of the first preachers of the Christian Gospel, the Divinely authorized founders of the Christian Church. He shows a certain eagerness and exultation in asserting it. He asserts it in the very first sentence of his letter : he is *not* an Apostle

---

[1] Preached in City Road Chapel, London, on Wednesday morning, March 4th, 1891, in connection with the celebration of the centenary of the death of John Wesley.

"from men;" his commission was from heaven; and his commission had not come to him "through men;" he had not received it through the intervention of any Church rulers to whom Christ had delegated any part of His power; but direct from "Jesus Christ" Himself, and "God the Father who raised him from the dead."

He will stand in no succession. This, for which his enemies reproached him, is the secret of his power; in this he glories. In the text he expands the declaration with which the letter begins. It was the "good pleasure" of God—God's free, spontaneous, unsought, unmerited grace—that had made him an Apostle; and this grace had been manifested in several ways.

(1) First, he says, From my very birth God "separated" me to this work. As Paul looked back upon his life he could see that the Divine purpose had been controlling his personal history from the very beginning, and preparing him for a service of which he had no thought, and which, if it had been proposed to him, he would have regarded with horror. His birth, by which he inherited the rights of Roman citizenship, though he was also "of the stock of Benjamin, a Hebrew of the Hebrews"; his early years in Tarsus, a great Greek city, famous for its wealth, its commerce, and its schools of learning and philosophy; his life as a student in Jerusalem; his zeal in mastering the doctrines and methods of the Rabbis; the earnestness and fidelity with which he

had submitted to the discipline of the most austere of Jewish sects, so that "touching the righteousness which is in the law" he was "blameless;"—all these had contributed in various ways to his fitness for the work to which God had destined him.

(2) God Himself — without the intervention of Apostles, without human intervention of any kind— had spoken to him the strong and gracious word which had broken his heart to penitence, and which had drawn him to Christ. There had been no movement towards Christ on his own part. He was on his way to Damascus, vehement, passionate in his hatred of the new sect; resolved to suppress it; it was God's "grace"—what else?—that "called" him to receive the Christian redemption and to preach the Christian Gospel. At that point, indeed, his own free response to the grace of God came in: till now, all that God had done to prepare him for his apostleship was done without any free concurrence of his in God's great purpose; he had known nothing of it: but now he might have thwarted and defeated the Divine love; but, as he says elsewhere, he "was not disobedient to the heavenly vision."

And (3), he adds, "It was the good pleasure of God . . . to reveal His Son in me that I might preach Him among the Gentiles." The revelation came, not for his own sake merely, but for the sake of the heathen men to whom he was to preach it; and it, therefore, came to him in a form which was determined by their condition as well as his own.

I.

These three manifestations of God's free, spontaneous grace to Paul have their parallel in the history of John Wesley, whose great and venerable name has drawn us together this morning.

(1) He, too, might have said that from his very birth God had "separated," set him apart, for the work of recovering large masses of the English people from irreligion and vice, and founding a religious society which would extend to all lands. There was an heroic strain in his blood ; his parents, on both sides, were the descendants of Puritan ministers, who had endured persecution for their fidelity to what they believed to be the will of God. But he was saved from the peril which comes upon men who are the heirs of great religious movements which have spent their strength. He was not to attempt to re-kindle the glorious fires of Puritanism, and so he was born in a country rectory. In the discipline of his childhood and youth, that reverence for authority and that care for the external institutions and aids of the religious life which are characteristic of the great Anglicans, were blended with the traditions of Puritanism. His father, a High churchman, was a man of courage and zeal ; he was deeply moved by the condition of heathen countries, proposed a scheme for carrying the Gospel of Christ to the remotest shores that had been reached by English trade, and offered to go out among the first missionaries. For his mother John Wesley had always the profoundest

reverence. She was a woman of remarkable natural sagacity, and he had almost unmeasured confidence in her judgment. She had a vigorous and cultivated mind, and there was great depth and strength in her religious life.

As he was passing from youth to manhood, the best elements in the Oxford of those days and the worst,—the zeal for righteousness of the small group of young men of whom he became the leader,—the scorn, the mockery, the insult which their zeal provoked,—all these were part of the discipline by which he was prepared for his work. His experience in Georgia was part of it. By God's grace he had been separated to his work from his birth.

(2) By God's "grace" he was "called," if not with the accompaniment of visible miracle, as Paul was called on the road to Damascus, yet by a movement of the Divine love, not less free, not less supernatural. For John Wesley would have said with an earnestness as deep and passionate as that of the most faithful disciple of John Calvin : " I sought God because God sought me. I found God because God found me." The saints are divided by their theologies, but they are one in their faith, and they all confess, " We love Him because He first loved us."

(3) It is, however, to the third illustration of God's grace in Wesley's history that I propose to direct your special consideration. He, too, could have said with Paul, " It was the good pleasure of God to *reveal His Son* in me, that I might preach Him."

You will understand at once that I refer to the experience through which he passed on the evening of Wednesday, the twenty-fourth of May, 1738, when he was thirty-five years of age, an experience so remarkable that for many years he was accustomed to speak of it as his real conversion, the time when his sins were forgiven, the beginning of his life in God through Christ. That wonderful experience, that revelation of Christ, had a direct and vital relation to all that has given the name of John Wesley an enduring place in the history of Christendom. But for *that*, there would have been no Methodist Revival; but for *that*, the great sisterhood of Methodist Societies represented at this commemoration, belonging to many races, speaking many tongues, and which might be described, with pardonable rhetorical exaggeration, as gathered out of every country under heaven,—but for that great experience, that revelation of Christ in John Wesley, these Societies would have had no existence. The "good pleasure" of God, the purposes of His grace in relation to England and the world, might have been fulfilled in other ways, but not by you.

II.

Nor is it the Methodist Societies alone that have reason to look back with deep and devout interest to that memorable hour. As you have done me the great and unmerited honour of permitting me to be here this morning, I desire to acknowledge with devout gratitude the grace of God which through you has reached many Churches having an earlier origin than yours, and a polity different from your own; Churches which for more than two generations were widely separated from yours by mutual distrust—distrust created in part by serious theological differences, in part by differences in relation to evangelistic methods and the discipline of the spiritual life.

The obligations which, under God, the older Nonconformist Churches of England owe to Methodism cannot be measured. When John Wesley began his work their strength had been seriously diminished. There were complaints that congregations were wasting away; that the sons and the daughters of the wealthier Nonconformists were passing over to the Episcopal Church. It was said that between the accession of George I., in 1714, and the year 1731, more than fifty Dissenting ministers took orders in the Establishment. Those who contested the accuracy of the stronger statements concerning the decay of the Dissenting interest, and who insisted that if in some parts of the country Dissenting Churches were declining, in others their strength was growing, acknowledged that the Dissenters were discouraged; that they were suffering from a want of buoyancy and energy in their religious life; that the stricter manners and the severer morals of an earlier generation were disappearing; and that the movement of theological opinion among them gave occasion for great anxiety To you for a long time our fathers did not look for deliverance. Wesley's Arminianism filled them with alarm. Nor was their alarm without reason. There had been a great drifting among the Nonconformist Churches during the first thirty or forty years of the eighteenth century from the central articles of the Christian Faith, and this was one of the principal causes of their weakness. The Divinity of our Lord had been denied, and the atonement which He achieved for men by His death; and these grave and ruinous errors had almost always begun with a surrender of the characteristic doctrines of Calvinism. Even where Arminianism had not come to these disastrous issues, it had paralysed the strength of Christian faith, and quenched the fire of spiritual earnestness.

But creeds which coincide in some of their principal articles may cover wholly different systems of religious thought, and wholly different conditions of the spiritual life. The Arminianism of many of the Nonconformists, at the beginning of the eighteenth century, appears to have been the result, in part, of that cold and powerless conception of God which is given by Deism, a conception which removes Him to an infinite distance from all His creatures, and leaves man to work out his own destiny in an environment of unchanging and mechanical laws. It was the result of a decaying sense of the energy and freedom of the life of the Eternal and of God's immanent presence and activity in the material universe and in man. It affirmed that man was free, partly because it conceived of God as remote.

Wesley's Arminianism had a wholly different root. For him the Universe was not a wonderful mechanism which had been projected into being by a succession of creative acts, and then left to work according to the laws of its structure ; for him God did not live apart from His creation, reigning on heights of inaccessible majesty. He believed that in God we live and move, and have our being. And yet in the strength of his own moral life he had a most vivid consciousness that he was morally free—free to receive or to reject the infinite grace which the living God was pressing upon him ; and therefore he was an Arminian. For a time the more serious Nonconformists did not discover the immense moral and spiritual difference between the old Arminianism and the new. The walls of mutual distrust which separated your fathers and mine stood firm and without a breach till long after George III. was king.

But the fires which were kindled on your side were burning so fiercely that the heat came through. The flames rose high and sparks fell over. You made the very atmosphere so hot that dry timber took fire, we knew not how. We listened—at first reluctantly— to Whitefield and the leaders of the Calvinistic revival, and discovered that God was doing a wonderful work before our very eyes, though it was not being done according to our traditions. Then we began to listen to you ; it was not far from the Tabernacle to the Foundry. A little later we began to draw closer to each other. I could give you a considerable list of eminent Congregational ministers who, towards the close of the last century and the beginning of this, brought to the service of the Congregational Churches the religious life which had been originated, the religious zeal which had been kindled, among Methodists. William Jay, of Bath, discovered the glory and grace of the Christian redemption at a Methodist service. My colleague and predecessor, John Angell James, did not attribute his religious decision to Methodist preaching; but he says in his autobiography, that when he was a boy at Blandford, the only religious fire in the town was among the Methodists; he was taken by his mother to Methodist meetings on Sunday nights, and there was a touch of Methodism in him to the very last. He always smelt of that fire. Thomas Raffles, of Liverpool, in his early life was a member of the Wesleyan Society. John Leifchild, of Craven, was originally one of your preachers. The great Revival which originated Methodism restored life, vigour, courage, fervour to the Congregational Churches of England.

III.

And, as I have said, Methodism owes its existence, under God, to that great experience through which John Wesley passed in a little room within a mile of this place on the evening of May 24, 1738. You all know the story. I am conscious of presumption in venturing to speak about it in such an assembly as this; but I ask you to bear with me, I care to speak of nothing else.

Wesley became a Fellow of Lincoln in 1726, and from that time his great concern was to live a religious life. During the following twelve years the earnestness with which he endeavoured to carry out his purpose was constantly becoming more intense. He began by setting apart an hour or two a day for prayer and religious meditation. He received the Lord's Supper every week. He fasted on Wednesday and Friday. His method of life was severe. He visited the prisoners in Oxford gaol; he went from house to house among the poor and the sick of the city, and denied himself not only the "superfluities"—to use his own words—but "many that are called necessaries of life," that he might do what good he could by his presence or his little fortune to the bodies and souls of all men. He diligently strove against all sin. He pursued "inward holiness"—the "union of the soul with God." He became the leader of a number of devout young men who were of the same mind as himself; he was their counsellor and their strong support. He had a passion for the conversion of the heathen, and went out to Georgia with the hope of being able to preach the Gospel to the Indians in that part of America. The attention of the whole University was drawn to his extraordinary zeal.

But when he returned from America he was in an agony of distress about his own salvation. He had gone to Georgia to convert the heathen; and he had learnt—so he thought—that he himself was not converted. In his later years he modified his opinion concerning the true nature of the experience through which he passed in May, 1738. He came to the conclusion that he was not, as he had supposed, "alienated from the life of God" till then, "a child of wrath," "an heir of hell;"[1] and I think that most thoughtful readers of his *Journals* will be of the same judgment. But he always retained the belief that that great experience was of transcendent importance. In this he was wholly right. If not critical for Wesley himself, in the way he had once supposed, it was critical for Methodism.

Immediately after he had passed through it he wrote this explanation of what he believed to have been the fatal defect of his previous religious life:—

"In my return to England, January, 1738, being in imminent danger of death, and very uneasy on that account, I was strongly convinced that the cause of that uneasiness was unbelief, and that the gaining of a true living faith was the 'one thing needful for me.' But still *I fixed not this faith on its right object. I meant only faith in God, not faith in or through Christ.* Again, I knew not that I was wholly void of this faith; but only thought I had not enough of it."[2]

---

[1] *Journals*, vol. i. page 76.
[2] *Ibid.*, page 101.

As the result of his conversations with Peter Böhler he came to see that he must renounce all dependence, in whole or in part, upon his own works or righteousness, and seek by continual prayer what he describes as "justifying, saving faith, a full reliance on the blood of Christ, shed for *me*, a trust in Him, as *my* Christ, as my sole justification, sanctification, and redemption."[1]

The faith came. Listen to his own account of what happened on that memorable evening:

"I went," he says, "very unwillingly to a society in Aldersgate Street, where one was reading Luther's Preface to the Epistle to the Romans. About a quarter before nine, while he was describing the change which God works in the heart through faith in Christ, I felt my heart strangely warmed. I felt I did trust in Christ, Christ alone for salvation. And an assurance was given me that He had taken away *my* sins, even *mine*, and saved *me* from the law of sin and death."[2]

Tell me whether he might not have described all this in Paul's words:—"It was the good pleasure of God to reveal His Son in me?"

Is there any account to be given of the nature and sources of the change through which he passed on that evening? I will make the attempt.

It is apparent that at the very core of Wesley's

---

[1] *Journals*, vol. i. page 102.
[2] *Ibid.*, page 103.

nature there was an immovable conviction that his will was morally free. This made him an Arminian. His acts were his own; they were not determined by blind fate or any Divine decree. It is also apparent that to him the Divine law was august, awful. He saw, as few men have ever seen, the infinite significance of the contrast between obedience and disobedience, sin and righteousness. He had sinned, and his sense of his guilt sometimes became intolerable. During his misery he felt that it was God's own hand that was heavy upon him; and that the condemnation of conscience revealed, but only partially revealed, the more appalling condemnation of God.

Further, it is apparent that he believed that our knowledge of God is real as far as it goes; and that what we call His attributes are not mere subjective representations of Him determined by the structure and laws of our own minds, but answer to something real and objective in the life of the Eternal; that as His Will is not identical with His Knowledge, His Justice is not identical with His Grace. In one of his Sermons he speaks of men who quiet their fears "by saying 'God is merciful;' confounding and swallowing up all at once in *that unwieldy idea of Mercy*, all His Holiness and essential hatred of sin; all His Justice, Wisdom and Truth."[1]

He knew that God was merciful. His mercy had

---

[1] "Sermons": *Works*, vol. v. page 100.

been revealed in Christ who had come to seek and to save the lost, and who had set forth the freedom of the Divine grace in the parable of the Prodigal Son. Yes; but God was just; and to Wesley the justice was as real as the mercy and as essential an element and force in God's eternal, unchangeable, absolute life. Indeed, apart from Justice, Mercy cannot even be thought; any more than the finite can be thought apart from the infinite, the relative apart from the absolute.

There is no Mercy where there is no guilt. If sin is nothing more than a transient though necessary incident of human development, or if it is nothing more than a disease of the moral life, it needs no forgiveness; there is nothing to forgive. If a disease and nothing more, it appeals—not to the Divine Mercy to pardon—but to the Divine Compassion and Power to cure. If a necessary incident in the development of the moral life of man, then, again, as it cannot be the object of Divine hostility and resentment, there is nothing in it for the Divine Mercy to forgive; it will gradually disappear in the pre-determined processes of that Divine movement by which the race is advancing towards perfection.

But to Wesley his own sin was a violent and voluntary disturbance of the ordered relations between man and God. It was not a misfortune but a crime. The responsibility for it was his; the guilt of it was his; and he believed, and believed rightly, that his sense of guilt was in truth his apprehension and sense of the Righteousness of God condemning him for his sin, and menacing him with awful punishment. It was because he was *justly* condemned, and because he was *justly* menaced with punishment, that he was in such sore need of Mercy. He had heard, he had received, he had preached the Gospel of Divine Grace, offering to all men the remission of sins, but his conscience demanded a Gospel of which during the twelve years preceding 1738 he had no real grasp, and this prevented him from finding peace. Justice condemned him, if Mercy forgave him. In his conception of God he could not suppress the Divine Justice even in the presence of the strongest assurances of the Divine Mercy. To him the two ideas, each necessary to the other, were irreconcilable contraries. He found, not their transcendent, but their actual and concrete synthesis in Christ—in Christ whose "blood was shed for him;" in Christ, who was his "sole justification, sanctification, and redemption." Till now, to use his own words, his faith had not been fixed on "its right object;" it had been "faith in God, not faith in or through Christ." Now his faith rested in Christ, and, as he says, "an assurance was given me that He had taken away *my* sins, even *mine*, and saved *me* from the law of sin and death."

It is no part of my duty this morning to offer any proofs of the fact that Christ died for the sins of men, or to attempt any illustration of the mystery.

It is enough that I should remind you that in John Wesley's personal discovery of the reality of the Atonement—the synthesis of Justice and Mercy in the death of Christ—he found the inspiration and the force which, under God, created Methodism. Methodism has its roots in a living faith in Christ as a real and objective Atonement for the sin of the world. Surrender that faith, and the roots of your life are destroyed.

IV.

Wesley proclaimed his new discovery with vehement energy. Within a month he was at Oxford, preaching before the University in the pulpit of St. Mary's on the text, "By grace are ye saved through faith," and insisting that the death of Christ is "the only sufficient means of redeeming man from death eternal," and that His resurrection is "the restoration of us all to life and immortality."[1] In a later sermon, also preached before the University, he gives his definition of Faith, a definition drawn from two separate sentences in the third of the Homilies of the Church of England appointed to be read in churches in the time of Queen Elizabeth. Wesley's definition reads thus:—

"The right and true Christian faith is not only to believe that Holy Scripture and the articles of our faith are true, but also to have a sure trust and

---

[1] "Sermons": *Works*, vol. v. page 9.

confidence to be saved from everlasting damnation by Christ. It is a sure trust and confidence which a man hath in God, that, by the merits of Christ, his sins are forgiven, and he reconciled to the favour of God; whereof doth follow a loving heart to obey His commandments."[1]

He repeats the substance of this definition in several of his sermons. It is a formal statement of the nature of that faith which had made so immense a difference in his own religious life. I do not propose to criticize it. The dullest intellect in Christendom might see that it is apparently open to one very elementary objection; if saving faith is a condition precedent of the forgiveness of sins, and restoration to the favour of God, saving faith can hardly be a belief that we are forgiven and restored to His favour already. But as this objection is so very obvious that it must occur to the dullest of men as soon as the definition is stated, modesty requires us to assume that it probably occurred to John Wesley himself, who was one of the acutest. Indeed there is evidence that it did occur to him.

In his old age, as the result of a deeper knowledge of the ways of God and of the religious life of man—not for mere logical reasons—he modified his judgment concerning the nature and contents of what the theologians call "saving faith."

---

[1] "Sermons": *Works*, vol. v. page 23.

"Nearly fifty years ago," he says, "when the preachers commonly called Methodists, began to preach that grand Scriptural doctrine of salvation by faith, they were not sufficiently apprised of the difference between a servant and a child of God;" and now, with a breadth of thought which is not commonly attributed to any of the men of the Evangelical Revival, he defines faith as, "Such a Divine conviction of God as, even in its infant state, enables every one that possesses it to 'fear God and work righteousness.' And whosoever, in every nation, believes thus far, the Apostle declares, is accepted of Him. He actually is, at that very moment, in a state of acceptance. But he is at present only a *servant* of God, not properly a *son*. Meantime let it be well observed that 'the wrath of God' no longer 'abideth on him.'" [1]

But Wesley still insisted on the power and blessedness of the nobler faith, which he describes as, "a Divine conviction, whereby every child of God is enabled to testify, 'The life that I now live I live by faith on the Son of God, who loved me and gave Himself for me.'" He still presses upon those whose faith is of the lower kind, the obligation to seek the higher; and he confidently assures them that if they seek it they will sooner or later possess it.[2]

---

[1] "Sermons": *Works*, vol. vii. page 199.
[2] *Ibid.*

In the earlier years of the movement he had refused to recognise the distinction implied by the terms "faith of adherence" and "faith of assurance." He found no such terms in the Bible. There were not "two faiths in one Lord;" but "one faith in one Lord." He said that he had never known a man saved from outward and inward sin without what was called "the faith of assurance"—"a sure confidence that by the merits of Christ he was reconciled to the mercy of God."[1] If he allowed any distinction between "the faith of adherence" and "the faith of assurance," he insisted, to the confusion and astonishment of theologians, that "the faith of assurance" came first.

There were good reasons, no doubt, for revising his original definition. It was true, as he said, that the earlier teaching made "sad the hearts of those whom God had not made sad;" and had led to the discouragement, perhaps the fatal discouragement, of many sincere penitents. And yet that paradoxical definition of saving Faith as "a sure trust and confidence which a man hath in God, that, by the merits of Christ, his sins are forgiven, and he reconciled to the favour of God" is perhaps truer than it seems. It is a paradox; for if faith is the condition precedent of salvation, how can it be a belief that we are saved already? But the definition is the result of a violent effort, breaking through the forms of

---

[1] *Journals*, vol. i. page 261.

the logical understanding, to express transcendent spiritual realities. For is it not true that God has already given us—has given to all men, believers and unbelievers alike,—eternal redemption in Christ? Is it not true that we can trust God for nothing, ask God for nothing, that lies beyond the wealth of blessing which in Christ is already ours? Does not the gift of Christ, according to the Divine thought and purpose, include all gifts? And when we find Christ, do we not discover that in Him we already possess—and had always possessed—all things?

Yes, it may be answered, But until we have faith in Christ, Christ is not ours, nor are the infinite blessings of His salvation ours. Is that true? You, surely of all men, are not going to say that Christ died for those only who, as God foresaw, would afterwards believe in Him. You, surely, are not intending to introduce into your hymn-book the famous verse of the great hymn-writer of Congregationalism :—

> "My soul looks back to see
> The burdens Thou didst bear
> When hanging on th' accursed tree,
> And *hopes* her guilt was there."

You do not hope; you know; and what you know is true for yourselves you know is also true for every man, saint or sinner, heathen or Christian, in every country and in every age; for Christ is "the Propitiation" for the sins "of the whole world." There is a relation between Christ and man antecedent to man's faith and independent of it. Faith does not create that relation—it accepts and consciously realizes a relation which exists before Faith, and apart from which Faith would be impossible; a relation wonderfully and mysteriously modified by the Death of Christ for our sins, but which is part of the Divine order of the Universe. For in Christ " were all things created, in the heavens and upon the earth "—sun and stars, mountains and seas, angels and men; and " in Him all things consist "—hold together and endure through all the millenniums of created existence. When I find Christ I do not find One who, till now, has been far from me. I find One who has always been the very ground of my being, the very root of my life. By faith I take up my citizenship in the Kingdom of God; but the citizenship was already mine by God's gift and God's purpose. By faith I accept and realize my sonship in the Divine household; but I was created in Christ to be a son. By faith I receive and rejoice in the forgiveness of my sin; but the forgiveness was already mine in Christ Jesus my Lord.

Wesley's paradox, by the very revolt to which it provokes the logical understanding, compels us to confront the transcendent mystery of the real relations of God to the human race in Christ.

V.

Finally, his original definition of Faith was organically connected with the great doctrine to which Methodism has given such magnificent emphasis—

That the Spirit of God bears direct witness to the spirit of man, and assures him of the forgiveness of his sins, and his Divine sonship. Indeed, the Faith which the definition demands is impossible, and was seen by Wesley to be impossible, apart from this "witness."

From the very first—from the time, I mean, that he passed through his great experience in May, 1738—Wesley saw that for the power as well as the joy of the Christian Life it was necessary that a man should have the complete certainty that he was no longer a "child of wrath," but a child of God. In this he was of one mind with Luther. For in maintaining the doctrine of Justification by Faith, it had been Luther's aim to recover for men that full assurance of their personal salvation which had been discouraged, if not rendered impossible, by Romish doctrine and by the Romish discipline of the spiritual life. To the nations of northern Europe which received the Lutheran Gospel there came a sudden burst of glorious sunshine; the clouds were driven away to distant horizons, and men rejoiced in the light of God; it seemed as if the age of gold had begun. But it was not possible for Christendom to break at once with its past. The clouds gathered again too soon. The iron times returned.

When Wesley began his work, the religious life of England—its best religious life—was wanting in buoyancy, courage, vigour, adventure, and even among devout men that joy of the Holy Ghost which can never be known apart from the certainty of personal salvation, was not general. But he knew that he himself had received from God the direct assurance of the forgiveness of his sins and of his Divine sonship. He refused to believe that this was an exceptional privilege, inaccessible to other men. What *he* had received, every man that believed in Christ might receive; for the glorious blessings which God has given to men in Christ are the common inheritance of all believers. From the very first, therefore, he insisted that no man should rest until the same Divinely authenticated certainty came to him.

By the testimony of the Spirit, he means "an inward impression on the soul, whereby the Spirit of God immediately and directly witnesses to my spirit that I am a child of God; that Jesus Christ hath loved me, and given Himself for me; that all my sins are blotted out; and I, even I, am reconciled to God." [1]

After twenty years' consideration he sees no cause to retract any part of this statement. This doctrine seems to him one "grand part of the testimony" which God has given to the Methodists to bear to all mankind. He says that it is by God's "peculiar blessing upon them in searching the Scriptures, confirmed by the experience of His children, that this great evangelical truth has been recovered, which had been for many years well-nigh lost and forgotten." [2]

---

[1] "Sermons": *Works*, vol. 5, page 124.   [2] *Ibid.*

Yes, *confirmed by the experience of His children.* That was the strength of Wesley's position. In the religious life of the early Methodists there was exhilaration, vigour, triumph. Their joy was irrepressible. It broke out in shouts of Hallelujah! It sang exulting songs. The old Dissenters were perplexed—sometimes scandalized. They heard of irreligious men, vicious men, who were writhing in an agony of repentance yesterday, and who were rejoicing in the certainty of forgiveness and in the sure hope of eternal glory to-day. It was not only the suddenness of the transition that confounded them, but its completeness. A fulness of assurance had come to penitents which, as many of them supposed was hardly possible to saints.

This "assurance" was a large part of your power. It gave to Methodism its hosts of preachers—preachers of many kinds and bearing many names. Personal testimony to the power of Christ to restore men to God, this can be given by every man to whom the witness of the Spirit has come. For this no protracted training at college is necessary; no Hebrew, no Greek, no mastery either of Arminius or Calvin. The man who was drunk in the streets a week ago, if he now knows Christ for himself, can stand under a tree or against a wall to-day and say to every one that will listen to him, "Christ Jesus came into the world to save sinners, of whom I am chief." He needs no hours of leisure to think over that text. He has no occasion to consult commentators as to its meaning;

the carpenter can put aside his saw and his plane, the blacksmith can throw down his apron and his hammer, and begin at once to expound the words; his own sin, his own salvation—these have revealed to him their wonderful contents. But for Wesley's doctrine of the Witness of the Spirit, Wesleyanism would never have had its great army of lay-preachers and class-leaders; if the power of the doctrine is ever lost, that army will gradually break up and melt away.

But the doctrine did something more than give you your preachers. If the new form of the religious life, illustrated by Methodism, perplexed the grave and thoughtful Christian men of the older Churches, the common people found in it an irresistible attractiveness. It seemed to them now that the Gospel was true after all—a real discovery of some infinite good that was within the reach of every man—the revelation of an actual redemption which had been wrought for the human race. The loud Amens which came from your people confirming the words of your preachers, the glad outcries of "Glory to God," "Praise the Lord,"—these carried home the Gospel to the hearts of multitudes who might have been almost unmoved by the testimony of a solitary man.

Nor was it on Sunday only, or only when engaged in religious services, that the Methodists had this abounding joy; it remained with them all the week through; there was a light resting upon their common path; their hearts were filled with music when there was no song on their lips. And so weary men and men who had been discouraged and broken down by trouble ; and men who had come to despair of themselves because they had been defeated in every attempt to live a better life ; and men who were miserable because they hated and despised themselves for their vices, and knew that others hated and despised them, too ; and men who had become lethargic and dull because their horizons were narrow and their occupations and thoughts monotonous—men whose imaginations had never been kindled, whose hearts had never been stirred ; and men who were happy as yet, but who had begun to see that the streams of earthly happiness soon run dry ; all sorts of men were charmed, excited, by the discovery that people like themselves had found the springs of an immortal gladness and strength. There was mystery in it ; but mystery itself has an eternal power over the hearts of men. The Methodists said that they were filled with joy because they had found God ; and is there not a secret conviction in the heart of every man, that to find God is man's supreme blessedness?

It was largely in the strength of your testimony to the witness of the Spirit that you won your early triumphs. I have said, that if your faith in this doctrine ever declines you will lose your preachers. I say now, that even if you kept your preachers their great successes would be over, for it is the common experience of the Methodist people, confirming every declaration of their preachers concerning the reality and greatness of the Christian redemption, that, under God, gives to the testimony of the preachers pathos and power.

VI.

I have spoken with a freedom which, as a minister of another Church, I had no right to assume; and yet it is not another Church, for we are all one in Christ. In your strength Evangelical Christendom is strong: in your weakness Evangelical Christendom would be weak. If I have ventured to appeal to you with unbecoming and presumptuous urgency to be loyal to our common faith, it is because I am so deeply conscious that the fortunes of the Congregational Churches of England cannot be separated from yours.

You are the heirs of great traditions. You stand in a noble succession. But—

> "They who on glorious ancestry enlarge,
> Produce their debt instead of their discharge."

You have awful responsibilities to the nations in which your societies are already planted, and to the nations to which you have still to make known the unsearchable riches of God's grace. Keep faith with your fathers; keep faith with Christ; keep faith with your children and your children's children; transmit to coming generations the Gospel which has already won such splendid triumphs. That "Word of God" which Wesley preached "liveth and abideth for ever." It is translated into new tongues; it is conceived in changing forms by the changing minds of men; every deeper discovery of the relations between God and man adds to its wealth and power; but it remains—that living word of God—the same in its substance through all centuries, its strength unspent, its glory undimmed.

It is a great Gospel which you and your fathers have preached during the hundred and fifty years of your history, a Gospel which declares the love of God for all men. Preach it still with the same confidence of faith and the same passion of joy. Tell men, that while they inherit by their birth the infirmities and sins of the race they also inherit by their birth the salvation which Christ has achieved for all mankind. Tell them that they live—not in a lost world, but in a redeemed world; a world lost by its revolt against God and its alienation from the life of God, but redeemed in the blood of Christ, and with powers in Christ and in the Spirit of Christ which render all righteousness possible. Tell men—all men—that they were created in Christ, and that when they discover and accept their true relation to Him they will live under new heavens and on a new earth, and will know the greatness of the sons of God. Tell them that they are blessed with every spiritual blessing in Christ; that God chose them in Him before the foundation of the world, that they should be holy and without blemish before Him in love; charge them not to defeat the purposes of the Divine grace; but to work out their own salvation with fear and trembling, and so to make their calling and election sure. See to it that through God's grace you know for yourselves that, through the merits of Christ, your sins are forgiven, and that you are indeed, and of a truth, the children of God; that your testimony to the Christian redemption may not rest on tradition but on your own personal experience.

Assembled for this sacred commemoration, the hearts of millions of men in many lands are drawn to you; and they trust that in these services a Divine flame will kindle that will spread over the whole world. I think I see descending upon this assembly the glorious forms of millions of men of other generations who through the ministry of your fathers escaped from eternal destruction, and whose home is in the fair city of God above. We are encompassed by a great cloud of witnesses. In their presence, in God's presence, over the very ashes of your founder whose death we commemorate, but who lives for evermore in the light of the Eternal, I call upon you to resolve, with all the solemnities of an oath, that you will stand fast until you die, in your fidelity to the truths which have given to Methodism its power and glory; and that henceforth you will pray with a deeper earnestness and a firmer faith that the fires of Methodism may never be extinguished. I call upon you to invoke in this great hour the good help of God, that you may surrender yourselves to His Will and to His grace with a consecration so complete and unreserved that it shall be possible for you to receive the fulness of His Spirit : and let your hearts wait on Him in confident hope, till the fulness of His Spirit shall be yours.

X.

THE MINISTRY REQUIRED BY THE AGE.[1]

IT is among our traditional usages, that when a minister is ordained to his first pastorate a sermon is preached to the Church and a solemn charge is delivered to the minister. This, however, is not an ordination; it is a recognition service. Dr. Goodrich has had a long experience of the duties and responsibilities of the Christian ministry, and he has discharged them honourably. He has drawn to himself the love and confidence of the Congregational Churches, both of England and Scotland. He knows already far better than I can tell him, the sorrows of the ministry, its labours, its perils, its anxieties, and its joys. He knows the eternal fountains of light, of consolation, and of strength.

---

[1] This discourse was prepared for the service held in the Congregational Chapel, Chorlton Road, Manchester, on Monday, November 3rd, 1890, in connection with the settlement of the Rev. Dr. Goodrich as Pastor of the Church meeting in that place. The discourse proved much too long for the occasion, and the whole of Part I. was omitted in delivery; the transition from the introductory paragraphs to Part II. was made by a few brief sentences.

It would be singularly presumptuous if I were to attempt to address to your minister anything of the nature of a charge. I can but express my affection for him, and the earnest hope that the large success of his ministry in this place will more than justify his retirement from the great position which he held in Glasgow.

Though I cannot deliver a charge, I have been requested to speak on a subject which might, perhaps, in hands strong enough to deal with it, suggest the materials for a charge—*The Ministry required by the Present Age.*

The subject is not of my selection, nor are the terms in which it is defined. I have no liking for subjects of this description—so large, so far-reaching. Their horizons are too remote. Their limits escape me. They are beyond my strength. And yet, since I have been asked to speak on this subject, I will do what I can.

But to discuss it at all, I must dismiss, at starting, a very large part of the life and work of the minister, and limit myself to his preaching ; and to discuss even this province of the subject to any good purpose, I must think of *you*—the Church and the congregation—rather than of the minister. For you have very much more to do with the substance and with the form of your minister's sermons than you probably suspect. When the eye is dim and the tongue falters and becomes indistinct in its utterance, the cause of the evil is not always to be found in the eye itself, or in the tongue itself; the root of the mischief may be in some remote organ of the body, or in a deficiency of general constitutional vigour. And the Church is a living body. If the minister does a great deal to form the life and determine the work of the congregation, the congregation does a great deal to form the life and determine the work of the minister. The strong currents of thought and feeling which are flowing in the congregation may carry him, without his knowing it, several points to the east or the west, when he is steering due north or south, and he may get on to dangerous rocks; or they may add, without his knowing it, to the speed which he is making on the right course. A strong and conscientious man, loyal to Christ, looking forward to that awful hour when he must give account of his ministry, will never try to preach so as to *please* his people; the more he loves them the less will he try to please them merely; but their conception of the kind of preaching which they really need will have a large influence on his own thoughts of how he ought to preach.

It is my belief that when Churches have discovered what are the true elements of power in a minister, and, disregarding all inferior and adventitious attractions, care supremely for what is supremely worth caring for, they will have a powerful ministry.

I.

What, then, should you desire in your minister's preaching? And, more definitely, how should you wish the Present Age—of which my subject requires me to think—to affect his preaching?

In answering these questions it is necessary, first of all, to grasp firmly a very obvious and commonplace truth :—Your minister is a *Christian* minister: as a preacher he is a preacher of the Christian Gospel. The Christian Gospel was given to men by the Lord Jesus Christ, and by those whom He commissioned to unfold its contents. It has been verified in the experience of the Christian Church, an experience which now extends over more than eighteen hundred years. You yourselves constitute a Christian Church, and are the heirs, trustees, and defenders of the faith which was once for all delivered to the saints. To you the ultimate secret of the life of man, and of that divine and eternal order in which man stands, has been revealed; you are not voyaging across unknown seas of thought in order to discover it. Your minister, therefore, has not to receive a revelation from the new age in which we are living: he has a revelation to deliver to it—a revelation from God—a revelation which is at once old and new; old as the sun and stars which have been the wonder and delight of men from the beginning ; new as that fresh and immediate vision of sun and stars which comes to the men of every new generation. We have something more than a tradition or an historic record of those celestial glories; we have seen them for ourselves, and can speak of them at first hand ; and yet they are the same that shone above Chaldean shepherds and the builders of the pyramids. The Christian Gospel is the Gospel of Christ, of Paul, of John, of Peter, of James.

To include its infinite contents within the limits of a few sentences is impossible; they are inexhaustible. But it is clear that the Christian Gospel assumes that man was created to share the life, and the righteousness, and the blessedness of the Eternal; that he has fallen short of this great glory; has fallen short of it by sin, has incurred guilt, and therefore needs the Divine forgiveness. The Christian Gospel also assumes that the moral and spiritual perfection of man cannot be attained by the development and discipline of any powers in man himself, but only by the inspiration of the Spirit of God, with whose grace man has freely to co-operate.

Is there anything in these assumptions to suggest an answer to our question as to the Ministry required by our Age? I think there is.

(1) These assumptions are categorically denied by certain theories of human life, which have been fighting hard for ascendency during the last thirty or forty years; and, what is more important, the convictions on which the assumptions rest are enfeebled by the general spirit and temper of our contemporaries.

For example, the doctrine of heredity, as it is very commonly held, is much more fatal to the sense of personal responsibility for life and conduct than the old doctrine of Original Sin, as it was commonly held by persons who professed the Calvinistic theology. Some modern theories of the power of environment, and especially of the social environment, over the personal life are more fatal to the sense of moral freedom than the Calvinistic doctrine of the Divine decrees. Just at the time when Calvinism had been very generally surrendered by the Churches, its least noble elements were re-asserted by the philosophers. The philosophers have picked up fragments of the creed which the theologians had cast aside—and the worst fragments. For what is the theory of human nature which includes the ethical and spiritual life of man within the region of natural law but a theory of Necessity? And the philosophical theory of Necessity is Calvinism without a God. The greatness of God, who to the Calvinist was a Living Person—a Living Person with an infinite love of righteousness and an infinite hatred of moral evil—with a Free Will, supreme, unbound by any authority beyond itself—the greatness of God, I say, as a Living Person, with transcendent moral perfection, invigorated the personality of a devout Calvinist, and gave new force to all the most robust elements of his moral life. In the presence of an unconscious Necessity human freedom is crushed; in the presence of an august Person, though unlimited power over all created things is in theory attributed to Him, human freedom rises to heroic energy, and becomes capable of heroic achievements.

It is not only the drift of scientific thought that

enfeebles the sense of moral freedom and moral responsibility. Large numbers of people have just discovered the sins of *Society*, and in the freshness of their penitence are declaring that Society, and Society alone, is responsible for the wickedness and misery of individual men. Create, they say, a new and just and gracious social order, and the wilderness will blossom as the rose; the vices of men will vanish; all men will be virtuous. Society, not the individual, is made responsible for the lying and the lust, the dishonesty, the cruelty, the selfishness, and the ambition of mankind.

These conceptions of human life strike at the very root of the assumptions of the Christian Gospel. The Christian minister, if he is to be successful in drawing men to Christ, must take account of them. That there is a measure of truth in them is certain, but the most fatal falsehoods are precisely those which are not wholly false; the truth which is in them is largely the secret of their power.

The Christian minister, in our time, has to consider how with God's help he can awaken that sense of personal responsibility which has been drugged by poisonous theories of life, and stifled by an atmosphere which is heavy and foul.

He may sometimes make an intellectual assault on the theories which are working the mischief, but his real success will come from other methods. He himself must have an awful sense of the *guilt*—not merely the *evil*—of sin; he must be vividly conscious of his own personal responsibility, and then there will be a wholesome, stimulating power in the masculine energy of his own moral life; virtue will go out of him. He must recur again and again to lines of thought and appeal, to which the natural conscience of every man is most likely to respond. He must rouse it to condemn with fierce indignation the crimes of other men; and while it is all aglow must turn its fires against the man's own sins. He must never forget that he has an ally in every man's heart—imprisoned, chained, its force broken, its eye dim, its voice feeble—but alive still, and still capable of giving answer to any message in which there is the accent of God.

He must insist on the true nature of sin as a crime deserving punishment—not merely a disease requiring to be cured; as an offence needing pardon—not merely a calamity like blindness, needing pity. He must bring home to every man his own part in determining his conduct, and not suffer it to be supposed that character is wholly the creation of birth and circumstances. While frankly recognising that certain regions of human life are within the dominion of necessity, he must insist on the reality and awful dignity of that inner sanctuary which is the province of freedom. He must distinguish between the occasions which make it *possible* for a man to sin—the pressure of forces both within and without which *move* him to sin—and his own consent to sin. He must show that the social order cannot be held responsible for the vices and irreligion of large numbers of our people, while there are large numbers, who are in exactly the same social condition, living an honest, upright, temperate, and Christian life. He must appeal to the Judgment to come, and to its awful, its glorious issues.

You must not suppose that your minister has forgotten the temper and requirements of the Age if he insists on these austere aspects of truth which the Age regards with hostility. They are in my judgment precisely what the Age requires to inspire it with a more masculine and robust moral temper, and to induce it to listen to the Christian Gospel.

(2) Closely associated with the tendencies of modern thought and feeling of which I have just spoken is the demand for a social order based upon the principles of the Sermon on the Mount.

I may say, in passing, that it seems to be very generally forgotten that the precepts of that discourse are addressed to the disciples of Christ, and that they are intended to regulate their conduct as citizens of the Kingdom of God—their conduct towards each other, and their conduct towards other men. There is nothing in them which directly illustrates Christ's conception of the State. Elsewhere in the New Testament there is an explicit application of the Christian law to political life. As citizens of the Kingdom of God we are bound to feel no resentment against those who injure us, and not to avenge ourselves. But are grave offences to go unpunished? That is not the Christian idea. " Avenge not yourselves, beloved. . . . vengeance belongeth to Me; I will recompense," saith the Lord. It is *our* blessedness to be called to show mercy and pity even to those who do us great wrongs ; the penalty of the wrongs—if they are not repented of and forgiven— God Himself will inflict. And in the social order these penalties are to be inflicted in God's name by judges and magistrates. For "the powers that be are ordained of God." The earthly ruler "beareth not the sword in vain, for he is a minister of God ; an avenger for wrath to him that doeth evil." Human life, under its present earthly conditions, approaches the Christian ideal when no personal resentments are felt against those who injure us, but when all crimes are equitably punished by the magistrates. Mercy is the great duty of the private citizen; of the magistrate, justice.

But this by the way. The great thing to insist upon is, that a Christian social order is impossible except to a Christian people. The arrangements proper in a college for young men would be mischievous in a school for boys. Institutions which are foreign to the spirit and character of a nation can have no real authority ; they will not work. Between the political and economic order on the one hand, and the temper and moral habits of a people on the other, the relations are vital. As long as the great desire of large numbers of our people is for material prosperity, a social order in harmony with the spirit of the Sermon on the Mount is impossible. Men must seek *first*—that is, as the supreme object of life—the Kingdom of God and His righteousness, before they can have an economic organization of society corresponding to the spirit and laws of Christ.

What, then, is a Christian minister to do in the presence of the demand that the whole force of the Church should be used in promoting urgent social reforms? Is he to avoid in the pulpit and elsewhere all those questions which in many noble hearts are creating a passionate enthusiasm? Is he to do nothing towards improving the material conditions of human life, and to be content with speaking of things eternal and divine? I do not believe that you will impose on your minister any such restraints.

You should rather wish him to remember the historic conditions under which the successive changes in the economic order of Christendom have occurred. They have been the results—in many cases the wholly unforeseen results—of new forces which have acted on the intellectual and moral life of nations; or of great geographical discoveries; or of great inventions. They have not been the fulfilment of the programme of any social reformers. The results—the beneficent results—of the partial triumphs of the Christian Faith in Europe—and let it never be forgotten that its triumphs have been very partial—were not foreseen by the Apostles and the early generations of their converts. Aided by economic forces it abolished the institution of slavery; but this effect of the new Faith was neither consciously intended by the early

Church nor foreseen. Nor was the change it has effected in the position of women intended or foreseen; nor the results—partly beneficent, partly disastrous—which have come from making pity and compassion for the poor a form of religious service. The leaven worked; no one foresaw how it would work.

Take another illustration. The results of the immense triumph of the principle of Individualism in France in the last century were neither intended nor foreseen. Great evils were swept away by the Revolution; but within a century, evils—new in their form and new in their magnitude—have sprung up in the place of those which have disappeared, and these are so great that the tide of a strong reaction is running to flood, and many compassionate men are crying out earnestly for the restoration of restraints on individual freedom—restraints differing in form for the most part from those which were removed—but still restraints; and yet the dissolution of these restraints was one of the chief ends and glories of the Revolution. The leaders of the Revolution did not intend or foresee the results of their work.

I do not believe in large schemes for changing the whole order, either of our political or economical life. If I am asked to accept a scheme and to work for it, which would transfer all the materials and instruments of production to the State, and am assured that only by such a revolutionary method as this can the miseries of considerable masses of the people be removed, I am obliged to reply, that the conditions which determine the economical prosperity of nations are so complex that I have not the confidence and the courage to determine whether such an immense reconstruction would on the whole be beneficial; that the equation contains so many unknown quantities that I cannot solve it; that the greatest and most beneficent improvements in the social and economic condition of nations have not hitherto been the working out of a complete and systematic theory of the true social and economic order; that, judging from experience, the destruction of our present organization and the attempt to reconstruct our economic life on the principles of Collectivism would not work as its promoters anticipate, and that very possibly the evil results would greatly outweigh the good.

And if I am told that the Christian faith is irrevocably pledged to the cause of justice and mercy, and that while the social order is unjust and unmerciful, Christian men are unfaithful to Christ if they do not attempt to reform it, I answer, Yes; but I must first be sure that the new order would be more just and more merciful than the old, and that the methods proposed for abolishing the old order would at the same time provide for the secure establishment of the new. And, further, the *first* object of the Christian faith is not to secure justice and mercy in social institutions, but to make Christian men merciful and just. It does not wait till the social order is Christian before it requires and enables Christian men to obey the law and illustrate the spirit of Christ. It has required and enabled men to love and honour each other as brethren under social conditions wholly antagonistic to the spirit of human brotherhood. The law was imperative in the old Roman times on masters and slaves; in mediæval times on lord and serf; and, with the law, power was given to fulfil it. It was by the assertion and partial fulfilment of the law under these adverse conditions that conditions more favourable to the true idea of human life were rendered possible. In our own days the same law is imperative and the same grace is given. It requires employers to care for their men in the spirit of Christ, and men to care for their employers in the spirit of Christ. It says to both, "Seek first the Kingdom of God and His righteousness." It requires, as I have sometimes said, the tradesman, the manufacturer, the merchant, to carry on his business under the competitive organization of modern industry as *if Christ were the Head of the firm*. It requires the clerk, the manager, the foreman, the workman, the porter, the errand boy, to do his part as *if Christ were the Head of the firm*, "as unto the Lord, not unto men." It offers power to all of them to enable them to do it. We should desire that the more merciful and equitable social order to which the present is only a transition should come as the natural result of a great change in the temper and character of the nation; should be the new and outward sign of a new and invisible grace; should come, not from the outbreak of the passions

of men violently demanding a larger share of the
material prosperity of the world for themselves, but
as an achievement of that love which "suffereth long
and is kind," "envieth not," "seeketh not its own."

Meanwhile every change in methods of production and distribution which promises to lessen the suffering and precariousness of human life, to add to its ease, security, comfort, and brightness—whatever is likely to lessen the fierceness of social and economic conflict and bind together—not one class of the community as an organized army to fight another—but all classes of the community, as a brotherhood for the welfare and safety of all; every social reform that will contribute to the dignity of the less fortunate of the people, and induce the wealthy and the powerful to discharge their responsibilities and duties, should be sustained, and heartily sustained, by every man that desires to see the will of God done on earth as it is done in heaven.

Some of these proposals may be so manifestly reasonable and practicable that you may wish your minister to advocate them in this place ; with regard to others, about whose reasonableness and practicability men of clear intelligence and of a just and generous spirit may be doubtful, you may prefer that he should be silent. But if the great hindrance of all economic and social reforms lies in human selfishness, in the passion for material prosperity, in the spirit of ambition, whether it is the ambition of a man for himself, or his ambition for his family, or his ambition for the class to which he belongs, the ministry of the Gospel in this place, if it is penetrated with the spirit of Christ, will render the kind of aid which is most necessary to every movement for improving the condition of the people; and in many cases the aid will be most effectively rendered to movements which are not explicitly advocated, and about whose wisdom your minister himself may be uncertain. The good leaven will work, and will work in ways which he neither intends nor foresees.

II.

But I suppose that when I was asked to speak of the Ministry required by the Present Age, it was intended that I should say something of the way in which the ministry should be affected by the present condition of the *Church* itself—its intellectual, ethical, and spiritual condition. An impossible subject! I approach it with despair; but I say again that I must do what I can.

(1) First of all, I think that you should wish your minister to recognise very frankly that immense intellectual movement in which all the Churches of the West have been involved since the Renaissance of the fifteenth century and the Reformation of the sixteenth. It has affected the theology of the Church of Rome as well as of the Protestant Churches. In the Protestant Churches there came a very powerful reaction, in the course of two or three generations

after the great revolt against the Roman authority; but very soon the tide turned again, and it has been flowing—with some checks—ever since. The Protestant attempt to recast theological thought in scholastic forms has broken down. It had broken down before your time and mine. The Evangelical Revival of the last century was one of the forces which contributed to break it down. Forty—thirty—years ago, perhaps later, there were men among us who exhorted us to be faithful to the theology of the Puritans, and by the Puritans they meant the Calvinistic Puritans; but these very men, though they were hardly conscious of it, had travelled very far from the position of the Puritan theologians. For good or for evil—partly, as I think, for both—they had ceased to hold the Puritan creed. Compare the Declaration of Faith and Order which was accepted by the ministers and representatives of the Congregational Churches of England and Wales in 1833—nearly sixty years ago—with the Westminster Confession; or compare it with the Declaration agreed upon by the elders and messengers of the Congregational Churches in England who met at the Savoy just after the death of Cromwell, which was substantially identical with the Westminster Confession; and you will see how immense was the transition from the theology of the Puritans to the theology of our immediate ecclesiastical ancestors. The elaborate and stately system of theological belief which had been created by the theologians of the Reformed Church, of whom Francis Turretin is the best representative, has been sinking into decay for two centuries. And, as yet, no other organized theological system has taken its place.

That seems to me a great evil. For it shows that we have no intellectual expression of the contents of faith which satisfies us, or which even approximately satisfies us. There are many who regard this condition of things with exultation. They triumph in their freedom. They seem to imagine that they are displaying heroic courage in insulting and trampling under foot traditional creeds. There is no heroic courage in *that*. I see the ruins of a fortress, stern and mighty in other centuries, but tenantless for generations; it shows the traces of successful siege; it has been wasted by wind and rain and frost, and long neglect; the strong men, with nerves and muscles of iron, who once held it against hostile armies, have long since turned to dust; the roof has fallen in; the walls are rent; many of its stones have been carried off by the neighbours, to build, not another fortress, but very humble homes to shelter them from the weather. The men who assaulted it in its strength must have had courage; the people who are mocking at the ancient garrison and are dancing triumphantly in the grass-covered courtyard, require none.

Indeed, the mocking and the dancing are rather frivolous occupations. Would it not be well, instead of dwelling very much more on the decay of old forms of theological belief, to attempt to construct new? While the intellect has no part, or very little part, in the religious life, the religious life will never have in it the elements of enduring vigour. The work of reconstruction must, I think, be done piece by piece. We may be satisfied if in a generation we make one or two great doctrines clearer and are able to define them with more precision. Our methods may as yet be imperfect; but we shall not be wise to wait till they are perfected; by putting them into practice we shall discover their defects and shall gradually amend them.

A strong intellectual conception of the great truths of the Christian faith is a real aid to moral and religious vigour. Where thought is vague, character is likely to be feeble. And do not be misled by the popular cry against the tyranny of exact theological thinking. Our present doctrinal controversies are, for the most part, not about the definitions of transcendent truths, but about the transcendent truths themselves. Definitions may be necessary in order to make the real issue clear. Athanasius defined because the Arians shuffled.

You should, in my judgment, wish your minister's preaching to be instructive. You should wish him to teach you something—something clear and definite—something that may not, indeed, be a final statement of the truth, for no statement of the truth can be final—but something which shall be sufficiently near the eternal fact for which it stands to serve you and to last your time.

The old maps of the country may be more or less

inaccurate; they may have become untrustworthy; but this is generally acknowledged, and nothing is to be gained by further attacks on them; give us another map that shall more truly represent the outlines of the coast, the lie of the mountains, the course of the rivers; if you can only give us a fairly accurate map of a single district, this will be more to the purpose than your demonstration of the untrustworthiness of the old maps of the continent. It is always easy to interest large numbers of men in attacks upon the beliefs of other people; try to create in this congregation a general and earnest desire to learn what you should believe yourselves. To people who have never had, or who have lost, the faculty for clear thinking, and to people who will not take the trouble to think, an instructive preacher will sometimes be dull; let your minister know that you like him to be dull in that way—at least now and then. Encourage him to respect the rights of the intellect; do not ask him always to preach sermons which can be understood by everybody, and understood without effort. As long as men are unwilling to serve God with their understanding, they withhold from Him half His claims.

(2) You will probably expect your minister to discuss the questions which have been raised concerning the dates and authorship of the books of Holy Scripture. In a congregation like this it is hardly possible for him to pass them over. As far as the books of the New Testament are concerned,

I think that we are within sight of the practical close of the controversy. After a century of struggle the historical trustworthiness of the Four Gospels and the genuineness of, at least, all the important epistles are secure. But with regard to the earlier books of the Old Testament—their sources and the times at which they received their present form—the battle is at its height. He would be a rash man, I think, who ventured just now to speak with absolute confidence on some of the questions under debate. Do not be alarmed if you find that your minister is uncertain about them—if he speaks with hesitation, if he declines to commit himself to a definite judgment. I cannot doubt that the issue of this controversy will, in any case, be to enlarge and exalt our conceptions of the method of Divine revelation; but the good which is certain to come of it will be immensely increased if, while it lasts, you and all other Churches wait patiently for its final results, and see clearly that no uncertainties with regard to investigations of this kind should lessen the strength or diminish the joy of your own consciousness that in Christ you have been restored to God.

(3) But it is certain that while our doctrinal uncertainties last, and while the debate on the literary and historical questions relating to our sacred books is still going on, there is serious peril to the spiritual life. I will not at this moment attempt to determine whether the peril is greater than that which has to be reckoned with when the Church is disturbed by no

serious intellectual conflicts. It is enough for us to consider our own dangers.

There are large numbers of people in our Churches whose chief intellectual interests—I mean their chief intellectual interests in religion—lie remote from the central truths of the Christian Gospel. They are deeply concerned, for example, in questions about the future of those who die impenitent—a question, no doubt, of immense importance, but one on which they will never reach a right conclusion, except by accident, as long as they have no corresponding intellectual interest in *all* the main truths which are implicated in the Incarnation of Christ and His death for the sins of the world. Others, again, are chiefly interested in literary, historical, or scientific questions relating to the Old Testament; these, too, are questions important in their place. But this diversion of intellectual and even moral interest from the central facts of the revelation of God in Christ—this absorption in a special set of questions, some of which are purely speculative and are remote from life and practice—is a grave evil, and must be taken into account by the minister.

You should wish him to speak, not merely on those subjects upon which you are always thinking and reading and talking, but on those great things about which you think very little; and you should wish him to speak of them in a manner that will, through God's grace, give them their right place in your thought and life. You should wish him to speak of these forgotten truths, not as a theologian merely, but as a minister of Christ; of the Incarnation, not so as to enable you to construct a theory about the limitations of our Lord's knowledge or His real accessibility to temptation, but so as to fill you with awe and wonder in the presence of the actual assumption of human nature and human life by the Eternal Son of God; of His sufferings and death, not so as to resolve hard questions about the theory of the Atonement, but so as to bring home to you the greatness of the redemption which His sufferings and death achieved for mankind; for in Christ "we have our redemption through His blood," and His blood was shed "unto remission of sins." You should wish your minister to make real to you, by God's grace, Paul's exultation in being "justified by faith" —the boundless joy, the new vigour, the large freedom which came to Christian men when that great truth, covered for centuries with thick clouds, shone out once more in its old splendour at the Reformation. You should wish him so to speak of Christ that you may know for yourselves that He who died is alive again and liveth for evermore; of the Spirit of God, that you may be able to bear witness, on the strength of your own experience, that He has come to the Church, and that He abides with it for ever.

(4) Finally, there is a great deal in the ethical and religious life of the Churches of our times which requires special and serious treatment by the Christian ministry. We have escaped from the power of tradi-

tion, not only in our theological thought, but in our personal habits and in the order of our homes. This freedom, like the theological freedom, is also spoken of by many persons with exultation, as though it were altogether a good thing, and had no evil in it.

That the tradition of conduct was outworn—that its passing away was, therefore, inevitable—is no doubt true. But this is our misfortune; we have no reason for rejoicing in it. It is an immense loss not to inherit by birth a method of life; for this means that the experience of past generations conveys no guidance to us as to the conduct and habits which contribute to form an ideal Christian character. It means that we have to begin afresh and to learn everything for ourselves. It is like being born into a country in which there are no roads, and in which we have to discover by exploration how to get from one point to another. Even after the exploration the roads have to be made, if we are to travel safely and easily. Human life is so complex that in the absence of definite traditions as to how it should be ordered, we are sure to make the gravest mistakes—mistakes which can never be remedied. If parents, for example, inherit no tradition as to the best way of ordering the lives of their children, they are sure—even the wisest of them—to go wrong, and to go wrong on some very important points; and the injury which their children suffer cannot be undone. If young men and women form habits which experience shows them to be injurious—and they are likely to form such habits ignorantly unless a wise tradition of conduct has great moral authority over the people with whom they live—the habits, even if at last they are broken, permanently affect the power and grace of character.

We had a traditional method of life at one time; indeed, we had it within the memory of many people now living; but it has disappeared; and now every man does what is right in his own eyes. We have the Sermon on the Mount; but the application of the Sermon on the Mount to the details of conduct is difficult. The old method had become hard, mechanical, artificial; but still it was a method, and it contained—though in a half fossilized form—the results of the experience of several generations of devout Christian men and women. For example, the traditional method of life gave us a certain conception of Sunday, and of how Sunday should be kept; how often we should attend public worship; what kind of books we should read at home; what occupations were lawful on Sunday, what were unlawful, to a Christian man. The old method has gone. Every man has now to find out for himself how it is best to keep the day; at present I do not think that the general results of the experiment can be regarded with satisfaction.

Take another example: Within the memory of many of us, works of fiction were peremptorily excluded from the homes of large numbers of Congregationalists. To read a novel, was a mark of unregeneracy. I very well remember preaching a sermon in which I incidentally defended novel-reading; it was in the early days of my ministry, and it greatly troubled some of the older members of my congregation—venerable, saintly men and women, whom I *often* troubled, but who showed great generosity and magnanimity in their treatment of me. Now, young and old, we are all reading novels. But at a Church meeting at Carrs Lane, held a fortnight or three weeks ago for conference on the hindrances to Christian living, I read a letter from one of the members—for we allow those to write who shrink from speaking—in which the writer said that for nineteen years her passion for works of fiction had been one of her greatest hindrances; that she had fought hard with it, but was not even now sure that it was finally mastered. And there can be no doubt that excessive novel-reading has an effect upon the moral and religious life analogous to that of excessive drinking; it weakens moral fibre, makes the will irresolute, destroys self-restraint, renders impossible many of the nobler virtues.

Take another example: The old method of life forbade a large number of amusements which we regard as innocent; and we scoff at its irrational rigidity. But at another Church conference, held a week later than that to which I have just referred, we had a conversation on the interest of the Church in Missions; and in a letter from another member of the Church, it was said that thirty years ago our young people were very generally interested in Foreign Missions, but that now large numbers of them are so occupied with lawn-tennis and other outdoor amusements in summer, and with pursuits of other kinds in winter, that they have neither the time nor the disposition to read about Missions or to care for them.

The old method of life, I repeat, cannot be defended. It declared many things to be wrong in themselves which are right in themselves. It was technical, external. It reminds me of the rabbinical interpretations of the Fourth Commandment. It is a sin, the rabbis argued, to work on the Sabbath; to lift and to carry a heavy burden—a burden weighing a hundredweight, to use modern terms—is to work, and therefore is a sin; but to lift and to carry a burden weighing ten pounds less than a hundredweight is also a sin, for a few pounds in the weight of a burden cannot make any difference in the morality of carrying it; and to lift and to carry a still lighter burden is also a sin; and at last they concluded that it was a sin to pick up and carry a piece of string. And some of the severer interpreters of the law maintained that since all work is muscular exertion, there should be no muscular exertion of any kind on the Sabbath—a case of "undistributed middle"—and that to keep the commandment perfectly a man should remain absolutely motionless through the whole of its twenty-four hours. The method of life which was once authoritative among us had this technical rabbinical character. You ought not to make a shirt on Sunday; therefore, you ought not to sew on a button.

And yet there was more of philosophy than we sometimes suppose in those rigid rules, which absolutely forbade any common work on the Sunday, and the writing of letters, and the reading of newspapers and "secular" books; declared all novels contraband; and condemned all exciting amusements. Things which are innocent, perhaps helpful, in moderation, are ruin and death in excess. The old method of life rested upon the same principle that is the reasonable ground of the Total Abstinence movement in our own times; to large numbers of persons total abstinence is easy—total abstinence from billiards, from dancing, from novels, from occupations on Sunday which are not strictly religious—but moderation is difficult. Our fathers insisted on total abstinence.

Apart from these definite and rigid rules, the whole conception of life which was traditional among us till within recent years was different from our own. Our strength has always been largely derived from the merchants, manufacturers, and prosperous tradesmen in the great towns and cities of the kingdom; and I think that, as a rule, in the early part of this century a merchant, a manufacturer, or a tradesman, who was a member of a Congregational Church, was satisfied to live in a smaller house than a merchant, manufacturer, or tradesman with the same income, who was what he would call "a man of the world"; he had less "glass" in his grounds; he kept fewer servants and fewer horses and carriages; he gave less costly entertainments. His whole way of living was simpler. There was a larger margin between his income and expenditure. There was a certain restraint upon indulgence in the pleasant things which were within his reach. All this came from a traditional theory—not perhaps very exactly defined—of the difference between the Christian and the worldly life. The theory has disappeared, and with the theory the practice. The very word "worldly" has almost ceased to be used. "Old times are changed; old manners gone"; and it might be worth while to consider whether the change is altogether for the better.

In literature a certain self-restraint, a pruning of a too luxurious growth of imagery and style, is necessary to perfection; in every form of art—in painting, sculpture, architecture—the decline from the nobleness and grace of the great masters begins with the relaxation of this restraint: and a similar relaxation is followed by the corruption of eloquence and its degradation to a worthless and pernicious rhetoric. And so in the conduct of life a certain moderation, a voluntary limitation of expenditure and enjoyment, is the condition of power and grace and dignity. Under even the silken robe there should be the leathern girdle. It is not the "body" merely which has to be kept under if we are not to be castaways.

The old method of life has disappeared. Is it not time for congregations to ask their ministers to assist them in constructing a new method, wiser and better than the old? for a new method is urgently needed.

The Christian ideal of life and conduct in this present century—what is it? The Christian ideal on the exchange, in the mill, in the workshop, in the counting-house, in Parliament, in the City Council, in the home—what is it? The Christian ideal for the employer, the Christian ideal for the employed—what is it? The old ways are out of repair, going to ruin; it is time to make straight paths for our feet.

To construct the Christian ideal of life and conduct we must be filled with the Spirit of God, must live under the full power of that transcendent revelation which has come to us through Christ, and in the conscious possession of that redemption which He achieved for the human race, once for all, by His Incarnation, Death, and Resurrection. We must see and know for ourselves that He has made all things new; that we are living in a new earth and under new heavens. Eternal things must enter into the solution of the problems of the hour. In determining how we are to live we must remember what we are—children of God redeemed by Christ, destined to an endless life of righteousness, wisdom, blessedness, and glory, and that we have to make our calling and election sure.

And so in this age, as in all past ages, the ministry

which the Church supremely requires is a ministry filled with awe and strength and tenderness by the immediate vision of God in Christ. And this is the ministry which is also supremely required by the world. If we know God in Christ for ourselves, men will listen to us with confidence when we tell them that they too may have redemption through the blood of Christ, even the forgiveness of sins, and that through Him they may share the life and the joy of God.

XI

THE CONGREGATION HELPING THE MINISTER.[1]

"Ye also helping together on our behalf by your supplication; that, for the gift bestowed upon us by means of many, thanks may be given by many persons on our behalf."—2 *Cor.* i. 11.

WHEN Paul wrote this Epistle, he had been recently passing through great troubles; and indeed, they were not yet over. His sufferings,—he does not explain what they were,—had exhausted his strength. He felt that he must die; this was his own judgment—the answer which his own heart gave to the severity of his sufferings. "We ourselves," he says, "have had the answer of death within ourselves"; and, he adds, that he was brought into this desperate condition, "that we should not trust in ourselves, but in God, who raiseth the dead." His agitation shows itself in his agitated words. There is hope, but no buoyancy; hope, but hope struggling

---

[1] Preached in Allen Street Congregational Chapel, Kensington, on Sunday morning, October 20th, 1889, in connection with the ordination of the Rev. C. S. Horne, M.A., as Pastor of the Church meeting in that place.

with the consciousness of complete prostration; and he appeals—the strong, courageous man who has left the impression of his noble personality on the life of great nations, an impression which, after eighteen hundred years, is still clear and deep—he appeals to the sympathy and asks the prayers of the Christian people at Corinth. He hopes, but he relies in part for the fulfilment of his hope on their intercession: "Ye also helping together on our behalf by your supplication; that, for the gift bestowed upon us by means of many, thanks may be given by many persons on our behalf."

There is something infinitely pathetic in it. These Corinthian Christians were not men of a very saintly kind. Some of them had not dealt with Paul at all generously; many of them had cared much more for the rhetorical glitter of some of their teachers, and for the airy philosophical speculations of others, than for the depth of his knowledge of God and of unseen and eternal things. They had no suspicion of his transcendent greatness. They had brought dishonour upon *him*, the founder of the Corinthian Church, and upon the Christian name itself by sanctioning immorality. And yet in all seriousness and earnestness he entreats them to pray for him. It may depend upon their prayers, whether his life is to be prematurely brought to an end, or whether he is to recover strength.

His appeal reminds us, that under God we are all in each other's keeping. No man stands alone. The greatest are in the keeping of the humblest and obscurest; and the greatest in their turn control and determine the lives and fortunes of the humblest and most obscure. That is largely true in cities, in nations; no class in the State can be strong and prosperous, or reach the ideal of life, if it is separated from other classes by mutual hostility and distrust, or even by mutual indifference. It is still more true in the Church. No man liveth to himself. It is hardly a figure to say that we are members one of another. We need never pray that if one member suffer all the members may suffer with it, and that if one member is honoured all the members may share the dignity and the joy. It must be so. We have a common life. The strength of one makes us all stronger, and by the weakness of one we are all made weaker.

And while God deals with us one by one, He also deals with us as Churches. There are some prayers, I suppose, which He will not answer unless many unite in them. When the blessings which are asked for relate—not to individuals, but to a whole community—it may be contrary to the settled principles and laws by which God acts, to answer the prayers unless a considerable number of those who form the community make the prayers their own. For anything we know, Paul's life and work may at this time have depended on the supplications of the Corinthian Christians; had they refused to listen to his appeal, it is possible, we cannot tell, that his own prayers for strength might have been unavailing. When a Christian Church ceased to care, and ceased to pray for the Apostle from whom it had first learnt the Christian Gospel, principles lying beyond the reach of our thought may have required that his earthly work should come to an end.

Last Thursday evening the pastor of the Church meeting within these walls was solemnly ordained to the Christian ministry; and he was reminded of its duties, its glories, and its perils. This morning I have been requested to preach to the Church and congregation on their relations to the minister.

You have already discovered the truth, a very grave truth, on which I propose to speak. Your minister cannot stand alone; his real force, the effectiveness of his work for its highest ends, depends largely on yourselves. If you on your side are faithful to your duties, his ministry may be a perpetual revelation of the presence and power of God in this place, and week after week the glory may become more glorious. Your minister's whole life may be transfigured; it may be apparent that he dwells in God and God in him. He may receive fresh and fresh discoveries of the Divine thought, speak with constantly increasing power and pathos of the Divine righteousness and love. You and your children and strangers may be conscious whenever service is held within these walls that eternity lies round our mortal years, and that God is very near to man. But you, I repeat, must do *your* part if he is to do *his*.

I.

You have to do your part in the *Worship*. What wonder, what mystery, there is in a congregation that has met to worship God! There is no other assembly in the world so august. The parliaments of mighty nations, conferences of statesmen, emperors, and kings who have met to discuss the affairs and to determine the fortunes of half a continent are inferior in dignity, and they illustrate less impressively the awful greatness of man. Here we stand on heights that pierce the very heavens. Here we know that we are children of the eternal and shall outlive the stars. Here we rise to those transcendent glories which the Son of God has made our inheritance by descending into the dark abysses of our ruin, our guilt, and our shame. Christ Himself, in some unique and wonderful way, is among us, drawing us into closer union both with each other and Himself, that we may share His own consciousness of living in God, and His own blessedness in God's love.

The hours of worship are the great, the sacred hours of life. Should there not be some preparation for them—on your part as well as on the part of the minister? For the minister, the free prayers of the Nonconformist Churches are by far the most difficult part of the service; they are sometimes, I suppose, the poorest and the meanest; but when minister and congregation are touched with the fire of God, they are the noblest. Therein lies their justification.

Sometimes, indeed, it may be that while a prayer has a great charm, the charm of it comes from the genius of the man who offers it. It has the music, the pathos, and the loftiness of a poem. It soothes, consoles, exalts. In form an appeal to God, in substance and real intention it is an appeal to man. But genius which can create prayers of that kind is uncommon. Usually, if the heart of a congregation is not filled with awe, and devout fear, and joy, and infinite hope by the consciousness of God's presence ; if there is no deep sorrow for sin and no yearning for the Divine forgiveness ; no intense longing for the consolation of God's pity and for the direct assurance of His love; no keen desire for Divine light and strength and peace; no consciousness that the Spirit is bearing witness with our spirit that we are children of God; no passionate desire, caught from near access to the heart of Christ, for the salvation of other men and for the restoration of the whole world to God;— usually, I say, if these are altogether absent, our free prayers are wearisome, sometimes they are intolerable. Happily, there is nothing to conceal their unreality and their worthlessness ; there is nothing to deceive us into the impression that we are praying when we are not praying ; illusion is hardly possible.

Should there not, I ask again, be preparation on your part as well as on the part of the minister? You, too, have received the life of God ; you, too, are a holy priesthood ordained to offer spiritual sacrifices acceptable to God through Jesus Christ ; you, too, have received the Holy Ghost. The worship is to be yours as well as his. That in our free prayers you take no audible part should bring home to you the more closely and the more forcibly, that unless you worship in spirit and in truth you are not praying at all. Would it not be well if, when Sunday morning came, you thought of the wonderful goodness of God in permitting us to worship Him; if you brooded over it, if you endeavoured to fill your whole mind and heart with the thought of it; if you dwelt on the glory with which it surrounds human life; if you were filled with awe as you thought of the congregation of which you hoped to form a part standing in the very presence of God, adoring Him in the majesty of His supreme authority, the steadfastness of His righteousness, and the infinite strength and tenderness of His love? Would it not be well that you should think, not merely of the blessings which, before the end of the day, were to come to yourselves, but of the blessings which were to come to other men in answer to your prayers? For the prayers which you offer here are common prayers. You do not approach God alone and on your own concerns merely, but as brethren in Christ, that you and they may pray together, and may together receive God's grace. Before you come here, think of men who are assaulted by strong temptation: resolve, with God's help, to put your very heart into the prayer that they may resist the temptation victoriously; you, in your turn, maybe delivered in the hour of sore danger by the intercessions of others. Think of men from whom the Divine light which once shone upon them has faded; make their sad condition your own; rejoice that they will be with you at the feet of God, and resolve that *you* will pray for them, though they may have no heart to pray for themselves. Think of restless consciences that, in answer to the common intercession, may receive peace; of weary, desponding hearts that may recover buoyancy and hope; of sorrow that may be soothed by the Divine pity; of anxiety which in God's presence may forget its solicitudes and cares. Think of those who are doing Christian work in your own Church and in other Churches, and of missionaries in heathen countries; be thankful that though you may not share their labours you can pray for them, and that in answer to your prayer their faith may be strengthened and their wisdom enlarged; that the endurance of some of them, sorely tried, may receive fresh support; the courage of some, almost gone, may rise to heroic vigour, and the zeal of others burn into an intenser flame.

Be in your place early enough to renew these thoughts before the service begins. Sit in silence; and let your heart be filled with wonder and hope as you remember that, as you are gathered together in Christ's name, Christ is among you, and that in union with Him you and the rest of the congregation may find God.

Do not come week after week expecting to have

the fire kindled by the songs of the Church or the
prayers of the minister; let it burn high and clear
before a word is spoken, before a hymn is sung. In
this way you will do your own part and help the
minister to do his. For ministers will tell you that
they generally know, not always, whether they are
praying alone, or whether there are many praying
with them; that sometimes, after the freest access
to God in private, they are conscious of obstruction
which they cannot overcome when they begin to
pray in the congregation; that after having ascended
into the very heavens on wings of faith before the
service, they find themselves dragged down to the
dust as soon as the service begins; and the less of
isolation there is in the life of the minister, the more
earnestly he endeavours to make the life of the
congregation his own, so that his prayers may be
theirs, and not his alone, the more completely is he
dependent upon them. Often, too, it is his joy to
discover, that though he was chilled when he was
speaking to God alone, a great warmth came to him
as soon as his life blended with the life of his people,
he caught the fire which was already burning in their
hearts. Resolve that, through God's grace, your
minister's part in the worship of this Church shall be
more devout in the power of your devoutness. Help,
do not hinder him.

II.

Help him in his *Teaching*. People often forget

that it takes two to make an effective sermon—the preacher and the hearer. A few years ago, after a minister had been preaching in a Wesleyan chapel not far from my house, one of the older officials of the circuit began to talk to him of the glories of a past generation, and said with some fervour, "Ah, sir, there were great preachers in those days." "Yes," was the reply of the minister, who perhaps felt just a touch of human irritation—"yes, and there were great hearers in those days." The answer was a wise and a just one. If preachers form and discipline their congregations, it is equally true that congregations form and discipline their preachers; and even those men who have a rigid strength which refuses to be bent and moulded by influences alien to their own ideal of excellence, and to their conception of what fidelity to their awful trust demands—even they find their work limited and conditioned by their people. For example, if a minister knows that his people, or a large majority of them, are impatient of intellectual effort; are unwilling or unable to bear the strain of continuous thinking for ten minutes at a time; if they become restless, or look at him with blank faces which show that he has lost their interest, when he is giving them an exact and careful account of the movement of thought in some difficult passage in Paul's epistles, or is endeavouring to define with accuracy some great Christian doctrine, he will be discouraged. He may be strong enough to resist the discouragement and to give them the best teaching he can, whether they want to be taught or not; but his very eagerness to secure the highest moral and spiritual ends of his ministry may, under such conditions, lead him to the conclusion that to do his congregation any real religious good he must always be simple and must never make any demands on their intellect. It is the people quite as much as the ministers who are responsible for whatever want of intellectual vigour may be charged on the modern pulpit.

It is vain to hope for the return in our time of the great days when a preacher could take an hour and a half or two hours, or even three, to build up a massive exposition and demonstration of one or other of the great doctrines of the Christian faith; working into its solid foundations text after text, each of them carefully explained, and the use of each carefully defended; then defining with painstaking accuracy the terms in which the doctrine was stated in one of the great confessions, or was stated afresh by himself; then distinguishing between the true definition and those defective forms of stating the doctrine by which well-meaning but unwary souls had been led astray; then placing in position on the summit of his granite walls his heaviest artillery of Scripture and of logic, and directing its thunder against Churches and theologies by which the truth had been openly denied;—it is vain, I say, to hope for the return of these great days. Even those loyal and devout hearts among us that still cherish veneration for the sanctity and faith and courage and fortitude of Puritanism would never consent to listen to Puritan preachers ; and perhaps some of them forget that the moral and spiritual vigour of Puritanism came in part, came largely, from the intellectual vigour with which Puritanism dealt with Christian truth. People now insist that the sermon should not exceed thirty minutes "with a leaning to mercy"; that was about the time that the great preachers often spent on the preliminary considerations through which it was necessary to approach their subject; and they spent another thirty minutes in deductions and practical applications when they had finished with it. Some well-disciplined congregations concede forty minutes, or even forty-five ; on special occasions they concede an hour, and then they think themselves generous. But the larger and ampler treatment of the great subjects of our ministry can be rarely, if ever, attempted. If we extend the treatment of one subject over two or three sermons, the congregation think themselves hardly dealt with ; for then they are required to recall to their memory on one Sunday what was said on the Sunday before,—perhaps two or three Sundays before,—and the effort is too much for many of them. Well, we must do what we can. We may at least endeavour to avoid that vagueness of thought which encourages intellectual indolence. We may at least refuse to be satisfied with mere pious sentiment which has no root or support in strong and clear conviction. We may at least resolve that the knowledge of grown men and women shall pass beyond those simple truths, and those simple aspects of simple truths, which might serve for the spiritual outfit of a child. We may at least resolve that we will do our best to protect our hearers from what Coleridge describes as those "numerous artifices by which austere truths are softened down into palatable falsehoods," and those other artifices, not less numerous, by which truths, not austere, but full of moral and spiritual energy, of joy and boundless hope, are reduced to an ineffective feebleness.

And yet it depends on our congregations whether even these things are possible. There can be no teaching by the preacher unless the congregation consents to make an effort to learn. You can help your minister by making that effort. You will soon find your reward. There is incomparable intellectual interest as well as incomparable spiritual power in the contents of the Christian Gospel; and the heart is never likely to feel the fulness of its power if the intellect is not fascinated by its interest. Do your part, and you will find that the preacher will do his part better every year. Let him see that you are interested in his endeavours to put you in possession of the ruling ideas of the Old and the New Testament, and that your mind works with his when he is illustrating and establishing some great Christian doctrine. Talk to him about these great themes. Tell him, when he has made some great subject clearer to you than it was before; when he has invested with fresh and deeper interest and fuller meaning some familiar story in Holy Scripture or some familiar text. Tell him, too, what still remains obscure, what he has left unexplained; let him know that you not only move to the very verge and outermost boundary of his own thought, but are looking beyond, and would be glad to be led further.

You can help him in his teaching, by doing what you can to secure for him the chance of learning more. To master the contents of this library of books, the Bible, a minister needs time. He will never master them; but as his own knowledge grows, his teaching will grow in depth and variety. To construct exact and definite conceptions of the great truths of the Christian faith, to organize them into a coherent system of thought, he needs time. He must return to them again and again; he must brood over them; he must read what theologians have written about them; he must examine and re-examine every passage in our Lord's teaching, and in the teaching of the apostles, that has any relation to them. As the result of this patient and laborious work his preaching will gain in solid strength, his thought will become more robust; he will not exaggerate one truth into falsehood, and wholly forget other truths which are equally necessary to the development of the perfect life. You will gain, and gain largely, by the increasing wealth of his knowledge of Divine things. Give him the chance of increasing that wealth, and of increasing it without spending at his desk the hours which should be spent in sleep. Be no parties to the frittering away of his time in innumerable occupations and engagements, which contribute nothing to your real profit. Relieve him as far as you can by taking into your own hands the details of Church business. Do not press him too early to undertake serious engagements outside the Church. Check him in a kindly manner if he is too eager. "Say to Archippus, Take heed to the ministry." Protect him against unnecessary encroachments on those golden hours of the day in which his best work can be best done. Help him, I say, in his teaching by giving him the chance of learning more.

III.

Help him in *his work as pastor* of the Church. That is a very large subject. I could find a text, if I wished to treat it, in Paul's words, addressed, —not to the Church officers, observe,—but to the Christian commonalty of the Church at Thessalonica: "We exhort you, brethren, admonish the disorderly, encourage the faint-hearted ; support the weak ; be long-suffering toward all. See that none render unto any one evil for evil ; but alway follow after that which is good, one toward another and toward all." That is an outline of the mutual duties of Church members written for a Church which had just escaped from heathendom. The duties ought not to be beyond the spiritual sagacity, and courage, and tenderness, and sympathy of a Church with a history like yours. But I wish to remind you of duties less delicate and less difficult—duties of a simpler and more elementary kind.

You will greatly help your minister as pastor of this Church if you will do your part in endeavouring to make it a real Christian society, instead of an assembly of individuals and of separate families sharing no common life and no common interests, bound together by no personal friendships, and no memories of mutual kindnesses. The minister, whatever his personal force, cannot, unhelped, draw into living and organic unity a Church of this magnitude; the members themselves must do it. What I mean is, that the Church should be a pleasant society to belong to. The members should be gracious and kindly to each other; the graciousness and kindliness resting on your common relations to Christ, for you are all one in Him—on your common hope of immortal glory and your common fidelity to this particular Church to which you belong. You should sympathize with each other's sorrows and joys, and show the sympathy. There should be a warm recognition of personal excellence, of generosity, and of zeal in good works. There should be cordiality and mutual consideration and respect. Every man cannot be the intimate personal friend of all the rest, but every man should have some personal friends in the Church—friends whom he knows well, for whom he cares a great deal—

friends who cannot be absent from worship without his noticing it—and who cannot be in trouble without his knowing it—friends to whom his heart clings, and whose hearts cling to him—friends for whom he constantly prays and in whose Christian life and work he is deeply interested. No man in the Church should ever have a sense of isolation; no man should feel that he is a stranger. When young men and women who are away from home are received into fellowship, special care should be taken that they are really received. Do not be satisfied with entering their names on the Church-roll—that is not receiving them; or with telling them of a Bible-class or a young people's society of which they can become members—that is not receiving them. Receive them as you would wish your own boys and girls to be received if they were in a great city a hundred miles off among strangers. Your personal kindness to them may do even more than the minister's preaching to defend them against the perils which threaten them, and to give them strength to attempt the highest kind of Christian living.

IV.

Now, passing, in conclusion, from the various forms of ministerial service in which you can help him, to claims which, in a sense, are more personal, and which yet are intimately related to his ministerial efficiency, I ask you, first of all, to help him by *praying* for him, and praying for him constantly.

This was the way in which the Corinthian Christians were asked to help Paul. I have already spoken of how you ought to prepare to take part in the prayers of the Church—I am now speaking of the prayers you should offer in your solitary approaches to God day after day all the week through.

We believe in the Holy Ghost; we believe that personal sanctity and powers for spiritual service come from Him; and that apart from His mysterious and gracious action on the hearts and consciences of those whom we are endeavouring to restore to God, and to assist in living the perfect life, all our work, even the best of it, even that which we do in His strength, is powerless. And we also believe that although the Holy Spirit dwells in us so that we have not to wait for His coming as the disciples waited at Pentecost, He reveals His presence and His power more gloriously in answer to our prayers; and that if we cease to pray, the manifestations of His grace are likely to cease.

Pray, then, for your minister as you expect him to pray for you. You are in his keeping, under God; he is in your keeping, under God. Pray that he may be defended from sin, as you pray that you yourselves may be defended from sin; that he may be filled with the life whose springs are in Christ, as you pray that you yourselves may be filled with that life. So intimate are the relations between you and him that if there is any relaxation in the authority of *his* conscience *your* moral vigour is likely to decline. If *he* sins in his heart, *you* are very likely to sin in your outward conduct. Pray for him that his courage may be high, that his faith may have the fortitude of granite rocks ; that the fires of his love for God may burn higher and higher, and with a clearer flame, as the months and years pass by ; that his zeal for your righteousness and your full realization of the Christian redemption may grow in intensity; that his joy in the vision of God may become fuller and richer. In answer to these prayers his ministry will increase in spiritual force, and your courage, your faith, your love, your zeal, your joy will be continually augmented. Think of him in his solitary hours when he is trying to reach the innermost depth of the meaning of the words of Christ and His apostles, trying to find his way to those eternal truths and facts which are to be the substance of his preaching, and then trying to give them an intellectual form that will assist you in finding them. Pray that the same illumination that was given to apostles, the same Holy Spirit that rested on Christ, may be with him. By your prayers make even his solitary work your own, and let the harvest of his solitary thought be as much yours as his.

Pray that when he speaks he may speak in the power of the Spirit. Let his best and highest words come from the Divine light and energy that have descended on him in answer to your intercessions ; and so make his very preaching as much yours as his.

Pray that those who listen to him may have their hearts opened to the grace of God by the power of the same Spirit; that Christian men may come here longing for and expecting fresh discoveries of their blessedness in Christ—fresh discoveries concerning the righteousness and the service which that blessedness renders possible; and pray that their longing may be satisfied and their expectation fulfilled. Pray that men who have drifted into "sunless seas of doubt" may be filled with wonder and faith and infinite hope by the vision of the glory of the Eternal. Pray that those who have been baffled in the endeavour to fulfil in conduct their own ideals of goodness may learn that the power of God is near them, and that in Christ they may reach a loftier righteousness than they have aimed at. Pray that those who come here restless, weary, desolate, their strength spent, their illusions all vanished, their hopes all quenched, may so listen to the preacher that soon they shall cease to listen to *him*, and long before the sermon is over shall begin to listen to another Voice —the Voice of Him who is among you when you are gathered together in His Name; and shall be drawn to His feet by His gracious words: "Come unto Me, all ye that labour and are heavy laden, and I will give you rest." Pray that men troubled by the consciousness of sin, agitated by the sense of guilt, may learn that the blood of Christ was shed for the remission of sins, and that the unjust are justified in Him. Pray that all who come here may discover the open mystery of the Christian Gospel, that we never find ourselves till we find Christ; and that the peace, the harmony, the strength, the joy, the perfection for which we were created are impossible until we reject and deny ourselves that Christ may become the true root, the central spring of our life. Pray—believing that your prayers will really contribute to these great results, and that these great results may not be achieved unless you pray; and then my friend's ministry will be followed with glorious success, and the success will not be his alone, but yours.

V.

Be *magnanimous, generous, kindly* in your treatment of him. You have shown a large confidence in him by inviting him to become your pastor; you have placed in his hands a great trust; but if he is to discharge the duties of that trust he must see and know that the confidence remains unshaken. The relations between a minister and his congregation are so fine, so delicate, that if on either side there is even a transient disturbance of mutual affection and mutual confidence, the power of the minister and the life of the people are at once impaired. Trust him. Very early in my own ministry I preached some sermons which created a great panic in the congregation. The people thought that I had forsaken truths which they regarded as part of the substance of the Christian Gospel. But it was my felicity—a felicity for which I can never cease to be grateful—to be the colleague of one of the most venerable and saintly men in the Congregational ministry, a man who was regarded with honour and affection by all the Congregational Churches in this kingdom, and by his own Church, of which at that time he had been the pastor for nearly fifty years, with unmeasured affection and devotion. After his death, I did not know it before, I learned that when the panic was at its height he went round privately to family after family in the congregation, and said to them: "Let him alone; the root of the matter is in him; the young man must have his fling." Your minister is, I think, less reckless, less aggressive, more considerate than I was in the days of my hot youth. He is gentle as well as strong; he is modest as well as resolute; he is not likely to try your confidence as I tried the confidence of my people more than thirty years ago. But if now and then you find that he is unwilling to state familiar truths in familiar terms, if he rejects a formula which seems to you an adequate statement of some great element of the Christian Gospel—a formula consecrated perhaps to your hearts by the memory of the peace and strength it gave you in some of the most awful, most pathetic, and most sacred hours of your personal history—do not be impatient; remember "that the root of the matter is in him." It may be, after all, that the new intellectual conception of the truth which to you is strange and powerless is the fittest for the new time, and will be more likely than the old to secure the acceptance of the truth by your children. You may discover that some truths which to yourselves are infinitely great and precious seldom appear in his preaching. Trust him, and give him time. We learn,—we really learn, —the contents of the Christian Gospel by life, by its struggles, joys, sorrows, and by the gradual illumination of the Spirit of God. If your minister were content to speak to you on the strength of a secondhand knowledge of eternal things, he might discourse on all the articles of the fullest and richest confession of faith ever adopted by any Evangelical Church; but if he is to speak at first hand he must speak only of those truths which have passed into his life. At fifty, at sixty, many of you must know for yourselves some things—you ought to know many things—which he cannot as yet know after that manner. And yet even those of you who know most may learn much from him; for every man that has a direct vision of God in Christ, and of the mysteries of the unseen and eternal order, can tell other men, wiser than himself, of some things that they have never seen. But truths that have come to you from agonies through which he has never passed, from an experience both of joy and sorrow more varied than he has known—can hardly as yet have come to him. Trust him, and give him time.

Never let him be discouraged by the sense of isolation in his work. Make him feel that you care for it, and are keenly interested in it. His strength will be doubled if he is conscious that he is not fighting a solitary battle, but that all of you are his comrades. Do not quench his ardour. Let him try his own methods. Some of them are likely to fail. It is better that he *should* fail sometimes than that he should be saved from failure by the too constant and authoritative pressure of the advice of more experienced and less adventurous friends. There are limits, of course, to that suggestion ; but if you are generous you will be able to determine the limits for yourselves. What I mean is, let him have the chance of doing some things in his own way rather than in yours ; and be as heartily sympathetic when he does them in his own way as when he does them in yours. It was said of some man, that he wanted the Lord's will done, provided he could be on the Committee of Ways and Means. There are many men of the same sort ; I trust that my friend will find very few of them here.

Encourage him. There are times when the most buoyant sink into despondency, when a grey, chilly mist creeps over the soul of those who have the largest happiness in the service of God, and then they feel as if all their strength was gone. Not very long ago—if I may venture once more to speak of myself —one of these evil moods was upon me ; but as I was passing along one of the streets of Birmingham, a poor but decently dressed woman, laden with parcels, stopped me and said, "God bless you, Dr. Dale!" Her face was unknown to me. I said, "Thank you, but what is your name?" "Never mind my name," she answered; "but if you could only know how you have made me feel hundreds of times, and what a happy home you have given me!—God bless you!" The mist broke, the sunlight came, I breathed the free air of the mountains of God. When assurances come to a minister, not that he has preached a fine sermon, but that through God's grace he has enabled some of his hearers to find life and strength and infinite hope in Christ,—has lessened their sorrows, dissipated their fear, given them a clear vision of duty, resoluteness in translating the vision into conduct,—his faith, his courage, his force are at once augmented. On the other hand, when those who receive religious help from him are silent, he is likely to begin to ask whether he has not missed his true vocation, and there will be neither brightness nor vigour in his ministry.

Surround him with affection. Let him know that you love him; then he will love you the more, and will put more of heart and strength into all his service for you. He is beginning his ministry among you, and it depends largely on yourselves whether the trembling hopes which have filled his heart as he has looked forward to his work will be more than fulfilled, or whether they will be miserably blighted. Kindly men have been made cynical by meeting with coldness and reserve where they looked for affection and frank confidence. You will not—I know you will not—inflict this fatal harm on your minister. By your own kindliness you will encourage and perfect all that is most kindly in him. You will rejoice in all his successes as though the successes were your own. You will not add to his discouragement when he is discouraged. You will sustain, by your hearty confidence in him—confidence expressed and manifested as well as felt—the vigour of his loyalty to Christ and the ardour of his devotion to your service. And may God grant that when many of you who have invited him to the pastorate of this Church have entered into the glory of God, your children and your children's children may still be listening with affection—affection which will then be deepening into veneration—to his teaching ; that by God's grace resting on his ministry they may live the perfect life, and, through all the vicissitudes of what are likely to be troubled times, may continue faithful to the great truths which are the very fibre of your own strength and the perpetual springs of your own joy!

XII

THE UNITY OF THE CHURCH.[1]

"And the glory which Thou hast given Me I have given unto them; that they may be one, even as we are one; I in them, and Thou in Me, that they may be perfected into one; that the world may know that Thou didst send Me, and lovedst them, even as Thou lovedst Me."—*John* xvii. 22, 23.

THESE words, it is clear, do not refer to the Apostles alone. Our Lord has just said, "Neither for these only do I pray, but for them also that believe on Me through their word; that they may all be one; even as Thou, Father, art in Me. and I in Thee, that they also may be in us: that the world may believe that Thou didst send Me."

How it may be with you, my Christian friends, I cannot tell; but for myself I am conscious that, although these words are so familiar, the truth on which they rest is so remote from the whole range of ordinary Christian thought that the more I think

---

[1] Preached on behalf of the London Missionary Society in the Congregational Chapel, Allen Street, Kensington, on Sunday morning, May 16th, 1886.

of it the more strange and the more wonderful it seems. It comes to me, whenever I recur to it, as though it were a fresh revelation from heaven.

That we should reach the perfection of righteousness, knowledge, power, blessedness, in union with God, is a truth which has become part of the substance of our life. It governs our religious belief; it organizes our theological thought; it inspires our prayers; it regulates our personal discipline. And if, when Christ was offering His great intercessory prayer, He had asked that all that believe on Him might become eternally one with Himself and with the Father, the prayer would have expressed the profoundest longing of our own hearts. At such a time, when His earthly work was almost done, when the awful shadow of the cross was upon Him, when His heart was breaking, not with agony as yet,—but under the pressure of an infinite love for those who loved Him—we feel sure that He would ask for us the very greatest blessings, and we know of none greater than this—to be one with Him and one with God in Him.

He asks for that in other parts of this prayer, but that is not what He asks for here, or, at least, it is not all that He asks for. It is not what He asks for first. His first prayer is, that all that believe in Him may be one with *each other*, that their union with each other may correspond to the union between Himself and the Father; and this unity of the Church is to be realized in God. It is as if our union with God were not an end in itself, but simply the means of our union with each other. Of course it is not really so, but it is clear that the end of Christ is to make us one with each other as well as one with God.

I repeat, the end of Christ is to make us one with each other as well as one with God. In the natural order of the world there are clear indications that we were not created for an isolated perfection—that no man can stand apart from the race—that isolation is death. If we are separated from *God* we die. If we are separated from the *race* we die. As our physical life depends upon the maintenance of our just relations to the physical world, and death comes when our fellowship—our communion—is broken with the air and water and food by which we are environed, our higher life depends upon the maintenance of our just relations to the intellectual and moral world, and death comes when our fellowship —our communion—is broken with the thought, the virtue, the joy, and sorrow of our race. The roots of our life are in God; yes; but a plant does not live by its roots alone, but by its whole environment. *God* is necessary to us. We are also necessary to each other. Individualism is true as an assertion of the sovereignty and infinite worth of the individual man against the encroachments of society and of the State, of ecclesiastical rulers and the Church; and yet the order of the world is not built on the principle of individualism, but on the principle of the unity of the race. Every man was made for his brother, every man's brother for him.

There are obvious illustrations of this law in the constitution of the world—in the natural order—which we did not create and cannot destroy. But the highest illustration of it is in the diviner life of man. We find perfection in our union with those who are in Christ, as well as in our union with Christ Himself; and, according to this prayer, our union with them is to be like the union between Christ and the Father. The institution of the Christian Church rests on this great fact. It is contrary to the Divine idea to save men, to perfect men, one by one, in isolation from each other; and the Church is not merely a wise expedient for the cultivation of religious thought and life; it is necessary to the complete power and glory of Christian perfection. We are to be one with each other, as Christ is one with the Father.

But how is this union—this personal union with all that believe in Christ—a personal union corresponding to that between Christ and the Father—possible? Is not every man in his own personal life separate from all other men? We live apart in a loneliness which is necessary and inevitable. We move through eternity like stars through infinite space. We never touch. Every one of us is alone. We are islands in an infinite ocean. We see each other from afar. By words, by actions, by innumerable means of communication, we maintain intercourse with each other, more or less perfect, and we have intercourse with men of all ages and of all lands. The dead speak to us as well as the living, and we can send on our thought to the generations that are to come. But still our life is isolated; it is altogether our own. It seems so, and yet it is not so. The common order of human life does not, after all, rest on the principle of individualism. The stars move in their separate orbits, but planet is linked to planet, and sun to sun, and system to system, and there is not a solitary orb that is not controlled in its motions by all the spheres. The islands lift themselves above the desolate waters which separate them, but the depths of the ocean are not infinite. Drain the waters away, and the islands are the mountain summits of a submerged continent.

We were created that we might be eternally one with each other. Not Individualism, but Communism, extending through the whole of the interests and activities of human life, is the Divine idea of the universe. The Divine idea has not been achieved. It has been thwarted, its fulfilment delayed, by the abnormal history of the human race; but Christ came to destroy the sin which separates us from each other as well as from God, and to draw the race into the unity for which it was created. Listen to His own account of the way in which He is doing it. It is very wonderful. It is a part of the Gospel which few of us, I imagine, have ever heartily received; but when once we receive it all our thoughts of man and of God, and of our relations to both, are changed : "The glory which Thou hast given Me I have given them, that they all may be one." The glory is given in *this* life to those who believe in Christ ; for one of the effects of giving it is declared to be the discovery by the world that Christ was sent of God ; the success of Christian missions at home and abroad, according to the words of Christ, is to be the result of the unity of the Church ; and He makes the Church one, by giving to all that believe in Him the glory which the Father had given to Him. The glory must, therefore, be given here and now—not merely as a future inheritance, but as a present possession ; not merely as something secret and mysterious, suspected or known only to ourselves, but as something so conspicuous, that it is to change the unbelief of the world into Christian faith.

What, then, is the glory which the Father gave to Christ, and which Christ has given to us that we may all be one ?

I will not attempt to enumerate the separate elements of it ; but I suppose that all the glory of Christ, all the glory that the Father gave to Him, is included in His eternal participation in the life of the Father—a participation so intimate that He is eternally one with God. "In the beginning was the Word, and the Word was with God, and the Word was God. The same was in the beginning with God." The life of the eternal Father is given to the eternal Son ; and between Son and Father there is eternal union ; and so the wisdom of the Father is the wisdom of the Son, the power of the Father the power of the Son, the righteousness of the Father the righteousness of the Son, the blessedness of the Father the blessedness of the Son, and the glory of the Father, the glory of the Son. When Christ became man He still retained this eternal union with the Father. " The Word became flesh," but remained the Word " and dwelt among us, and we beheld His glory ; glory as of the Only Begotten of the Father, full of grace and truth." The eternal life of the Father was eternally His ;—" The life was manifested," John says, " and we have seen it, and bear witness and declare unto you the life, the eternal life, which was with the Father, and was manifested unto us."

And from the beginning of our Lord's ministry to the end of it, in forms perpetually varying, He was continually saying that He had come to give men the eternal life which dwelt in Himself, and which He had received from the Father. Do not imagine that this is some great mystery to be reserved for those who, as the result of long years of fellowship with God, have touched the heights of Christian knowledge and of Christian achievement. This was the gospel that He preached to the woman of Samaria when He told her about the water of life. This was the gospel that He preached to the crowds that followed Him after He had multiplied the loaves ; He was the bread of life, the living bread, and if any man ate of that bread he was to live for ever. It was of the fatal result of refusing this supreme gift that He warned those who rejected His claims: "Ye will not come unto Me that ye might have life." It was to rescue His sheep from death that He died: "My sheep," He said, "hear My voice, and I give unto them eternal life, and they shall never perish." It was on the necessity of this life that He spoke to Nicodemus when He said, "Except a man be born anew, he cannot see the kingdom of God." Birth is the beginning of life; by our first birth we come into this visible world, but when another and a higher life comes to us in the second birth, we pass consciously into the invisible and eternal kingdom of God. It was of this community of life between Himself and those who believe in Him, that He was speaking, when He told His disciples that He is the vine, and that they are the branches—that only as they retain their union with Him, can they truly live and achieve the righteousness of God.

The glory of Christ, I repeat, is that eternal life which, as the eternal Son of God, He receives from the Father and by which He is eternally one with the Father; the life which was obscured and yet revealed during His earthly ministry, and which will be perfectly manifested to us when we see Him beyond death. This eternal life and this union with the Father He has given to us. He and the Father are one—one by eternal fellowship in an eternal life, and yet personally distinguished from each other. He has drawn all that believe in Him into fellowship in that same eternal life. We remain personally distinct from each other, and yet we are one in Him; and, as our union with each other is perfected, Christ declares that the world will come to believe in Him, and will be restored to God.

But what are the relations between this unity of the Church in Christ and the recovery of the world from unbelief? These may be included under two principal divisions.

I.

The elevation of those who believe in Christ into union with each other and with God, is a wonderful manifestation of the power of Christ as the Saviour of the world. It is a present revelation of God to mankind. You remember that Christ assumed that men ought to have recognised God in Him, apart from His miracles. They ought to have discovered that He had a unique glory, a diviner life than theirs, a righteousness which had its roots in the eternal righteousness of God. They ought to have seen that He was nearer to God than they were; that, while He shared the common infirmities and woes of men, He lived in God and God in Him, so that to have seen Him was to have seen the Father.

And there were some whose vision was clear enough to perceive His glory and who believed in Him for what He was—not merely for the miracles He worked. You and I know the difference between the life of an animal and the life of a plant, except when the life of an animal is of so low a kind that it hardly emerges from the inferior order. We know the difference between the life of a man and the life of an animal, except when the nobler elements of human life are so undeveloped that the man hardly rises above the brute. And men should be capable of recognising the difference between the eternal life which you and I have received from Christ, and the common life of the race; and they will recognise it unless it is so feeble that its glory is unable to penetrate and to transfigure us.

There can, I imagine, be little doubt that the actual growth of the Christian faith is due principally to this revelation of the Divine in the spirit and lives of Christian men and women. Those who have not received the supreme gift of Christ are drawn, they cannot tell how, to those who have received it. They find in Christian men and women something that lifts their thought to the eternal and Divine. There are elements in the Christian character which they are sure must have come from God. Those who believe in Christ have their true home in regions which lie beyond the frontiers of this visible and transitory world. In other words, they have received eternal life. The glory which the Father gave to the Son, the Son has given to them. They are under the authority of the laws of an eternal kingdom. Their hopes are built on eternal foundations which are unshaken by the most violent convulsions; no reverses of fortune crush them, for their treasure is laid up in heaven; the springs of their highest joy are in the eternal life of God, and they are happy in His eternal love. Men are conscious that this is the true and ideal life of the race, and when they find it realized, however imperfectly, in individual Christian people, they come to believe that Christ was sent of God to save the world.

But the illustration of the redemptive power of Christ and of the union with God of those who believe in Him, is incomplete when it is given only in the individual life. We want, and the world wants, the impression which comes from the power of a Divine society. Looking back upon the history of Christendom, this impression does actually come to us when we think of the saints. We can see that they share a common life—that their home was under the same eternal heavens—that in their faith, their sorrow, their joy, their righteousness, they were one. They belong to the same race; they speak the same tongue. They did not know it themselves, but now it is all plain. They are all one—saints of the Eastern and saints of the Western Church, founders of rival orders, bishops of rival sees, hermits and monks, schoolmen of the Middle Ages and puritan theologians, fathers of the early centuries and leaders of modern reformations—they are all one ; they share, and obviously share, the same supernatural life, and are the witnesses that the kingdom of heaven has been established among men. The unity is so central and so vital, that differences of country, of civilization, of language, of creed, of Church, cannot conceal it. Sharp and bitter controversies, mutual anathemas, cannot destroy it—cannot even obscure its glory, or in any way diminish its force and value as a demonstration that they were all born of God. Let the time come when the proof will be equally decisive, that the commonalty of every Church in Christendom, the unnumbered millions of those who believe in Christ, are one with each other, because they are one with Him, and there will be a visible miracle before the eyes of men—the sign of a Divine presence and of a Divine power, that Unbelief will find it hard to resist.

That time is not to be brought nearer by great movements for the suppression of ecclesiastical and doctrinal differences—by the confederation of separate Churches—by skilful diplomacy for securing the celebration of a common worship, and the acceptance of a common creed. All the separate religious communities of this country might be drawn into one great ecclesiastical organization; but their external unity would have nothing in it to fill men with awe, and to compel them to say that it was the work of the Divine Spirit. All Western Europe might be restored to union with the Papacy, and the long-standing quarrel between Rome and Constantinople be healed; and still there might be no sign that Christian men are really one with each other in the high supernatural sense of Christ's words—one with each other because they are one in God. It is not of the unity of an external ecclesiastical organization that Christ is thinking, but of the unity which comes from the complete triumph of a common life.

To realize that unity, we must dwell in God and God must dwell in us; and yet our life must not be a solitary life in the Eternal. We must escape from that spirit of individualism which in its excess has been one of the chief evils of the modern Church. In the discipline of the Christian life there must be as serious an attempt to perfect our communion with each other as to perfect our communion with God. We must draw together—man to man, every one of us to his Christian brother in the same Church, —that in the actual Christian society to which we belong, the Divine idea may be fulfilled; and then the larger, wider unity would begin to be revealed.

I know of some Christian people who think that they illustrate the unity of those who are in Christ by separating themselves from the Christian brethren who are nearest to them and cultivating the intimacy and sharing the work of those who in creed and Church associations are most remote. Not so will the prayer of Christ be fulfilled. We must begin where we are; and must recognise the truth that if anything separates us from communion with the Christian man who is nearest to us we should be almost as eager to remove it as to remove what separates us from communion with God. The world will not believe that in God we are one with all Christians until we are one with the brethren who are at our side.

Remember, that Christ did not pray that, in order to convince the world that He came from God, there might be raised up in every age great scholars who with unanswerable proofs should demonstrate the reality of His miracles and of His resurrection. He prayed that the Church might be perfected into one, that the world might know that the Father had sent Him. *You*—you are to supply the evidences of the truth of the Christian Faith by which our own generation is to be brought to God. In you—in your union with God, in your union with each other, you are to illustrate the Divine results of the work of Christ, and these will demonstrate His Divine mission. In your union with God, in your union with each other, you are to reveal the greatness of the Christian redemption and so to awaken in the hearts of men a deep and vehement desire to share your blessedness.

II.

But there is a second way in which this unity of the Church in Christ would contribute to the creation and extension of Faith. If we were all one with each other and one with Christ, it would be because the eternal life which is given us in Him had energy enough to subdue and to reduce into permanent subordination all mere individual interests; we should care supremely for the common interests of the Church, for the honour of Christ and for His final triumph over the sin of the human race. We speak of a *nation* becoming one when all classes and orders in the State, men of all occupations and of all creeds, glow with the fires of a patriotic passion which, for the time, consume all sectional and all personal interests. Such a passion throbbed in the heart of the English people when the vessels of the Spanish Armada were nearing the English coast. Catholics and Protestants, nobles, merchants, mechanics, peasants, were all aflame together. They ceased to care for themselves, for their personal distinction, for the advancement of their families, for their ecclesiastical party; and they cared only for the independence of their country. That glorious unity made England invincible. But such a national unity is only a symbol of the unity possible to the Christian Church in Christ. We have to strive to achieve it. As it comes it will show itself, not, as I imagine, in any gusts of vehement passion, not in any violent disarrangement of the common order of human life, but in the gradual elevation of those who are in Christ into perfect sympathy with Him in His thoughts and purposes in relation to the human race. Christian men will remain in their trades, their professions, their homes, their public life, but they will be gradually penetrated, inspired, possessed, with Christ's own compassion for those who are not yet restored to God. As the consciousness of their union with each other in Christ becomes more vivid, the consciousness of their blessedness in each other and in Christ will become richer and stronger, and they will long more and more earnestly that all men should share the blessedness. A great evangelistic spirit, intensified by communion with Christ, intensified by communion with those in whom the evangelistic spirit is already strong, will be revealed in the Church; through every Christian man will be manifested the infinite mercy which brought Christ from the throne of God to accomplish the salvation of the world. Why, the woman who touched the very garments of Christ was healed by the virtue that went out of Him. When *we* are perfectly one with Him every Christian man will be a channel of grace to those who come near him—a sacrament with regenerating power—a sacrament made holy and effective by the real presence of Christ.

There will not only be eagerness to save men. In the strength of this unity with each other, as well as with Him, there will be the power to do it. I was reading the other day an explanation of what constitutes effective Christian preaching, and the writer said, "It is not the words of the preacher that produce the impression, but the man behind the words." That is not even half the truth. It is *Christ* behind the man that produces the impression; and this holds true throughout the whole range of our Christian activity; holds true not only of my work, but of the work which those of you are doing who are engaged in connection with the various agencies of this Church. You want to become more effective Sunday-school teachers. Come into such close communion with your fellow teachers and with the Church that it shall be possible for you to be one with Christ; and if you are one with Him all those you teach will be dimly conscious that behind you there is an august and gracious Presence; and many will discover who it is—will discover that it is Christ. You want to reach the grown men and women about you who know nothing of the blessedness of the Christian faith. Come into such close communion with the Church and with those who are willing to share your work that your work shall not be your own, but the work of the body of Christ filled with the Spirit of Christ; so that the words you speak shall be the good seed sown by the Son of Man Himself; some of it may fall on rocky ground, some among thorns, but much of it will fall on good ground, and will bring forth fruit thirty, sixty, or a hundred fold. Wonderful will be the power of the Christian Church when filled with this eternal life, and when its members are thus one with each other and one with Christ, even as Christ is one with the Father.

Those who are troubled, as many are troubled, by what seems the amazing method which the Divine love has elected for the redemption of the world, would find their trouble cease if once they discovered the truth which I have been endeavouring to illustrate this morning. "How is it," men ask—and they have been asking through age after age—"How is it that to human infirmity God has entrusted this great work of making known His infinite love to the human race? Why did He not call in higher and more effective agencies than those on which He has relied for the victory of His grace over the sins and sorrows of mankind?" "Human infirmity!"—He has never trusted *that*. He has trusted those who are one with the eternal Son of God. "More effective agencies!"—where are agents to be had more effective than those to whom this work has been given, men who, by the power of His Eternal Spirit, are members of the body of Christ, penetrated with His life, ruled by His will, themselves knowing the blessedness and glory of that redemption which they have to make known to others? If He had sent shining archangels from their thrones in order to make this Gospel known, they could but have spoken of Christ's redemption at second hand. But you and I know it for ourselves. We are akin to God, having been made partakers of the Divine nature in Christ. Before you challenge the wisdom and grace of God in entrusting this great work to the Church, you must learn what the Church is according to God's own idea and conception of it, and what the Church will become as the blessed time approaches when this great prayer of Christ will be fulfilled, and heart after heart is drawn together under the inspiration of a common life, rejoicing in a common hope, realising the blessedness of restoration to God, and of restoration to all saints.

Have you considered what obligations are imposed upon you in the form of personal service, wherever personal service is possible, and in the form of gifts large and generous, according to your resources, as well as personal service? By the Divine method for the redemption of the world God trusts *you*, and there is no one else to trust ; and the world is looking to you for the discovery of the Divine grace ; and the silence must be unbroken, unless the word of the Gospel comes through your lips. We never learn how dear we are to God's heart until we discover that he has trusted us with the work about which He cares the most, and only in this service is it possible for us actually to realize the truth which seems to lie so far above us, and yet is so near, that we are one with Christ, and heirs with Christ of His eternal glory. It is all of a piece ; refuse to recognise and acknowledge, refuse to discharge, the great obligations of the Christian life, and its prerogatives will appear incredible. The duties and the glories go together. It is because we have received the life of God that we are able to bring the world home to God, and we shall never quite believe or half believe in the greatness that has come to us, until in actual effort and endeavour we fulfil the duties associated with that greatness.

You have an opportunity this morning of accomplishing God's thought in making you one with Christ. You are members of the body of Christ, and through your hands Christ gives to-day for the support of this great enterprise for drawing the world back to God. You acknowledge that you are

His not your property merely, but body, soul, and spirit His—and now, you being one with Him, He takes your hand and dips it into the resources of your poverty or of your wealth. Let Him have his way and give according to the impulses of His heart and not your own. Realize your union with Him not only in high and blessed sentiment which, when real, is indeed a prophecy of the eternal joy of heaven, but by giving this day to the propagation of the Gospel among the heathen as Christ Himself would have you give.

XIII.

PROPITIATION.[1]

"He is the Propitiation for our sins; and not for ours only, but also for the whole world."—1 *John* ii. 2.

THIS truth has the most intimate and the most obvious relations to the great duty which should hold the first place in our thoughts this morning. Christ is the Propitiation for the sins of the whole world. Then the whole world ought to know it, and it is one of the great ends of Christian missions to make this most startling, most mysterious, most glorious fact known to all mankind.

But do we ourselves believe it? Are we sure of the truth of our message? It may be doubted, I think, whether the idea of Propitiation retains its old position in our religious thought. There are very many Christian people who, without rejecting it, regard it with habitual indifference; their belief in it rests on authority and on nothing else; it has no deep roots in their conscience or in their conceptions of God and of God's relation to the human race. It

---

[1] Preached, on behalf of the London Missionary Society, in Union Chapel, Islington, on Sunday morning, May 17th, 1885.

is a belief that does not interest them ; it lies apart from the general structure and substance of their thought ; it exerts no real and effective influence over their lives ; if it were to disappear, they would lose nothing that contributes either to their faith in God or to their practical righteousness. It is a source of perplexity rather than of courage and of peace. If the authority on which the idea of Propitiation rests were to give way, there would be one mystery the less to baffle and defeat speculation and to place a strain upon faith.

There are others, who, while acknowledging the Lord Jesus as Son of God and Saviour of mankind, regard the idea of propitiation not with indifference but with hostility. They protest that God is love, that nothing is needed to induce Him to forgive the sins of men ; that Propitiation is not only unnecessary, but intolerable ; that the idea is an outrage on the mercy of God and a hindrance to the faith of man. But do they really mean what they say? Have they measured their words? Are they sure that they hold the principle for which they contend with so much earnestness, sometimes with so much passion, sometimes even with so much of moral scorn, for those who differ from them?

There is nothing necessary—this is your contention—to induce God to forgive the sins of men. Nothing? Do you really mean it? If a man has acted unjustly, ungenerously, basely, cruelly, do you not think it necessary that he should in his very heart acknowledge that he has sinned, be sorry for it, confess it, resolve to sin no more? However merciful God may be, is it not your conviction that there must be some reason of this kind—penitence, confession, amendment—before He forgives? Do you not believe that until there is penitence, confession, amendment, there is moral resentment in the heart of God against the man who is guilty of grave offences, a resentment very real, very deep, very serious, though it does not destroy love? If so, you, too, contend that Propitiation is necessary before forgiveness, only you say that a man's own repentance, his own confession, his own moral reformation, are necessary if perfectly happy relations between him and God are to be restored. You argue naturally enough from human relations and from human analogies. We condemn a man who has done a great wrong; and until he recognises his fault, confesses it, resolves not to repeat it, we feel a just, moral resentment against him; but when he frankly confesses it, and we see that there is proof of the sincerity of his repentance, our feelings change, and we are propitiated.

You say that it is the same with God: your real objection, therefore, is not to the necessity of propitiation; you allow its necessity, you contend for its necessity; you say that God will not forgive a man until he is sorry for his past wrong-doing, and has resolved to do better in the future; you say that since God is righteous as well as merciful, He must be moved with moral resentment against a man who feels no penitence for his neglect of duty, or for his positive acts of injustice and immorality; you do not deny, I repeat, that Propitiation is necessary before pardon; but you say that the Propitiation consists in a man's own sense of his fault, his own acknowledgment of it, his own determination to do better. John says that the Propitiation is *not* anything that a man feels, or says, or does, but that *Christ* is the Propitiation for the sins of the world. This is the great truth that Paul preached, preached with such earnestness and power that it provoked against him cruel slander and fierce persecution. Christ Himself taught it when He said that His blood was to be shed for the remission of sins; and to Christ this truth was of such central and supreme importance that He embodied it, enshrined it, in the most sacred and pathetic of the services of the Church.

There are three truths of such transcendent greatness, related so vitally to the salvation of the human race, that Christ would not trust them to the living teaching of the Apostles, or even to the written Scriptures which were to perpetuate the memory of His earthly ministry and to illustrate His revelation of the righteousness and mercy of God. The first of these truths is His sovereignty over the human race: in Baptism He claims every child that is born into the world as His own, affirms that He loves every man, is the Lord of every man, and is the Saviour of every man. In the Lord's Supper He declares that He is the Bread from heaven which God has given for the life of the world, that the life of God is made the inheritance of the human race in Him ; and in the same service He declares that His blood was shed for the remission of sins ; or, in other words, that He is the Propitiation for the sins of the world. These are the central facts of the Christian Gospel. They are the very substance of the revelation which God has made to us through Christ, and of these truths I know not which is of the greatest importance.

Let us now return to the one I am illustrating this morning We are agreed that before sin is forgiven, Propitiation, or a moral reason for forgiveness, is necessary. But, as I have said, there are some of us that believe that the reason for forgiveness is a man's own repentance ; by our own repentance we have to remove God's just resentment against us on account of wrong-doing. We have to do this, it is supposed, one by one. When *you* have repented, that is a reason for the forgiveness of *your* sin ; but it is no reason for the forgiveness of mine. I, too, have to repent before my sin can be pardoned. Each man has to repent for himself. But the Christian Gospel affirms that Christ is the Propitiation for the whole world.

Here is one of the fundamental differences between the Christian Gospel and the religious theory which we should construct for ourselves if the Gospel had never come to us. Let us see, for a moment, where these two theories agree and where they differ. Both these theories agree that God is merciful; that He loves all men; that He loves those who are guilty of the worst sins; that He is willing to forgive them, to make them eternally righteous, and to raise them to eternal glory. Both agree that, while God is merciful, He is righteous, and that He must and ought to feel moral resentment against sin, and against those who are guilty of sin. Both agree that something is necessary to remove this resentment, and both, therefore, agree in the necessity for Propitiation; for Propitiation is that by which resentment is removed. But at this point there is a difference which cannot be measured—an infinite difference; a difference which affects the whole development of our moral and religious life, our whole conception of God, and our whole conception of man. For some of you, as I have said, affirm that the resentment will disappear naturally and necessarily if you repent, if you sincerely and earnestly determine to do right, and that you will be more and more fully assured of your forgiveness as your reformation goes on towards complete moral perfection. *You* find the reason for the removal of Divine resentment in yourselves. But the Gospel says that the reason for the removal of it is in God, in Christ the eternal Son of God. It says that so intimate and so wonderful are the relations between Christ and us that *He*, not our repentance, not our amendment, is the reason, the ground, of our forgiveness. The Divine resentment against human sin has not to be removed by the repentance of men one by one, by their individual confession of sin, by their individual amendment; it is removed by Christ: He is the Propitiation for the whole world. Observe that John does not merely say that the sufferings of Christ and the death of Christ, are the Propitiation, but Christ Himself. It is largely because He has died that He is the Propitiation; but it is He, the living Christ, that is the Propitiation for the sins of men.

Suppose that the whole world had repented of its sin, that every drunkard felt bitterly ashamed of his drunkenness, and resolved to be temperate; that every dishonest man felt distress for his dishonesty, and began to make restitution to those whom he had wronged, and determined he would never rest till the restitution was complete; that every liar hated and despised himself for his lying, and was going from house to house confessing his fault to every one that he had at any time deceived; that every man that had been guilty of unkindness and cruelty was heart-broken, and was entreating wife and child, brother, sister, neighbour, workman, whom he had injured, to forgive him; suppose that every covetous man, every ambitious man, every vain man, every ill-tempered man, every selfish man, felt keen self-reproach and deep humiliation for his vice; that every irreligious man was troubled and penitent for his irreligion and was longing to become devout; suppose that from ocean to ocean, in every country, civilized and uncivilized, in great cities, among wandering tribes in the desert, among the rich, among the poor, there were a universal sorrow and anguish on account of past follies and past sins, and a universal determination to reform; you would find in this a reason why God's moral displeasure with the world should cease, a reason why His resentment should pass away; you would say that on the ground of this repentance all men might, with perfect confidence, trust in God to forgive them. But the Christian Gospel declares that the reason for the Divine forgiveness exists already. The world has not repented; but Christ is the Propitiation for the sins of the world, and on the ground of what Christ is in relation to God and in relation to man, all men may, with perfect confidence, trust in God to forgive.

But where is the place for *our* repentance? Let me appeal to your own experience. Have you never found that after a man has dismissed his resentment against you, resentment which you had provoked by some grave offence, you felt the inexcusableness of your conduct as you had never felt it before? While his resentment lasted, while he was cold and distant you were disposed to palliate your offence, to excuse it, to think that he judged you too severely; but when *he* ceased to judge you, *you* began to judge yourself; when *he* ceased to dwell on your fault, *you* began to dwell on it; when *he* made you feel that he was at peace with you, *you* discovered for the first time what reason there had been for his anger.

Christ inspires repentance by the assurance of mercy. This is of the very substance of the Christian Gospel. It is a declaration that the reason of God's forgiveness of human sin is in God Himself, not in man; in Christ the Eternal Son of God, not in ourselves; it is a declaration, not merely of the infinite love of God, for there may be love where moral resentment remains, and where moral resentment is active; but, as Paul puts it, the preachers of the Gospel are the heralds of God sent to proclaim to nations in revolt that God is at peace with them; at peace with them that are afar off; at peace with them that are nigh; at peace, not with the penitent merely, but with the impenitent; not with the devout Christian merely, but with those who do not yet believe in Christ; at peace with all mankind. We have not to explain to men the terms on which they can induce God to grant remission; but to tell them that He grants it freely for Christ's sake—that they have only to accept it. If they say, We desire the remission of sins, but are doubtful whether as yet our sorrow for sin is bitter enough to be a reason for the Divine forgiveness, we answer that the reason for the Divine forgiveness is not in their sorrow but in Christ. If they ask, When may we hope that our amendment will be sufficient to allow us to rely on the Divine pardon? we answer that the reason for the Divine pardon is not in their amendment but in Christ. If they are uneasy because they are not anxious enough for the remission of sins, and ask whether we think it possible that with so little anxiety God will forgive, we answer that the reason for the Divine forgiveness is not in their anxiety but in Christ.

This Gospel sweeps away every reason for distrust, drives before it, like great winds of God, every cloud of doubt and uncertainty that conceals the glory of the Divine love. If you could live a thousand years sorrowing all the time for the sins of yesterday, never repeating them, doing the will of God with unvarying loyalty, serving mankind with unsparing devotion; would that be a ground on which to rest the hope that God would be merciful? You have a stronger ground already: that sorrow would be your own, that loyalty your own, that generous service your own; you might still doubt whether it reached God's great ideal of what ought to be done to remove His just resentment against your wrong-doing, but the reason for your forgiveness is in God Himself, in the Eternal Son of God. "Herein is love; not that we loved God, but that He loved us, and sent His Son to be the Propitiation for our sins."

It is a wonderful Gospel—God was in Christ, God is in Christ still, not reckoning the trespasses of men against them. Christ is the Propitiation for the sins of the world. God has made peace by the blood of His cross. We may think that we have something better to tell mankind than this, something fresher, something more likely to awaken their moral interest and to give depth and animation to their moral life; and if we claim to be merely the teachers of a religious theory which we have created for ourselves by deep and prolonged meditation on the mystery of the world, and on the discoveries which man has made of the eternal universe that surrounds him, I suppose that we have a right to teach men what we please. But if we describe ourselves as Christian preachers, we must follow Paul's example, and be able to say, "I delivered unto you first of all that which also I received, how that Christ died for our sins according to the Scriptures." We must declare with John that "Christ is the Propitiation for the sins of the world." We may have many other things to tell men, but if we profess to deliver to men the contents of the Christian revelation, this must be among the very first elements of our message.

For according to Christ's revelation of God, the Father of all men wants His children to know—all His children, the worst, the basest, the foulest, the most profane—that He is at peace with them for Christ's sake; at peace with them before they confess their sin and before they forsake it; at peace with them, that they may be prevailed upon to confess their sin and prevailed upon to forsake it. We may think that this is a dangerous message; God is responsible for it, not we. We have no right to tamper with it, to qualify it, or to explain it away. Who are we that we should come between the heart of God and any child of His that He wants to make glad, and to make glad at once by the assurance of His mercy? Knowing that God is at peace with men, it is intolerable cruelty to conceal it from them.

You may say, preach *Christ*—not a theory of the atonement, not a doctrine of Propitiation. But, surely, one of the most amazing and most glorious things about Christ is this, that He is the Propitiation for the sin of the world. How can we preach Christ without preaching *that*,—that we have redemption through His blood, even the forgiveness of sins according to the riches of His grace?

It is only as we receive this truth into the very depths of our Christian consciousness, only as we permit it to penetrate, to inspire, to organize our whole religious thought, that we can even approach a true conception of what Christ is or of what His relations are to God and to ourselves. True conceptions of Christ are not built up on definite texts which can be quoted in proof either of His Divine greatness, or of the reality of His humanity. True conceptions of Christ are not to be created merely by dwelling upon the environment of His earthly life, and the manner in which He bore Himself to that environment. True conceptions of Christ are the slow growth of the Christian life, and they come from the gradual discovery of the contents of the Christian redemption. Who must He be that can describe Himself as the Giver of eternal life, the Vine of which all saints are the branches, and apart from whom they can do nothing; the Way to the Father, so that no man can find God except through

Him? What must be the relations of Christ to God for it to be possible for these great claims to rest on a solid foundation? We know for ourselves that the claims are true: we have verified them in our personal history; they have been verified in the personal history of sixty generations of penitents and saints. On the other hand, what must be the relations of Christ to man for it to be possible that His sorrow for the world's sin, His voluntary entrance into the agony, the darkness, and the death which are the result of the world's sin, should constitute the Propitiation for the sin of the world? You never discover how near God is to you till you learn that Christ, the eternal Son of God, has relations to every man so close, so intimate, that His acknowledgment of the world's sin is the ground on which God is at peace with all mankind. Christ is the eternal root of our righteousness—that is one half of the Gospel; Christ is the ground of the remission of our sins—that is another half. Reject either, and the glory of the Christian Gospel is clouded; it is in danger of being wholly quenched.

He is the Propitiation for the sins of the whole world. Then, I repeat, the whole world ought to know it. I plead with you this morning on behalf of men in heathen countries, how numerous we cannot tell, to whom the light that lighteth every man has revealed their moral faults, their moral ruin, and who have a vague and troubled consciousness that by their sin they have provoked the resentment of invisible and awful powers. I hear of such men who voluntarily submit to poverty, to hunger, to pain, prolonged through many years, to allay and to remove the Divine resentment which they dread. It is for us to tell them that there is no resentment, that it has been removed already, that they have not to propitiate the anger of God by their sufferings, that the Propitiation already exists in God Himself, and that they have now to thank God for being at peace with them and to rejoice in His infinite love.

I plead with you on behalf of unnumbered millions of men, who, if I may judge of the hearts of others by my own, shrink from the light that comes to them because the first dim rays of it reveal moral imperfections which alarm and torture them and fill them with despair. If they knew, as we know, that Christ is the Propitiation for their sins, multitudes of them would have the courage to let the light of conscience fall on all the moral evil which the light discloses; but knowing nothing of the Christian Gospel, the discovery of sin brings pain with it, and fear with it, and they turn from the light, refuse to receive it, and by their resistance the light becomes darkness. Let Christ be known as the Propitiation for their sin, and they too may be brought to repentance and may receive courage to attempt to do the will of God.

The inquiries which have attracted so much attention during the last thirty or forty years to the nobler elements of the great religious systems of the

F. C. 22

pagan world, have led some to imagine that the Christian Gospel is, after all, not so necessary to mankind as our fathers supposed. Underlying the superstitions and corruptions of heathen faith, there are the outlines of a noble theism and the elements of a noble morality, and there is a certain kinship, more or less remote, between the Christian Gospel and the higher forms of heathen speculation. To us there ought to be nothing surprising in this. The Christ, whose earthly history is told in the Four Gospels, is "the light that lighteth every man"; and light remains light, however it may be refracted and whatever may be the density of the medium through which it shines. But here there is something that heathen men do not know—that He, the eternal Fountain of law, is also the Propitiation for sin ; and the knowledge of this truth would give peace and hope and strength to those who have discovered their sin ; it would melt to penitence those who will refuse to think of their sin until they discover that it is already atoned for. We have to tell men that God is at peace with them for Christ's sake ; until they know this, many of them will refuse to think of Him altogether ; or if they think of Him, their whole moral and religious life will be a persistent effort to avert imaginary Divine resentment ; it will, therefore, move on false lines under the control of false assumptions and towards false ends.

To some of you, I fear that this great truth, that Christ is the Propitiation for the sin of the world, has long seemed nothing more than the obsolete dogma of a presumptuous, artificial, and cruel theology. You think that, in rejecting it, you are in sympathy with what has a right to call itself the advanced thought of an advanced age. Let me remind you that the alternative theory—the theory that it is in our own penitence, in our own amendment, that God finds the reason for the forgiveness of sin—is just as old as this, and older. There is no novelty in that—in the discovery that we are environed by law, and that what we ourselves are and do must determine our relations to God. Salvation by personal penitence, salvation by personal righteousness, the theory which seems to you the generous flower and fruit of the most advanced religious thought, was the theory of the Judaisers who followed Paul from city to city with slanders which his heroic sanctity could not shame into silence, with malignity which his glorious devotion to the honour of God and the salvation of man could not subdue to admiration and love. The theory which seems to you the result of a wider and deeper knowledge of God than that of your fathers, and of a freer religious thought, is in substance the theory of that powerful church which for a thousand years held the life of Europe in chains. You think that by making repentance and a good life part at least of the reason of the Divine forgiveness, you are strengthening the foundations of morality. That doctrine was tried through century after century, and multitudes of men who received it as the very truth of God were guilty of vices so shameless, so foul, that they have escaped the just infamy of their offences because the mere description of their deeds is an offence against Christian morals. And, on the other hand, it was this truth—free, unconditional forgiveness of sin, resting not on penitence, not on good works, but on Christ—that inspired the nations of northern Europe with the breath of a new and more vigorous moral life.

Look again, before we close, at the wonderful fact which lies at the root of the great truth that Christ is the Propitiation for the sins of the world. A crude and shallow individualism represents every man as standing alone and apart, the whole secret and mystery of his character and life being enclosed within the years that lie between his birth and his death. A deeper consideration of man's true position discovers that we cannot stand apart either from our ancestors or our contemporaries. Within a narrow area I am free, and the measure of my freedom is the measure of my responsibility; but I belong to the race. Apart from my choice I have a share in all its virtues and all its crimes, in its glories and in its shame. My personal history has been largely determined for me by the wisdom and the folly, the vices and the sanctity, of forgotten generations. I am a branch of a great tree whose roots lie back in a remote past; the men who lived in the morning of the world, before the foundations of the pyramids were laid, before the nations of Europe left the early home of their race in the central plains of Asia, and saw the Western seas—these have left me an inheritance of weakness or of strength which makes the achievement of duty easier or harder for me to-day.

The Gospel reveals to me another and more surprising fact : I am one, not with the human race alone, but with the eternal Son of God ; how intimately one I shall never know until I share His eternal glory. But already my personal righteousness is limited, not by my personal force, but by my capacity for receiving and appropriating the righteousness that dwells in Him. The life of the race is mine ; heroes and slaves, saints and sinners, of other centuries still live in me ; the life of the Son of God is mine ; and I touch the perfection of my nature only when I am able to say, It is not I that live, but Christ liveth in me. The union between Him and me is so perfect, that if I am righteous it is in the strength of His righteousness ; and if my sin is forgiven, it is because He is the Propitiation for the sin of the world. The great doctrine of the Christian atonement is one illustration of the intimacy of the union between the human race and the Son of God.

Be sure of it—for many of you this truth, if you received it, would be your moral and spiritual redemption. The difference between your present religious life, hesitating and uncertain in its faith, languid in its devotion, giving you neither consolation nor courage, inspiring you with no force for the duties of this world, with no splendid hopes of a glorious immortality, and a religious life strong in the strength of God and blessed in His eternal blessedness—the difference lies here: here is the secret of that vision of God which destroys doubt, kindles the fires of love, changes despondency into triumph, and gives the assurance that we have received the Divine life and that we belong to the Divine household. All that is characteristic of Christian morality has its roots in this great discovery,—the unselfishness, the cheerfulness, the frankness, the humility of the ideal Christian character. Joy and righteousness, the firmness of Christian faith, and the ardour of Christian charity, receive from it their inspiration and their support. To those who have found in Christ the Propitiation for their sins He also becomes, and necessarily becomes, the root of a transcendent, of a divine holiness.

And this truth, as it is a great part of the message of the Christian Church to mankind, is the eternal spring of that heroic generosity and that heroic zeal which find their noblest exercise in the evangelization of the world.

XIV.

THE DIVINE LIFE IN MAN.[1]

WE are assembled in the presence of God and in the name of our Lord Jesus Christ as the ministers and representatives of Christian Churches planted in many lands—in England, Scotland, Wales and Ireland; in the United States of America; in Canada; in the West Indies; in South Africa; in Madagascar; in Australia, Tasmania, and New Zealand; in the islands of the South Pacific; in India; in China; in Japan; and in several of the countries of continental Europe. Most of us inherit the ecclesiastical traditions of the Separatists, who in the time of Queen Elizabeth revived in this country the polity of the apostolic churches. In their courageous fidelity to the trust, which, as they believed, they had received from God, some of them suffered long and cruel confinement in the Fleet prison, on part of the site of which stands the Memorial Hall in which we met

---

[1] The address delivered by the President at the opening of the International Congregational Council, on the morning of July 14th, 1891, in the New Weigh House Chapel, Duke Street, Oxford Street, London.

yesterday. Some of them suffered death at Tyburn, not far from the place where we are meeting to-day. But the Congregational churches of Norway and Sweden, to whose representatives I venture in your name to give a special welcome, have a different history. They have grown into sudden strength during the last thirty years as the result of a special manifestation of the power and the grace of God; and they found the Congregational Church order for themselves in the pages of the New Testament.

The churches we represent have a common polity, and that polity has its roots in the central contents of the Christian faith. For the theory of Congregationalism rests upon the belief that in Christ the very life of God has been given to man, and that when those who have received that life are gathered together in Christ's name, Christ who died but is risen again is in the midst of them.

We are Congregationalists; but we rejoice in our kinship with all that recognise in Christ the Son of God and the Lord and Saviour of men. We give a hearty welcome to the representatives of other Christian communities who have honoured us with their presence this morning. We pray that in their ministry, as well as in our own, the great power of God may be revealed, and that their churches may, all of them, be manifestly the temples of the Holy Ghost.

The subject announced for this address is not my own choice. It was proposed to me by the English section of the committee which arranged the proceedings of this Council: and though I was conscious that it lies far beyond the limits of my strength, and requires for its adequate treatment a far deeper and richer religious experience than my own, I felt that it was my duty to meet their wishes. In discussing it I speak for myself. Although you have done me the great and undeserved honour of placing me in this chair, you have given me no authority to speak in your name. With a common faith in Christ as Son of God, Brother, Lord, Redeemer, Judge of men, there are wide divergencies among us in our intellectual construction of the contents of the Christian Gospel. The responsibility for what I may say lies with myself and myself alone.

The committee did not inform me of the reasons which had led them to the selection of this subject; but I can imagine that they judged it desirable that our deliberations should begin in those high and sacred regions where all to whom the grace and power of the Christian redemption have been revealed meet on common ground, and their ecclesiastical and theological differences are forgotten.

For it is the faith of all churches, and of all theologies that can be called Christian, that the end for which the Lord Jesus Christ came into the world is the realization by man of the righteousness, the blessedness, and the glory of the life of God. Here we are at one with great religious communities, with which we and our fathers have had grave, and sometimes fierce and bitter controversies—controversies on the nature and polity of the Church, and its place in the spiritual order; on the methods by which the Divine grace effects the salvation of men; on the ideal and discipline of Christian perfection; on the Authority which should determine the faith and practice of those who confess that Christ is their Saviour and Lord.

Among the men from whom we are divided by these cruel conflicts, but from whom our hearts should never be estranged, we recognise a saintliness shining with a glory that has its fountains in God; in their very contention and argument for errors which seem to us to obscure the light and impair the power of the Christian Gospel, we catch an accent which is the sign that they too are children of the Eternal. If they maintain with passionate earnestness a doctrine of the Priesthood and of the Sacraments which appears to us to be irreconcilable with the whole spirit and substance of the Christian faith; if they regard those who reject and assail this doctrine as the worst enemies of the human race, it is because for them the Sacraments, when duly administered, are the appointed means by which the grace of God first originates and then sustains the Divine life in man. It is this which in their judgment makes the sacramental and sacerdotal controversy so critical, so awful. In that controversy, as they suppose, the whole power and glory of the Christian redemption are at stake. They are contending for the sacredness and efficacy of the institutions by which they believe that the eternal life of God is made the actual possession of mankind.

I.

Whatever may be the nearer fortunes of this great conflict which has now extended over many centuries, it is not unreasonable, I think, to hope that the Church is on its way to a truer and deeper theological conception of that supreme truth which to all serious persons gives to the conflict its infinite importance. For it is apparent that during the last thirty or forty years the mystery of the Incarnation, with all that it reveals concerning God and man, has been exerting a new power, both over speculative thought, and over the religious life. There is a conviction which has grown immensely in strength during the present generation, that the solutions of the greatest and most oppressive problems concerning God, concerning individual men, concerning human society and the history of our race, and even concerning the material universe itself, are to be found in the Person of Christ. The deeper currents of theological thought have set in that direction. But any account of the Person of Christ, as He was revealed in the visible and natural order, must rest upon some conception of His eternal relations, both to the Father and the whole creation; and it is in those august and sacred heights that we are to find the real interpretation of the truth concerning the Divine life in man.

The Christian conception of this truth rests on the Christian conception of the Divine nature itself. It is immeasurably remote from that theory of the Universe which affirms the existence of an Eternal Power or an Eternal Spirit, whose nature is absolutely one and simple, and whose presence, by a process of eternal and necessary development, is revealed in the order and beauty of the visible creation, and in whatever is fair, noble, and gracious in the life of man. Pantheism, if it appears to have some correspondence with the Christian doctrine, is in its deeper elements wholly alien from it.

The Divine life in man, according to the Christian Gospel, is the life which dwells eternally in the Son of God, "who was in the beginning with God, and who was God; by whom all things were made, and without whom was not anything made that was made." It is a life which, because of its eternal relations to the life of the Father, could be manifested in submission and obedience to the Father's will. Theologians have spoken of the eternal subordination of the Son, and have sometimes so spoken as to suggest that they attribute to the Son an inferior glory. I shrink from speaking of subordination. But the Incarnation is a real revelation of God—a revelation interpreted and confirmed by the most certain experiences of the Christian life in every age. A reversal of the relations between the Father and the Son as illustrated in the

Incarnation and in the whole movement of the Divine love for human redemption is inconceivable; and these relations bear witness to eternal mysteries in the life of God.

For us the Son is no secondary Deity. He was in the beginning with God, and He was God. It could never be said that He was not, or that He began to be. We attribute to Him no inferior glory. But in the Incarnation, His eternal life and perfection were revealed in obedience and submission, as the eternal life and perfection of the Father are for ever revealed in Authority. Obedience, submission—these, also, are Divine. If in the Father there is the assertion of the supreme sovereignty of the eternal law of righteousness—if His will is the authoritative expression of that law—if this is His characteristic glory, the free acceptance of that sovereignty is the characteristic glory of the Son. In the Spirit there is the synthesis of the two forms of perfection; and in the power of the Spirit, Father and Son have a common blessedness, and are eternally one.

It is the life of the Son which God has made the inheritance of our race; and we ourselves know that this life reaches its complete union with the Father, and its perfect blessedness through the communion and grace of the Divine Spirit. Our relations to God as His sons are grounded on the eternal relations of the Son to the Father, and the life of the Son and the communion of the Holy Ghost have been made ours that we may realize our sonship.

II.

I have said that this life, according to the Divine will and purpose, has been made the inheritance of the race. As the Incarnation is no afterthought of the Divine mind occasioned by the entrance of sin into the world, neither is the gift of eternal life in Christ a mere expedient for restoring sinful men to holiness. That man should live his life in the power of the life of the eternal Son was included in the Divine idea of man. This was the perfection to which, according to the original constitution of our nature, we were destined. Through sin we have all fallen "short of the glory of God," missed, forfeited the transcendent honour, righteousness and blessedness for which we were created; but it remains true that we were created in Christ Jesus, and through the infinite grace of God and the power of the Christian redemption, all that was possible to us through our creation may yet be recovered.

There is a passage in Paul's epistle to the Colossians in which the truth concerning Christ's relations to the Universe—a truth which is sometimes attributed to John, as though it had been revealed only to him—is most wonderfully expressed. "In Him," that is, in the Son of God, the Son of His love, " were all things created, in the heavens and upon the earth; things visible and things invisible, whether thrones or dominions or principalities or powers; all things have been created through Him, and unto Him; and

He *is* before all things, and in Him all things consist," or hold together in their divinely determined order. That is the Christian account of the universe.

Who can doubt that Paul found in it the strong support, the ultimate interpretation of that mystery which had been concealed through all ages and generations, but was now manifested to the saints, that the Gentiles were fellow-heirs of the great promise which had been made to the Jews, and had their part with the descendants of Abraham in the unsearchable riches of Christ? To Judaizing teachers who insisted that heathen men could not share the blessedness of the Divine redemption and the Divine kingdom, unless in some sort they became Jews, I can imagine Paul saying, " Ah, you are strangers to the real glory of Christ. When I stand up to preach in these great heathen cities, in Ephesus, in Corinth, in Rome, I see above me the same shining heavens that bend over Jerusalem—in Christ they were created, in Christ they endure ; I see the same sun whose light falls on the temple in which our fathers worshipped — its fires were kindled by Christ, and apart from Christ those fires would die down and be extinguished ; at night there shine the same stars that shine over the hills of Judea—it is in the power of Christ that through age after age their solemn movement is unbroken, and their splendour undimmed. When I travel through heathen lands, I see around me everywhere the manifestations of Christ's presence and power, and goodness; in mountains, and forests, and shining streams; in the vine and the fig-tree, and the ripening corn, in every flower that blossoms from the earth, in every bird that sings in the air. The winds are His, and the rain, and the dew. In Christ were all these things created; in Him they are held together; and separated from Him they would fall out of their order, and the whole universe would become a chaos.

"But if the heavens which are stretched over these heathen men, and the earth beneath their feet, were created in Christ; and the wheat from which they make their bread, and the water which they drink, and whatever else sustains their life and adds to its comfort and delight; in whom were the heathen men themselves created? If it is only in Christ that these visible and material things endure, in whom is it that the men—men of every race and every tongue—endure? Have they an independent life? Does their existence rest on another foundation? Are they defended and sustained in being by some inferior Power? No; the men, like their country, were created in Christ. In Christ is the common root of the life of the race."

III.

Man was to find his perfection in sharing the life of the Eternal Son; the Eternal Son was to reveal His own perfection and achieve ours by sharing the life of man. I suppose that the consummate union between man and the Son of God would not have been possible apart from the consummate union effected in the Incarnation between the Son of God and man. Even if we had not sinned, I suppose that *He* would have come to *us*, in order that *we* might come to *Him*. The fellowship, the partnership between Him and us, was to be a fellowship, a partnership, on both sides. If the branches share the life of the Vine, the Vine also shares the life of the branches. He would not let us go when we broke away from Him, in revolt against the Divine authority and grace; He clung to us still; and so He came into the inheritance of all the woes that had followed from our sin. The fellowship, the partnership, I repeat, between Him and us, was to be a fellowship, a partnership on both sides. He had to share our sorrows as we were to share His joy. He had to be assailed by the power of our sin, tempted, hard pressed to maintain His fidelity, as we were to become perfect in the power of His perfection. He had to pass into the awful shadow of the world's sin, to endure the agony of Gethsemane, and the desolation and death of the cross, as we were to inherit through the golden ages of our immortality the blessed relations to the Father which illustrate the glory of His righteousness. When I have discovered that by the very constitution of my nature I am to achieve perfection in the power of the life of Another—who is yet not Another, but the very ground of my own being—it ceases to be incredible to me that Another—who is yet not Another

—should be the Atonement for my sin, and that His relation to God should determine mine.

IV.

"God gave unto us eternal life; and this life is in His Son." It is a gift to the world as Christ is the Propitiation for the sin of the world. But it is a free, ethical, spiritual life that is given; and such a life must be actually lived, if a man is to possess it. It cannot be passed into the human soul like a stream of electric force; the soul itself remaining passive. No sovereign act of the Divine power can effectively give it, apart from a free consent to receive it. What we call the potency of life, its germ, may be conferred by a Divine act; but if the life is to be more than a potency, more than a germ, we must live it. God Himself cannot make thought actually ours, except as we ourselves think; nor penitence for sin, except as we ourselves are penitent; nor love, except as we ourselves love. And the eternal life which He has made the common possession of the race in Christ cannot actually be ours unless we live it.

This life is not an indefinite force; it has certain ethical and spiritual qualities, which witness to its origin and its power. Where these are, the life is; where these are not, the life is not. In their highest form they are manifested in the transcendent perfection of the Lord Jesus Christ; but they are also manifested, though with less of completeness and of energy, in all that have received the life which God has given us in Him.

And so, that Divine sonship which is our inheritance in Christ, and which has its roots in the eternal relations of the Eternal Son to the Father, is always represented in the teaching of Christ and of the apostles as unrealized where the ethical and spiritual conditions of its realization are absent.

There are sharp contrasts drawn between those who are God's children and those who are not. "Behold what manner of love the Father hath bestowed upon us, that we should be called children of God; and such we are. For this cause the world knoweth us not, because it knew Him not." "In this the children of God are manifest, and the children of the devil: whosoever doeth not righteousness is not of God; neither he that loveth not his brother." "As many as are led by the Spirit of God, these are sons of God." And the realization of the sonship, like the realization of the life, is associated with faith in the Lord Jesus Christ. "As many as received Him, to them gave He the right to become children of God; even to them that believe on His name." "Ye are all sons of God—through faith— in Christ Jesus." "He that hath the Son hath the life: he that hath not the Son of God, hath not the life."

In Christ, God is the Father of all mankind. This is the glorious discovery of the Christian Gospel. This, according to the Christian faith, is the very foundation of the order of the world and of human life. To this truth, Christ bears witness in baptism, which declares that every child is by birth, not only the heir of the infirmities, and sorrows, and perils, and sins of the race, but also the heir of the life, and love, and righteousness, and joy of God. To this truth we bear witness in our preaching; for we do not tell men that God will become their Father, as the result of their repentance and of their belief in His mercy revealed through Christ; but that because He is already their Father, they should repent and believe.

Yes, on the Divine side the relationship of Fatherhood stands firm; but on the human side the relationship of sonship, and the participation of that Divine life which is inseparable from sonship, has to be freely realized by every man. Deny that God is the Father of all men; limit His Fatherhood to those who are already trusting in His infinite mercy, and are already endeavouring to do His will; and you disturb, if you do not destroy, the very grounds of that faith in Him in the power of which men receive the forgiveness of sin, and enter into the actual possession of the blessedness for which they were created in Christ. But on the other hand, tell men —all men—the covetous, the untruthful, the sensual, the profane, the proud, the envious, the uncompassionate, the revengeful, that they are already the sons of God, and you reduce Divine sonship to a merely natural relationship; you obscure its ethical and spiritual character; you contribute to the most fatal illusions; you encourage indifference to the august claims of righteousness; you suppress the most awful warnings of prophets and apostles, and of the Lord Jesus Christ Himself; and you paralyse the urgency of those mighty motives which should induce men to make it the supreme end of life that the great place and the great inheritance to which God has destined them in Christ may be actually theirs.

V.

The Divine life which God has given us in Christ—this is the point on which, for the moment, I am insisting—must be actually lived; it must be a power in character and conduct, or it is not realized. There are some who live it and realize it; there are others who do not. This is one of the ultimate principles of the Congregational polity. It has a place not merely in the historic creed of Congregationalists; it is one of the foundations of the Congregational Church order.

I said earlier in this address, that when we are considering the Divine life in man, we occupy ground common to Christian men of all Churches; and yet it is precisely here that we find imperative reasons for our own polity. Indeed I should regard with deep distrust any ecclesiastical or doctrinal peculiarities of Congregationalism which were not rooted in the common faith of Christendom. The only adequate justification of what is distinct and characteristic in the creed or polity of any particular Christian community—is the desire to assert in the most effective form the truths in which all Christian communities agree.

We are at one with all Christendom in acknowledging that it is the glory of Christ to have made the Divine life the inheritance of the human race. We are overpowered with awe and wonder by the transcendent greatness of the gift. For us the supreme question in relation to every man is, whether he has made this life his own. That he professes a true creed, that he has been baptized into the name of the Father and the Son and the Holy Ghost, that he is zealous in the discharge of what are called religious duties, that he bestows all his goods to feed the poor, that he gives his body to be burned—all this is nothing: has he received the Divine life? Is he living in the power of that life? It is this which divides those in whom the gracious thoughts of God concerning mankind are being fulfilled, from those in whom they are being defeated; those who have received the forgiveness of sin, from those who are still unforgiven; those who have received the right to become the children of God, from those who have not; those who have been translated into the Divine light and the Divine kingdom, from those who are in darkness and in peril of eternal destruction. And—if we have rightly understood the mind of Christ—it is this which should divide those who are within the Church from those who are without. We may not be able, in the confusions and perplexities of human life, to secure the perfect realization of this ideal of the Divine society; but for us on whom the splendours of that ideal have shone, to surrender it would be ignoble and base. We cannot be unfaithful to the heavenly vision.

We have been often told that according to Christ's teaching the wheat and the tares are to grow together till the harvest; but He interpreted His own parable; the field in which the wheat and the tares are to grow together is the world; it was not Christ's habit to speak of the world when He meant the Church. We have been often told that it is impossible to draw into the membership of the Church all those in whom the life of God is present, and impossible to exclude those from whom it is absent. We admit the impossibility. There was a Judas among the twelve, and yet, according to the ideal of the apostleship, the apostleship was for the friends of Christ, not for traitors. Divine ideals have never yet been realized in the life of either individual saints or of societies. For us, and in this world, the Divine is always the impossible. Give me a law for individual conduct which requires a perfection that is within my reach, and I am sure that the law does not represent the Divine thought: "Not that I have already obtained, or am already made perfect; but I press on, if so be that I may apprehend that for which also I was apprehended of Christ Jesus": this from the beginning has been the confession of saints. Give me a Church polity which is what men call practical—a polity which in its completeness can be realized—and I am sure that it is something different from the ideal polity of that Divine society whose Builder and Maker is God.

The Church—this is the Congregational ideal—is a society larger or smaller, consisting of those who have received the Divine life ; and who, with whatever inconstancy and whatever failures, are endeavouring to live in the power of it. All that is characteristic of Congregationalism lies in that ideal. The responsibilities and the corresponding powers attributed to the commonalty of Christian people are directly related to the assumption that they have received the life that dwells in Christ, and that they are one with Him. When they are gathered together in His name, whether they are but two or three or whether they are a thousand, Christ Himself is in the midst of them ; one of the company; inspiring their prayers, guiding their decisions : so that their prayers are His and their decisions His rather than theirs. If the ideal were realized, what things soever they bind on earth would be bound in Heaven ; and what things soever they loose on earth would be loosed in Heaven ; and whatever they agreed to ask, would be done for them of the Father. All this would be true if the ideal were realized. It is actually true in the *measure* in which the ideal is realized.

VI.

The Divine life in man is not to reveal its power exclusively in prayer and worship, in high spiritual experiences, in the vision of God, in the fervour of love for Him, in a confident faith in His mercy, in an exulting hope of eternal glory : nor is its force to be exhausted in the integrity, the purity, the grace of the personal Christian character ; nor in what is called, by way of distinction, Christian work—the preaching of the Gospel, the teaching of religious truth, the consolation of the sorrowful. There are no doubt in every age elect souls who receive a call from Heaven not to entangle themselves with the affairs of this life, and who cannot fulfil their vocation unless they "continue steadfastly in prayer and in the ministry of the word." But that was a false conception of sanctity, and it rested on a false conception of the order of the world, which permitted men to imagine that the heights of Christian perfection could be reached only by those who isolated themselves from the common affairs of mankind, and spent their years in the solitary discipline of personal holiness, in communion with the Eternal, and in work which in its form as well as in its spirit was religious. And though the Churches which we represent have largely escaped from the traditions which separated the religious from the secular life, it may still be necessary for us to maintain that in every form of activity to which man is divinely destined by the constitution of his nature and the order of the world, the Divine life which is God's great gift in Christ may be manifested. That life cannot alienate our interest from those great scientific discoveries which are the intellectual glory of this century; for since God is immanent in the material universe these discoveries disclose the Divine thoughts and the methods of the Divine working. It cannot make us look with an indifferent eye upon the creations of genius in literature or art, or upon any of the conditions which can contribute to the general development of the intellectual activity and power of our city, or our country; it is God who kindles in man the light of the intellect; and if the Divine life is in us, we shall rejoice in the splendour of the flame. I have heard of a devout Christian, living in our own times, who appeared to regard it as the note of a great advance towards Christian perfection, that he sailed up one of the most beautiful rivers in Europe without the faintest pulse of interest or delight in its broad and shining waters, in its banks which are covered with vineyards and orchards, in the neighbouring mountains which send down their torrents to enrich and swell the stream. If some evil power—some Ahriman—had created the beautiful river and the lovely country, this indifference might perhaps have been admirable; but that the presence in a man of the life of God should destroy for him the charm of the works of God—this surely is impossible; the charm should be heightened; the works should be glorified.

Nor should this life be regarded as inconsistent with a keen and vigorous activity in commerce and manufactures, and in the general affairs of society and the State. Is there a Divine ideal to be fulfilled in the whole order of the life of man? Is the commandment of God "exceeding broad"? Is every remotest province in the wide continent of human interests subject to His sovereignty? Is the will of God to be done on earth as well as in Heaven? If so, then the Divine life which dwells in us will, by its free and spontaneous power, impel us into comradeship with God in His great endeavour—traversed, resisted, thwarted—but persistently maintained through all the confused ages of human history—for He fainteth not, neither is He weary—to reveal His own perfect thought in the whole life of man.

There is a saintliness of the bank, of the exchange, of the newspaper office, of the court of justice, and of Parliament as well as of the cloister; of the laboratory, the painting room, and the university, as well as of the Church; a saintliness of the merchant, the manufacturer, the tradesman, the farmer, the mechanic, as well as of the apostle and the preacher; and we shall not discharge our full duty as ministers and churches unless we make it apparent that as the great forces of Nature, which are but forms of the eternal power of God, are present and active in every region of the material world—in phenomena the most splendid and imposing, in phenomena the most insignificant and obscure—so the Divine life which dwells in man should be present and active in all the infinite varieties of human effort and experience. Churches exist not merely for the consolation and ultimate salvation of their individual members, but that the Divine life which dwells in Christian men—developed, invigorated and disciplined by common worship, by ethical as well as by spiritual instruction, by the atmosphere and the traditions and the public opinion of a society which is the home of Christ and of the Spirit of Christ—may change and transfigure the whole order of the world.

VII.

Ours is a glorious conception of the Church, and should create in all those who are entrusted with it a calm and reverential enthusiasm, and a devout, patient, laborious fidelity. I wish to ask, in conclusion, a few questions which are not definitely raised in the programme of our proceedings—I shall put them very briefly—as to the extent to which the Congregational ideal has authority over our thought and life.

1. As the eternal Father and the eternal Son are one in the eternal Spirit, all those who have received the life which God has given men in the Son achieve their union with the Father in the power of the same Spirit. The Divine life—the life which has its fountains in Christ, and which is ours because of our union with Him—is consummated in its perfection by

the grace of the Spirit. Is it quite certain that this truth holds the great place that it should in the Congregational Churches of this generation? In England and Scotland—I do not know how it may be in other parts of the world—there have been held during the last thirty years numerous assemblies of Christian men and women associated with different Evangelical Churches—many of them associated with our own—for the express purpose of seeking a larger measure of the power of the Spirit of God. These assemblies, which are usually called Conventions for the deepening of the spiritual life, have of late been held in all parts of this country; some of them have been attended day after day by many thousands of people. It is no part of my present duty to offer any criticism upon them; but they seem to me to bear witness to a prevailing sense of want and dissatisfaction. Are we sure that in our churches generally there is a deep and vivid consciousness that the Church is the temple of the Holy Ghost?

2. It was the aim of our ecclesiastical ancestors, who revived the Congregational polity in England 300 years ago, to realize in the Church the communion of saints. This communion, as they believed, could not be realized unless Church membership was limited to those who had received the Divine life. It was their conviction that every man in whom that life dwells can contribute something to the light, and power, and joy of his brethren. The meetings of the Church were therefore, in part, meetings for mutual instruc-

tion, counsel, warning, exhortation. It was the duty, not of the elders merely, but of private members, to admonish the disorderly, to encourage the fainthearted, to support the weak, to see that none rendered evil for evil, to follow after that which is good, one toward another and toward all. I suppose that there was never so large a number of Christian people personally engaged in rendering service of many kinds to those who are outside the Church as in our own time; but I wonder whether there is a corresponding earnestness in the internal edification of the Church, in what Paul calls the "building up" of the body "in love."

3. I should like to ask whether, in our relations to the controversies of our times, the Congregational idea of the Church has exerted its proper and adequate influence. We believe that a Church is a society of men possessing the life of the eternal Son of God, and having direct access through Him, in the power of the Spirit, to the Father—of men knowing for themselves, at first hand, the reality and glory of the Christian redemption—of men to whom the truth of the Christian Gospel is authenticated by a most certain experience, the experience, not of an individual life merely, but of a Society. Is this consistent with the agitation, the heat, the panic, created by the assaults of critics on the historic records of the Jewish and the Christian revelations? We, of all men, should keep calm. These controversies leave untouched the strong guarantees of our faith. For us, every Church

is a society of original and independent witnesses to the grace and power of Christ. For us, the immediate manifestations of the eternal life that dwells in Christ are found not merely in the words and deeds and sufferings recorded in the four gospels, but in the company of the faithful. We know that Christ is alive from the dead, for He lives in them.

The Divine life in man—this is a truth to which, in common with the holy Catholic Church throughout the whole world, we bear our testimony; and, as we think, our testimony receives emphasis and strength from the very polity of our churches. In that life, we, who are assembled at this Council, are all one. We serve God and His people under different skies; we have been separated from each other and shall be separated again, by the breadths of vast continents and of immense oceans; but in our common union with Christ we are one. In our intellectual account of the contents of the Christian Gospel there may be wide differences: and yet we are one. For us, Christ is the eternal Foundation and the only Foundation, of the Church as well as of the individual life. I trust that through God's grace the meetings of this Council may assist us to build on that Foundation—not wood, hay, stubble, but gold, silver, costly stones. For "each man's work shall be made manifest; for the day shall declare it . . . and the fire shall prove each man's work, of what sort it is. If any man's work shall abide which he built thereon, he shall receive a reward. If any man's work shall be burned, he shall suffer loss, but he himself shall be saved: yet so as through fire." May God grant that both we and our work may endure the trial of that great day!

www.ingramcontent.com/pod-product-compliance
Lightning Source LLC
Chambersburg PA
CBHW020301240426
43673CB00039B/669